ONE NATION UNDER GOD

ONE NATION UNDER GOD

BY RUS WALTON

THIRD CENTURY PUBLISHERS

THIRD CENTURY PUBLISHERS, INC.

Library of Congress Catalogue Number 75-7975

To
ILA
My
Forever
Love

TABLE OF CONTENTS

PROLOGUE

Just A Few Words At The Outset . . .

This is a book about Christianity.

Applied Christianity.

It is a book about following God's laws and Christ's teachings in all of our dealings and doings . . .

. . . in all of our affairs, personal and public, spiritual and civic.

This is a book especially for Christians.

Christian Americans.

A book hopefully helpful to those who live in this land and walk in the laws and the light and the delight of The Living God. Those who are committed to the love, the truth, the power and the path of Jesus Christ. As Savior and King.

There is no sickly pretense of neutrality in its pages. Nothing lukewarm. This book refuses to hide the light of Christ under any bushel, or any ballot, or any porkbarrel. It suggests–it proclaims–that God is right, and God is relevant–for today, and always.

This is a book about the Great American Republic.

About its genesis and its foundations. About its dreams and its purpose. Not man's purpose but God's purpose.

And, it is a book about the false gods and strange prophets who have led us astray. Coupled with what must be done if America is to be once more One Nation Under God.

This is a book about freedom. Individual freedom.

Not the fractured, constrained, regulated and restricted freedom as we witness it and feel it in this land today.

But freedom in its truest and fullest measure:
Freedom under God.
Freedom through God.
Freedom for each and every individual.

Freedom in a land and in a society where all individuals are at liberty to do the best (or the least) that they can to pursue any calling, any trade, any profession—or none at all—so long as they do not trespass on the equal freedoms of others, or any other person.

This is not a book about license—or anarchy.

It is a book about the rights—and the responsibilities—of liberty. It does not propose, it does not condone, license. License—that which permits one to do what others may not do—leads to licentiousness. Licentiousness leads to anarchy. And anarchy is the jungle.

Some readers may be surprised at some of the concepts set forth, some of the applications and some of the responsibilities of freedom herein proposed. If so, perhaps that is because freedom is truly a startling concept . . . a concept that finds its origin and its sustenance in God. Thus it has dimensions and demands we too often overlook.

It has been a long time since we have truly had freedom in this land. A whole generation has grown up that knows not freedom as it was and as it should be once more.

This is not a book about groups, or sections or segments or however some would slice and slot our society today.

It is a book about individuals—and individuality.

About the God-likeness of each and every person.

The uniqueness with which God has endowed each of His children.

The primacy of importance with which each individual is cloaked.

As many Christians have preached and written: *"The ground is level at the foot of the Cross."*

So it is and so it should be likewise in all areas of life. Not the levelling of the anthill, but the oneness in the sight of The Lord and the oneness in the law of the land. This book refuses to engage in segregation of any kind—inverse, reverse, converse or perverse. Each individual must seek his own salvation through The Lord and each must attend to his own earthly destiny. Each must be accountable for his personal actions; each entitled to the reward of his labor, each responsible for the consequences of his wrongdoings. *No man is beneath the law, no man is above the law.* There should be no rubber yardsticks, no double standards, no improper barriers, no special favors.

Finally, this:

The writings in this book are offered with love and faith and concern and conviction. But the purpose of this book is not to promote conformity; it is to stimulate prayer and meditation and thoughtful study—*and constructive action.*

To call for Christian action.

Applied Christianity. In the home, in the community, in the nation, and in the world.

May The Good Lord bless you and may The Holy Spirit guide you as you walk through these pages.

CHAPTER ONE

The Christian Idea of Government

In the beginning . . .

At that point in God's good time when the Constitutional Convention had completed its work . . .

The lady sidled up to old Ben Franklin.

"Well, Dr. Franklin. What have you given us?"

Dr. Franklin turned to her and replied:

"You have a republic, madame. If you can keep it."

So it was, after thousands of years of false starts
and forbidden fruits
and wrong turns
and tyranny and license
man finally made a true beginning in human government.

No more graven images.

No more state shepherds.

No more kings, or empires, or emperors.

No more unrestrained authority
or state religion
or sanctioned appetite
or mob rule.
No more tyranny.
The Great American Republic!

Self-Government With Union

There had been other governments before that had gone by that description–that word, "republic".

But those were different. Different in origin. Different in nature. Different in structure. The best of that past was incorporated into this new and true republic. The rest–the evil, the excess–was rejected.

So this new creation stood unique. A system of self-government. By the consent of the governed. And, with union.

Not uniformity. Union. *Unity.*

One out of many. Mortared with the blood of patriots and constructed with the Spirit of The Lord wherein lies liberty.

A constitutional republic with individual liberty, elected representatives and limited government. A government resting squarely on Christian principles and limited by the inherent rights of the governed. A government with its powers nailed down; fastened and confined to the proper defense of the individual–to his pursuits of life, liberty, property and happiness, those unalienable rights endowed by The Creator.

A republic in which the power to govern was checked and balanced by devices designed to stop the tyrant in his tracks.

Four Fences

It was no easy task to get those early Americans, those individualists, to agree on government. Each in his own way and in his own freedom worshipped Almighty God. They were not about to submit to another king, or men, or mobs. These subjects-turned-citizens were not only mindful of their rights, they were jealous of them; determined that never again would their inherent freedom be usurped, abused, mis-used or denied.

And so these cagey sons of liberty joined to erect four fences around their government.

Four fences, so that it could not get out of hand or out of bounds:

The Executive
The Legislative
The Judicial, and
The Individual.

Each was to be a check, a balance, on the other. *And the final fence, the individual, was to be the greatest check of all.* No despot, no tyrant, not even a majority or a mob was to separate him from his unalienable rights. In the individual's hand was always to be the power to bring government to heel.

After God, the individual came first. Only by his consent could government govern—and then, only to protect his life, liberty and property. Not just his, but all men—*equally.*

"It is important to note that such toleration (of each individual's rights) comes about through Christianity—because only the Christian idea of man honors all men be they 'Greek', 'Jew', 'Barbarian', 'Scythian', 'bond' or 'free'. Christianity respects each individual because it honors God and gives the supremacy to Him." [1]

A Republic!

And so the founding fathers created a republic.

A monarchy? No way!

They had just been down that bitter road. They knew all about the misuse of those so-called "divine rights of kings". And, they knew the Scriptures. They were mindful of the Prophet Samuel's warning back when the nation of Israel had demanded an earthly king:

"This," said Samuel, "This shall be the manner of the king that shall reign over you:

> *"He will take your sons, and appoint them for himself, for his chariots, and to be his horsemen; and some shall run before his chariots. And he will appoint him captains over thousands and captains over fifties; and will set them to ear his ground, and to reap his harvest, and to make his instruments of war, and instruments of his chariots. And he will take your daughters to be perfumers, and to be cooks, and to be bakers. And he will take your fields, and your vineyards, and your olive yards, even the best of them, and give them unto his servants. And he will take the tenth of your seed, and of your vineyards, and give to his officers, and to his servants. And he will take your menservants, and your maidservants, and your choicest young men, and your asses, and put them to his work. He will take the tenth of your sheep;* **and ye shall be his servants.** *And ye shall cry out in that day because of your king whom ye shall have chosen; and the Lord will not hear you in that day."* [2]

The founding fathers knew, first-hand, the striking similarity between those excesses Samuel had prophesied and that bill of indictments against the King of England, as set forth in their Declaration of Independence. They were not about to travel that road again.

Collectivism? Communism? Absolutely not!

". . . ye taking away of propertie, and bringing in comunitie into a comone wealth." [3] The first Pilgrims had made that false start. They had tried collectivism "under the most favorable conditions, among a people conscientious and bound together by strong religious enthusiasm".[4]

And it failed, miserably. During the winter of 1620-21 it had almost done them in. "It resulted, as such sinking of personal interest must ever result, in dissensions and insubordination, in unthrift and famine." [5]

No more of that!

A democracy? Not on your life!

Democracy? Where half plus one can squash the rest? Where a fanatical majority can deprive the individual of his rights, his life, his property? Not for these men.

They knew democracy with its excesses, its levelling-down process, its inherent seeds of destruction. They knew Plato's warning that unrestricted democracy must result in dictatorship.

The very essence of democracy rests in the absolute sovereignty of the majority. Our founding fathers could never accept such tyranny. They recognized only one rightful sovereign over men and nations–*Almighty God!* And next to God? The individual–not the state, not the majority.

"Each religion has a form of government, and Christianity astonished the world by establishing self-government . . . the foundation stone of the United States of America." [6]

The Great American Republic!

A government of law, not men.

With a Constitution that set down certain ground rules. This was the law of the land:

- *–the rights of the minority protected*
- *–the rights of the majority upheld but not permitted to be destructive*
- *–the process of change provided for but in a manner that prevented capricious acts or wanton revision.*

And, wonder of it all, the safeguard of representative government that filtered passion and emotion through the checkgates and the balances and the divisions of local, state and federal government.

"Further excursion into the field of metaphysics would only emphasize what is too much ignored by contemporary Americans–that their Republic is far more than an administrative mechanism. The authors of the Constitution were eminently practical men. But to consider this political achievement critically is to see that they realized the distinction we have drawn between the *condition* of freedom and the *urge* to liberty;

"that they realized the impossibility of maintaining freedom unless those who are 'at liberty' are able to exercise self-restraint;

"that their consequent objective was a political system permitting a happy balance and conciliation between the dynamic and the static.

"In short, the problem to which they resolutely addressed themselves was how to integrate a liberty of divine origin with an order of human manufacture." [7]

The Golden Mean

Article 4, Section 4: *"The United States shall guarantee to every State in this union a republican form of government."*

There it is! Proposed, adopted and ratified: "a republican form of government".

Do you think for one moment the founders of this nation would have guaranteed this to the states without having the absolute intent of providing the same for the nation?

A republic!

"A form of government under a constitution which provides for the election of (1) an *executive* and (2) a *legislative* body who, working together in a representative capacity, have all power of appointment, all power of legislation, all power to raise revenues and appropriate expenditures, and are required to create (3) a *judiciary* to pass upon the justice and legality of their governmental acts and to recognize (4) *certain inherent individual rights.*" [8]

There it is–the golden mean, *the dynamic balance!*

"All through the realm of nature and of human activity we find examples of the trinity classification–*the two extremes and the golden mean.* A few of the more striking classifications (in government) are cited in order to emphasize this fundamental truth and to illustrate the importance and the soundness of the law of the golden means:

Extreme	*Golden Mean*	*Extreme*
AUTOCRACY	REPUBLIC	DEMOCRACY
Tyrants	Statesmen	Demagogues
Bondage	Liberty	License
Oppression	Reason	Impulse
Arbitrariness	Arbitration	Agitation
Submission	Contentment	Discontent
Coercion	Justice	Anarchy
Reaction	Progress	Chaos
Feudalism	Property rights	Socialism

"To my mind, the most important event that has occurred since creation was the coming of Christ, for He came to establish *the standard of right living for all mankind.* The next most important event was the founding of this Republic under the Constitution, because it provided for the standard form of right for government." [9]

Chained To The Constitution

That embryonic power that boldly had declared its independence from an Empire–and backed its words with blood and fortune and sacred honor–was not about to hand the keys of freedom to another tyrant, regardless of the guise. Not even one home-grown. They were tight-fisted with their liberty, and they meant to be.

They gave to this government just enough power to serve. Just enough and no more. The citizens were to be the master; the state the servant.

And even then, with all the checks and balances and fences of that Divinely-inspired constitutional document, it was not until the *Bill of Rights* was tacked on that the states consented to the union and ratified the federation.

Those precious first Ten Amendments, first drawn by men from Pennsylvania. Point by point those ten caveats detailed what government could do–*and what it could not do.* With the final whack of their hammer, free and independent men capped their holy affirmation:

The Ninth Amendment:

> *"The enumeration in the Constitution of certain rights shall not be construed to deny or disparage others retained by the people."*

The Tenth Amendment:

> *"The powers not delegated to the United States by the Constitution, nor prohibited to it by the States, are reserved to the States, respectively, or to the people."*

Take heed, all would-be Caesars!

Governments and men of government would be bound, and kept in bounds. Chained to their proper role by the Constitution. A government of laws, not men; of principles, not whim.

Bed-Rock

All those fences, all those checks and balances, were vital. *Are* vital. Vital to the core of the republic.

Yet in a way they were the superstructure. A wrought-iron superstructure embedded in a master rock.

A greater spirit.

A greater law.

A higher authority.

An eternal truth.

The rock, the power, and the beauty and the light that was the Spirit of the American Republic and its Constitution had been on earth since the beginning of time.

Since The Creation.

It was there when Christ, with God, created the heavens and the earth–and man.

It was there with Christ when God gave man dominion over the land and the sea and the plants and the beasts–**but not his fellow man.** In the image of God created He man. A free agent, with a free will. Not a robot, not a vassal; a steward, only a little lower than the angels. In the final reckoning man's accountability and dominion were God's.

The genesis–

the spark–it was all there, too, when Christ, with God, established civil government. When He ordained it after the flood, through Noah.

That power–

that righteousness–it was there when God gave us the law. There on Mount Sinai, through Moses. The Law and the ordinances to govern man's comings and goings here on earth.

And, surely it was there through the manifested power and purity and love and light and sacrifice of Jesus Christ, our Savior.

"For God so loved the world that He gave His only begotten son, that whosoever believes on Him shall not perish but have life–everlasting life." [10]

Free!

Christ died–and rose–to make men free. All men, all nations.

Through Christ we are freed from the wages and the death of sin. Eternal freedom.

Free from the ravages of appetite. Internal freedom. If we choose to be.

Free from the savagery of demagogues and kings. External freedom. If we choose to be.

Just as Christ brought us *internal freedom* (and a rebirth into a new life through Him) so He brought us a new direction for our *external freedom* (and a new purpose for our civil government).

If Christ would die for men, where did Caesar get off forcing men to live–and die–for him?

There! There was the spark, the flame, the beacon light of the American idea. The power of the Great American Republic. The sense of the Constitution of these United States.

"The concept of a secular state was virtually non-existent in 1776 as well as in 1787, when the Constitution was written, and no less so when the Bill of Rights was adopted. To read the Constitution as the charter for a secular state is to misread history, and to misread it radically. The Constitution was designed *to perpetuate* a Christian order.

"Let us consider the obvious rebuttal to such a statement, for it needs to be met: Why then is there, in the main, an absence of any reference to Christianity in the Constitution?

"The response must be equally blunt: There is an absence of reference because the framers of the Constitution did not believe that this was an area of jurisdiction for the federal government. It would not have occured to them to attempt to re-establish that which the colonists had fought against, namely, religious control and establishment by the central government. The colonists would not have tolerated power in the Federal Union which they had rebelled against when claimed by crown and parliament.

"The freedom of the first amendment from federal interference is not *from* religion but *for* religion in the constituent states." [11]

Separation of church and state? Absolutely!

Divorcement of God from government? Not so!

"Next to the Christian religion, of which America is the most influential advocate, the American government and Constitution is the most precious possession which the world holds, or which the future can inherit.

"This is true: *true because the American system is the political expression of Christian ideas* . . . a nation founded upon the rock of religion and rooted in the love of man." [12]

The Christian Idea of Government

Christ's Great Commandment?

"Love one another: just as I have loved you so you too should love one another." [13]

That is the very tap-root of self-government and individual freedom under God.

His Golden Rule for life?

"Do unto others as you would have others do unto you." [14]

That is the power that can make men free and force governments to seek their proper place . . . and live within those bounds.

His Great Injunction?

"Seek ye first the kingdom of God and all these things shall be added unto you." [15]

Once and for all that established the balance and the order.

"For what does it profit a man if he gain the whole world and lose his soul?" [16]

These were the ideals, the ideas, the principles, the spirit of the men who founded this republic.

"These texts, and many others of similar import, were as guiding lights to the resolute men and women who came to America not merely to worship as they wished, but even more to live, so far as humanly possible, in the manner Christ ordained." [17]

No single man had a greater positive influence on the framers of our Constitution that John Locke, English theorist and Christian philosopher of the 17th Century.* And in his writings, this:

"Our Saviour's great rule, that 'we should love our neighbors as ourselves', is such a fundamental truth for the regulating of human society, that, by that alone, one might without difficulty determine all the cases and doubts in social morality." [18]

Years later, in 1851, when Daniel Webster was reviewing the history of "this great American family", he reaffirmed the need and role of God in government:

"Let the religious element in man's nature be neglected, let him be influenced by no higher motives than low self-interest, and subjected to no stronger restraint than the limits of civil authority, and he becomes the creature of selfish passion or blind fanaticism."

"On the other hand, the cultivation of the religious sentiment represses licentiousness, incites to general benevolence and the practical acknowledgement of the brotherhood of man, inspires respect for law and order, and gives strength to the whole social fabric, at the same time that it conducts the human soul upward to the Author of its being." [19]

And, more than one hundred years after Webster, Charles Malik, one-time Ambassador to the United Nations from Lebanon, put it this way:

"The good (in the United States) would never have come into being without the blessing and the power of Jesus Christ.

"Whoever tries to conceive the American word without taking full account of the suffering and love and salvation of Christ is only dreaming.

"I know how embarrassing this matter is to politicians, bureaucrats, businessmen and cynics; but, whatever these honored men think, the irrefutable truth is that the soul of America is at its best and highest, Christian.

"When the tears and joy of Christ come to perfect fruition in this land, then America will utter her word."

---

* Locke's "Two Treatises on Government"–and especially his "Of Civil Government"–were read and studied and quoted by the thinkers and writers and movers of the American colonies. Next to The Holy Scriptures, they were probably the most influential documents in early America.

God First

Christ did, indeed, instruct us to "render unto Caesar that which is Caesar's."

But, was that not in part a challenge to seek that proper balance between God and government? Was it not to urge His followers to refrain from becoming entrapped with the things of earthly empire?

*And, just what is Caesar's?**

We are not to render unto him those things that are God's.

Our bodies, our spirit, our soul, our free will–those are not Caesar's. They are God's. Through the wondrous gifts of God they belong to us. *Each one of us. Every one of us.*

God had a purpose when He instituted (ordained) civil authority, in the days of Noah.[20] That purpose was to protect the lives and property and well-being of man from those whose inner strength was weak or non-existent; those whose lack of moral responsibility turned them to crimes and violence against their fellow men.[21]

Human government was instituted as a defensive agency. A protector not a provider. Its laws were to be in concert with God's laws–the laws of nature and nature's God.

And, what of those laws and what of the primary purposes of those laws and judgements? The Laws God handed down through Moses? They were given to make clear the imperative doctrine of man's personal responsibility to God. To make clear the purity and holiness that should characterize the life of people with whom the law of the nation was at the same time the law of God.[22]

Christians know that civil government is ordained by God. We are instructed to pray for our government officials and to seek God's guidance of their conduct of our public affairs.

In his book, *Shaping History Through Prayer and Fasting,* Derek Prince affirms that "Christian citizens of the United States should be forever thankful that the basic charter of their nation agrees so exactly with the purposes and principles of government ordained

---

* For a deeper consideration of this question, read Chapter Ten, *Taxes and The Power To Destroy.*

in the Scriptures."[23] Mr. Prince reminds us of Paul's advice in 1 Timothy 2:2. Roughly translated, that advice boils down to this:

"Good government is the will of God."

In Christ's teachings and in the counsel of His Apostles we find the keys to that proper balance between God's government and man's. And, also the road to restoration of that balance should it be lost.

The Law (Matt. 5:17)
The Great Commandment (John 15:17)
The Golden Rule (Matt. 7:12)
The Great Injunction (Matt. 6:33)
The Whole Spectrum of Love (1 Cor. 13:1-13)
The Whole Armor of God (Eph. 6:10-18)

Clearly it is affirmed, and reaffirmed:

Man is God's servant, God's steward; not the state's.

The state is to serve the law-abiding and to punish the law-breaker, not vice versa.

Under God, the individual is to be self-governing.

"Christianity is a stranger to despotic power."[24]

The First Christian Congregations

What dynamic ideas, these Christian precepts!

These Divine precepts that had been from the beginning and that burst forth as The Master walked and talked on earth and as His disciples and apostles spread the Gospel.

As these ideas spread and widened from individual to individual to family and group, a secondary transformation began to work. The power of the Spirit, first internal, also took external shape and form. It manifested itself in the Christians' daily lives. And it manifested in the structure of the early Christian congregations.

Consider the spirit, the structure, the lovely workings of those early Christian churches. The ones at Galatia. Philippi. Antioch. Thessalonica. Ephesus. Colosse. Corinth. Rome.

There was true self-government. *Christianity applied.* The seeds and fruit, the patterns, for other men to follow. To modify, perhaps, but to maintain.

"In the beginning Christianity was simply Gospel. Ecclesiastical organization was not the cause, but the effect of life.

"Churches were constituted by the spontaneous association of believers. Individuals and families, drawn toward each other by their common trust in Jesus, the Christ, and their common interest in the good news concerning the kingdom of God, became a community united, not by external bonds, but by the vital force of distinctive ideas and principles . . . in every place the society of believers in Christ was a little republic." [25]

"Christianity, in its essence, its doctrines, and its forms, is republican." [26]

Republican.

Not in any narrow partisan sense or meaning of that word.

Certainly not in any reference to the politics of today.

But, republican, meaning "that form of government which derives all its powers directly or indirectly from the body of the people and is administered by persons holding office with the consent of the governed." [27]

Consider the republican features of the churches then.

"These churches had officers, which were to be regarded and observed, in their proper spheres, as much as officers of any other republic. But the manner of their ruling was not to be as 'Lords over God's heritage'.

" 'Whosoever will be chief among you,' said the Savior, 'let him be your servant.' " [28]

The churches instituted by the apostles were local institutions only. Each local church was complete in itself, and was held responsible to Christ for its own character and the character of those whom it retained in its fellowship. The members of the congregation elected their own elders and deacons. Through prayer and study they sought God's will in their lives—and in their church affairs. They reached *UP* to imbue themselves with the love and light and spirit of Christ. In all things. The whole suit of armor.

Matters of congregational polity were attended to by the members through their elected elders and deacons. If, upon occasion, the church sought the Apostle's opinion or instruction, that was their decision.*

One Mind In Christ

There was *no regional body*
no state board
no national council
no self-annointed hierarchy to enforce dictums or edicts or decrees or tributes. Christ was Lord, and Master, and Governor of affairs both individual and congregational.

There were hundreds and hundreds of miles between those far-flung congregations. But there was unity. There was no central control; but there was a common bond. Many members; one body. Out of many, one!

It was a new heart, and a new mind; a new love through Christ. It was the power of the universe, the seed of Creation, in those souls on fire. And it spread!

Against all adversity it spread. In hidden rooms. By quiet shores. Through the marketplace. In darkest catacombs. Through martyrs, through persecutions; even when the score read Lions-Ten, Christians-Zero, it would not die. A glorious, unyielding, lifting faith that would not—could not—be denied.

Tyrants would try to snuff it out; hierarchies would try to subvert it; emperors would try to suborn it; demigods would try to pervert it, or divert it. But it would not die and it would not yield. Its truth, its purity, its power would prevail. It would find again its form in God's good time.

---

* "If the Apostle Paul, who was an inspired person, had not dominion over the faith of the churches, how came the Roman emperor, or other Christian princes, by such a jurisdiction—which has no foundation in the law of nature or in the New Testament?" Daniel Neal, *History of the Puritans,* 1731.

Westward To America

Others have documented the westward movement of that Christian light. Other volumes detail the rise and fall and contributions of the nations and the inquisitions of the dark Dark Ages.*

Suffice to mention here that each regime and transit added to man's constantly expanding sum:

> Pythagoris and Euclid, Aristotle, Socrates and Plato, Galileo and DaVinci; language, laws and logarithm, politics and science, art and architecture, navigation and introspection . . . the ability to examine and define the concrete, the intellect to conceptualize the abstract. . . . all were preparation for man's development and for his republican capacities.

And suffice to say the Christian light moved westward within the epochs. Persisting like a blade of grass that shatters through the boulder to flourish in a virgin land an ocean's span away.

It came through John Milton; through his *Paradise Lost* and through his other writings:

> "*(Pro Populo Anglicano Defensio)* Our liberty is not Caesar's. It is a blessing we have received from God Himself. It is what we were born to. To lay this down at Caesar's feet, which we derive not from him, which we are not beholden to him for, were an unworthy action, and a degrading of our very nature. . . ."

It came through Wycliffe. Wycliffe, the "morning star of the reformation", whose love of truth, of freedom and independence compelled him to give his English countrymen the open Scriptures as their best safeguard and protection during "the thickest darkness of anti-Christian idolatry." [29]

Wycliffe, who published his conclusions "that the new Testament or Gospel is a perfect rule of life and manners and ought to be read by the people".[30] And who then proceeded, before his martyrdom, to translate the New Testament into English.

It came, too—this light, through Tyndale, the father of the English

---

* Specifically recommended: Verna Hall's *Christian History of The Constitution.*

Bible.

Through Martin Luther, and John Calvin, and Thomas Cartwright and the Presbyterians. *God moved in wondrous ways His mysteries to perform!*

"That mysterious influence of that Power which enchains the destinies of States, overruling the decisions of sovereigns and the forethought of statesmen . . .

"A Genoese adventurer, discovering America

"An obscure German, inventing the printing press

"An Augustine monk, denouncing indulgences, introduced a schism in religion and changed the foundation of English politics

"A young French refugee, skilled alike in theology and civil law . . . entering the republic of Geneva, and conforming its ecclesiastical discipline to the principles of republican simplicity, established a party, of which Englishmen became members, and New England the asylum."[31]

It came with the growing thunder of a new age dawning. First the Pilgrims, then the Puritans. Followed by the Quakers, the Huguenots, the Catholics, and the Lutherans, the Presbyterians, Methodists and Baptists. Joined here in this uncharted land by Virginians who would raise their voice and lend their arms and give their sons as presidents.

It came on the written wings of Locke, and Montesquieu, Sidney and Blackstone, and Paine and Adams and Franklin, and the Committees of Correspondence.

It came through the crimson tyrannies of king and parliament and stamp acts and writs of assistance and quartered troops. Impelled by the Sons of Liberty in Boston, triggered by that shot at Concord, impassioned by a member of Virginia's House of Burgess speaking at St. John's Episcopal Church in Richmond:

"Is life so dear or peace so sweet, as to be purchased at the price of chains or slavery? Forbid it, Almighty God! I know not what course others may take, but as for me, give me liberty or give me death!"[32]

Thus, in the course of human events, it formed and marched and moved . . .

". . . with a firm reliance on the protection of Divine Providence".

The Pagan View of Man

So it arrived, that Christian light.

Not a birth, a rebirth!

A continuation, after so long a time, of the seed and fruit and the courage and persistence of preceding Christians. A propagation of the faith in things Spiritual, and things of civil government and liberty.

"Christianity then appeared with the central doctrine that man was created in the Divine image, and destined for immortality; pronouncing that, in the eye of God, all men are equal. This asserted for the individual an independent value. It occasioned the great inference that man is superior to the State, which ought to be fashioned for his use.

"This was the advent of a new spirit and a new power in the world." [33]

It met, head-on, another value placed on man.

The pagan view

> *"that the social order rested on the assumed natural inequality of men"; that the individual was "of value only as he formed a part of the political fabric and was able to contribute to its uses, as though it were the end of his being to aggrandize the state."* [34]

It was obvious that such a humanistic, nihilistic philosophy could not abide the Christian truth that man is Divine, and unique; that man is not a political unit or an economic digit, not an end unto the State.

"Socialism's government is the *external* control of the parts, as opposed to Christianity's *internal* control of the individual." [35]

And thus the battle is joined—even today, even at home as well as abroad:

Shall we have controlled citizens, or controlled government?

Is the individual the master, or the slave?

Is man Divine, accountable to His Maker? Or, is he a means to an end, subservient to the State?

It is the eternal struggle.

"For we wrestle not against flesh and blood, but against principalities, against powers, against the rulers of darkness of this world, against spiritual wickedness in high places." [36]

CHAPTER TWO

False Gods, Strange Prophets

There is nothing of survival inherent in a republic. Its longevity depends upon the Faith, the spirit, and the genius of the people within.

James Madison, one of the framers of the Constitution, explained the nature of the American republic in these words:

> *"We have staked the whole future of American civilization, not upon the power of government, far from it. We have staked the future of all of our political institutions upon the capacity of mankind for self-government; upon the capacity of each and all of us to govern ourselves, to control ourselves, to sustain ourselves according to the Ten Commandments of God."*

But, what if the Faith is weakened? What if the spirit of the people flags? What if the flesh grows weak? When that occurs, the republic goes unattended:

- –its *checks and balances* between the executive, the legislative, the judicial and the individual are rigged–or circumvented;
- –its *fences* between the federal, state and local governments are downed.

The system is then altered and subverted.

Part Of The Past

It would not be accurate to say the republic is dead. But, it would not be far off the mark to say that its workings have been shelved. The form remains. It is acknowledged on those national holidays and in those patriotic speeches. Then it is put back, under glass along with the other relics.

The fact is this:

this nation is now more of a democracy than it is a republic.

And, to those who will see behind the slogans and hear beyond the chants, another truth is clear:

with the passing of the republic also passes the power of the people.

The Vital Difference

What's that you say?

How can that be? In a democracy the power is the people!

Not so! In its last rites, democracy enslaves the people.

In a democracy, the power that prevails is the militant. The vocal, organized minority. And, perhaps, an occasional restive, fleeting majority.

Four hundred years ago Alexander Fraser Tyler, a professor in England, examined the fruits of a democracy and called them bitter:

"A democracy cannot exist as a permanent form of government. It can exist only until the voters discover that they can vote themselves largess out of the public treasury. From that moment on the majority always votes for the candidate promising the most benefits from the public treasury–with the result that democracy always collapses over a loose fiscal policy, always to be followed by dictatorship."

Check back with Madison again:

"A pure democracy . . . can admit of no cure for the mischiefs of faction. A common passion or interest will . . . be felt by a majority . . . and there is nothing to check the inducements to sacrifice the weaker party. . . . Hence it is that such democra-

cies have ever been. . . found incompatible with personal security or the rights of property; and have in general been as short in their lives as they have been violent in their death." [1]

There is the difference! The vital difference between the republic and a democracy.

In the republic, the majority will represent the individual and protect the minority. Because the checks and balances work. The fences are up. Representation is observed.

In a democracy, the majority can represent the group, the mob, the militant, the demagogue. The checks and balances are waived. The fences are down. Sound and fury can carry the day.

It was that vital difference that prompted the framers of our Constitution to give us the Great American Republic.

We have not kept it very well.

"To put the matter bluntly, there is under way in the United States at the present time a definite and determined movement to change our representative republic into a socialistic democracy. It presents itself in many persuasive and seductive forms. It uses attractive formulas to which men like to give adhesion; but if it is successful, it will bring an end to the form of government that was founded when our Constitution was made. . . ."

Those are the words of Dr. Nicholas Murray Butler, the president of Columbia University during the 1930s and 40s. He wrote them in his book, *Why Should We Change Our Form of Government?* Forty years ago he wrote them.

Where Have We Gone?

Forty years ago! A lot has gone since then. Think back. Check the politics and government in this land for the past twenty–thirty, forty–years.

What has happened?

Where have we gone?

Well, we have gone backward–and left the course of freedom.

Upon occasion and on specific issues, we–the people–voted a

reaffirmation of America.

"Get on with the republic." That's what we advised.

We voted for economy instead of extravagance. For liberty instead of license. For state's rights instead of centralism. For individualism instead of collectivism.

Did our will, or our vote, prevail. Did the course change? Or, did it remain the same?

During those years political party was exchanged for party; leader for leader; representative for representative. Yet, the drift remained. And the power of the people was passing with the years.

Revolutionary Intent

Consider the 1930s under Franklin Roosevelt. Consider especially those first 100 days under the "New Deal", in the early months of 1933. It was then, more than ever before, that socialism sank its roots deep into the nation's heart. It was then the republic took its hardest lumps.

Franklin Roosevelt was not elected on a platform of socialism. He did not run on the promise of a planned society or super state. His proposals to America went in the *opposite* direction. *The Democratic platform of 1932 would make today's conservative stand up and cheer!* The first three planks, to which FDR bound and pledged himself, were these:

"1. **An immediate and drastic reduction in governmental expenditures** by abolishing useless commissions and offices, consolidating departments and bureaus and eliminating extravagance, to accomplish *a saving of not less than 25 percent in the cost of Federal government.*

"2. Maintenance of the national credit by a **Federal budget annually balanced.**

"3. **A sound currency** to be maintained at all hazards." [2]

And in the run of his campaign of 1932, Mr. Roosevelt stated—not once but again, and again, and again:

"We are spending altogether too much money for government services which are neither practical nor necessary. In addition to this, we are attempting too many functions and we need a simplification of what the Federal government is giving to the people."

The American people loved it. They cheered in their anticipation.

But, the promises and speeches were sheer duplicity. Expediency at its zenith. Sham at its worst. Garet Garrett, a giant of American journalism, spelled it out. In his *The Revolution Was,* he wrote:

"What was concealed from the people was a general *revolutionary intention*—the intention, that is, to bring about revolution in the state, within the form of law. This becomes clear when you set down what it was the people thought they were voting for in contrast with what they got. They thought they were voting

"For less government, not more;

"For an end to deficit spending by government, not deficit spending raised to the plane of social principles, and

"For sound money, not as the New Deal afterward defined it, but as everybody then understood it. . . ." [3]

That is what the majority of Americans voted for, in 1932.

And this is what they got:

—*the number and the powers of federal agencies exploded* into an alphabetized nightmare (AAA, NRA, NLRB, PWA, WPA) and the shrapnel chewed into virtually every aspect of our daily lives (even today much of it is still there, embedded in the muscle of the republic).

—*the federal budget zoomed and the national debt increased* (in the first four years of the Roosevelt administration, spending increased 85 percent; the federal debt increased 72 percent and the number of federal employees rose 48 percent).

—*the sound, gold standard money was decimated* (citizens and companies were divested of their gold under penalty of fine or imprisonment; the gold redemption clause in all government obligations (contracts) was repudiated, the dollar was devalued and Washington pocketed a $2 billion "windfall" from the confiscated gold).

It was all done in the name of emergency; in the name of economic panic and the banking crisis. By Mr. Roosevelt's own admission, in his book, *On Our Way,* the banking crisis lasted only one week. . . . "But the full meaning of that word emergency related to far more than banks. . . . It could be cured only by *a complete reorganization and measured controls of the economic structure. . . . It called for a long series of new laws, new administrative agencies."*

Thus the republic was shunted backstage and "democracy" moved front and center. It came to the fore in the dark of night, flying flags to freedom, chanting praises to a new shepherd. Promises and praises. But, in 1940–after all the confiscations of liberty and property–14.6 percent of America was still unemployed, farms were still fallow, factories were still idle.

Different Pennants, Same Heading

It has been much the same since then but not as concentrated, not as blatant.

Consider those candidates who, elected on their promise to bring government back home, have voted to centralize its powers on the banks of the Potomac. Consider those candidates who, elected on their promise to reduce the size and scope and cost of government, have worked to fuel its fires and fan its flames.

And, consider the consequences:

In *only nine* of the past forty years has the federal budget been balanced; in *only six* of the forty has the federal deficit been reduced.

In every year but two since 1940, the value (the purchasing power) of the dollar has eroded; what was worth 100 cents then is worth 25 cents now, and shrinking. And, with the passing of the buck has passed much of the power of the people. It's not just the money, it's the principle; and with the money went our principles.

It took 172 years–from 1787 to 1961–for the federal budget to reach $100 billion. *It took only nine more years* to reach the $200 billion mark–actually $208 billion, in 1970. *In just five years* since then, annual spending by the federal government is knocking at the $400 billion door.

The projected federal deficits for fiscal 1975 and 1976 come close to $150 billion. *That two-year deficit–$150 billion–will exceed all the money spent by Uncle Sam in the first 142 years of this republic.*

Some politicians are committed to the left; to tax, to spend, to control and elect. At least we know just where they stand. Others say they are commited to the right and yet they vote to tax and spend. Challenge them and here's your answer:

"You just don't understand the pressures. You folks live in a world of theory. Politicians deal with reality; the art of the possible.

"Besides, half a loaf is better than none."

There's your answer, and there's the problem: the half a loaf they give away is yours. Not theirs, yours. And the next time it's half of your halfloaf, and then half of that. Before you know it, you're left with one thin slice and even that is stale.

So much for campaign rhetoric. So much for party platforms and promises. Partisan pennants changed but the course remained the same *and to the left.* We voted one way, most politicians went the other. We have wandered in their wilderness–traipsing along after elephants and donkeys–for more than forty years.

Power At The Base

The structure of the republic was pyramidal. Its base of strength was at the local level, in the counties and the states. from there the structure rose to the point of chief executive and even he was checked and balanced.

In the early days, and for the first one hundred years, that was the shape of the nation. For more than the first century, the county formed the basic unit of this republic. As important as the states were to the federation, they were not the basic unit.[4]

The county held the jurisdiction in those areas important to the workings of our civil government: [5]

- –the *property tax* was apportioned and levied at the county level so that the citizens could keep the lid on supervisors and tax assessors. With taxation went representation–or else.
- –the *criminal law* was first and foremost a matter of county jurisdiction and enforcement.
- –and *civil law,* to a great degree, was adopted by locally elected officials and enforced by local courts.

There was a time, not too many years ago, when elections to fill those local offices were regarded as just as important–maybe even more important–than state and federal contests. In those times, the state was more or less benign and Washington–well, Washington was miles away attending to its proper constitutional and limited duties.

But that has changed. Now Caesar calls the loudest tune and citizens are more entranced by his election.

The shift came long ago but it did not really manifest itself until the early 1930s. In 1934, and '35, and '36, you could measure the start of the change in this republic. Year by year you could see the power center move. You could measure it by the transfer of the people's money from the bottom to the top; from the counties and the states to Babylon.

The Inverted Pyramid

In 1902, all governments in the republic–federal, state and local–spent $1.7 billion of the people's money. More than 65 percent of that was raised and spent by local and state government. Only 34 percent was expended by the federal government.

In 1922, the total costs of government had risen to $9.3 billion but still the lion's share was expended at the local level:

–46 percent by cities and counties
–14 percent by the states, and
–40 percent was federal.

At that point the base was more-or-less intact, and fairly solid.

In 1934, it started to shift. That year the federal share of the expended $12.8 billion rose to 46 percent. The state and local portion was down to 54 percent. Not a big shift, but a shift. A sign of things to come.

In 1936 the pyramid turned. For the first time–except in years of war–the federal government spent more of the people's earnings than did the state and local entities, *combined.* Of the $16.7 billion in expenditures that year

–$9.2 billion (55%) was spent by Washington

–$4.4 billion (26%) was spent by local governments, and
–$3.1 billion (19%) was spent by the sovereign states.

That was the beginning. From then on Babylon became the font of money–and power. In 1950, the federal government spent 63 percent of all the public funds; in 1960, 64 percent; in 1970, 63.5 percent. The pattern had been established and the pyramid is now inverted, and it casts a long, long shadow.

The Lengthening Shadow

To get some idea of just how far that shadow has spread, how far across this land it stretches, get yourself a map of these United States. And, get yourself a crayon, a big red crayon.

Start with Hawaii and Alaska. Color them red.

Then start at the Mainland, at the Pacific Coast. Color the states red; from the Canadian border south to Mexico, color the states red. Then east, across the Sierras, across the salt flats, across the Rockies, across the Great Plains. Color all the states red. Color every state from the far Pacific to the Mississippi River–and then six states beyond: Wisconsin, Indiana, Kentucky, Tennessee, Alabama and Mississippi. *Color them red, too.*

That's thirty states, in all!

There are almost 100 million Americans living in those thirty states. In 1973, it would have taken *all* of the personal income of *all* of those 100 million persons living in *all* of those thirty states to equal the total tax take in this nation. The personal income of those 100 million Americans totalled $369 billion. The total tax take was $370 billion–*not counting the levy of inflation.* And, almost two-thirds of those taxes went to Washington.

Color the taxpayers blue!

From Guns To Give-Aways

It has been a steady and a growing drain, this siphoning of our resources to fatten Washington. But, it has seen its greatest increases during times of war; increases that have come, and remained.

After every war, government's expenditures rise to meet the bloated war-years income. Budgets do not return to pre-war levels; the money-spending fever drops—but never back to normal.

Back in 1916, before our boys marched off to make the world "safe for democracy", the federal budget stood at $734 million. To pay for World War I the budget swelled to $12.7 billion in 1918 and on up to $18.5 billion in 1919. When Johnny was safely home the budget dropped—and stopped at $6 billion, four times what it was before the war.

It was the same with World War II. In 1940, Uncle Sam was spending $9 billion a year. In 1945, when we were going all out to rescue freedom, spending was running at $98 billion a year. In 1948, with most of our men back home and our planes and ships in mothballs, the budget dropped and held at $33 billion—three and one-half times higher than pre-Pearl Harbor days.

It was the same with Vietnam—the "unwar". In 1960, when we were first being drawn in, the federal budget stood at $98 billion. As our involvement increased, so did the budget. By 1968, it was $184 billion. The fighting is over but not the budget bulge; it keeps growing. For 1974, it was almost $300 billion!

It's not just the guns, it's all that butter, all those give-aways, domestic and foreign. During the past twenty years, defense spending has increased 66 percent. *Over the same period, federal spending on health, education and welfare has soared 1,345 percent!*

In 1974, out of every federal dollar that was ours, 45 cents went to HEW and 30 cents went to defense. *That's not the whole picture!* Every time Uncle Sam increases federal spending for welfare, or education, or health, the states and the local government are forced to up their spending, too. It's known as "matching funds" but call it what it really is—"baiting the money trap". Small wonder so many states and counties and cities are in financial hot water while facing a taxpayer revolt.

Through constitutions and charters, citizens have prohibited most state and local government from indulging in deficit spending—which is, in its way, a form of taxation without representation. But, Washington has found a way to pre-empt such wisdom; *it is called revenue sharing.*

The question is, of course, what revenue?

Uncle Sam is already up to his hocks in red ink. More money, more revenues, must come from bigger deficits. There is no law prohibiting federal deficits, no law mandating balanced budgets; thus Washington can go deeper and deeper into the hole and citizens in states and cities are forced to share the burden—and the mortgage.

Call it what it is: *deficit sharing.* At least, we should be honest.

The Real Third Party

In a republic, the government is firmly of and by and for the people.

In a democracy, freedom is exchanged for promise; for "security", for "peace", for "succor". But, those who are succored will sooner or later be suckered. *Along the line, the people become of and by and for the government.*

And, has that not happened?

In 1929, the ratio was one government employe for every eleven Americans working in private industry. Today, by way of measurement, the ratio is one government employe for every four Americans working in private industry.

Congress, itself, is an example of the governmental mushroom. In 1954, the number of congressional employes was 5,600; in 1974 it was 17,000. The number of employes has increased at a rate six times faster than the increase in the number of constituents. In the late 1950s, the U.S. Senate had one office building and the House of Representatives had two. Today it takes five buildings to house both houses and plans are under way to convert a huge warehouse into additional offices and erect yet another House Office Building!

There are now some 14 million persons on our public payrolls—federal, state and local. There are more Americans working for government than all the men and women employed by the manufacturers of durable goods.[6] Those 14 million government employes outnumber *all* the Americans employed in the retail trades.

With tongue-in-cheek, the Morgan Guaranty Trust Company recently engaged in some fanciful predictions. Noting that the increase in public employment has been twice that of the rate of rise in the total labor force, the bank suggested:

"In the year 2049 everyone in America will be working for the government." It's a laugh but it's not a laugh. The 81,000-plus governmental agencies in the United States now employ one out of every five Americans in the nation's labor force.

The fact is, a new branch of government has evolved: the Government, itself.

Along with the executive, the legislative and the judicial, we now have the governmental. An entity unto its own. No longer a servant of the people and the other three branches–it is now an empire, a force unto itself. Invisible yet ubiquitous; the servant has become a master.

Years ago, when this new branch was still in its adolescence, Senator Paul Douglas of Illinois described it in other terms. He said there were three parties in Washington, D.C.–the Democratic party, the Republican party, and the Government party, representing the agencies and bureaus and departments and divisions. Senator Douglas observed that "no pressure group was more persistent and skilled in the technique of getting what it wants." [7]

And so it is. In the ten years from 1962 to 1972, while wages and salaries in the private sector were rising 66 percent, wages and salaries for federal civilian employes rose 88 percent. In the five years prior to 1975, salaries and fringe benefits for governmental employes increased 53 percent. In 1974, while the number of jobs in private industry declined by 678,000, the number of jobs in government increased 385,000.[8]

The Junking of America

The shift from republic to democracy was subtle. It was cumulative. Sometimes by accident, often by design. And together an avalanche gathering size, and speed, and power.

What brings about this junking of the American idea? What permits it to occur?

Is it a weakening of the individual will? The loss of self-reliance;

thus the abdication of self-government? People do, indeed, get the government they resemble.

Once this was the creed:

"I do not choose to be a common man; I choose to be uncommon, if I can. I seek opportunity, not security. I do not wish to be a kept citizen, humbled and dulled by having the state look after me. I want to take the calculated risk; to dream and to build, to fail and to succeed.

"I refuse to barter incentive for a dole. I prefer the challenges of life to guaranteed existence; the thrill of fulfillment to the stale calm of utopia. I will not trade freedom for beneficence or my dignity for a handout. I will never cower before any master or bend to any threat. It is my heritage to stand erect, proud and unafraid and act for myself; to enjoy the benefits of my creation and to face the world boldly and say, 'This I have done.'

"All this is what it means to be an American!"[9]

Whatever happened to that soul song?

What happened to that uncommon common man? And to his Faith?

Is that it? Have we lost the Faith? Replaced it, perhaps, with the "new" faith that goes with the "new" politics and the "new" economics? Dr. Ivan Bierly, former head of the Volker Fund, suggests so:

"A new faith has arisen opposite to that which inspired our country's beginnings. It is a faith in man, as man, and in man's reason, as the regulator and the determiner of right and wrong. In biblical terms, man has turned from Christian orientation to anti-Christian, man-oriented, secular leadership. The problem there is, which 'man' is 'right'?

"In the process of the transition we have kept the 'language' of freedom under God but the roots have been severed. We have lost conscious contact with our historical Christian roots. While we have kept the language we fail to realize that we have lost the spirit that those roots require. This is the source of our 'tower of Babel' today. Parenthetically, it is also the reason we find it difficult to understand that the Russian Dialectic with respect to freedom is practically the opposite from that on which this nation was founded. Is it any wonder we come out second-best in 'detente' situations?"

The Pagan View Exhumed

It was not the intolerance of those who put God first that brought the change, the transition. Indolence, perhaps, and excessive tolerance; *but not intolerance.*

It was the intolerance of those who hold the pagan view. Those to whom the State is king and human reason the holy grail. Those to whom man's value rests in his contribution to the State and to its institutions. When they slammed the door on the Christian idea—that each individual is divine, unique, and sacred—they opened the gates to paganism.

By belittling God they paved the way for Caesar.

"In proportion as Americans let go of faith in the absolute power of God, they accepted the belief in the all powerful state. This is true of peoples, or nations, for their idea of God determines the form of their civil, political, religious and social institutions." [10]

There are those who hold, perhaps with good intent, that if the Lord Jesus were on earth today He would be a socialist. *Be not deceived.* Socialism is paganism. It makes of the State an idol, a graven image, a golden calf; *and, it puts that ahead of God.* Thus, over-and-above its secondary sins, it commits the unpardonable:

It violates the First Commandment.

"Thou shalt have no other gods before Me."

God? Or, Caesar?

Who can say, in honesty, that God's laws are now the applied law of this land? That they are the basis of the workings of our institutions?

If that were so, how do we then account for the rise of Caesar and the growing glorification of the State?

Who can say, with honesty, the statist schools advance the cause of freedom or the bedrock of religion? Or morality? Or ethics? If that were so, how do we then account for the fact that the theory of evolution, for example, is given first place and the story of creation is cast aside as myth and fable? Thus to the young, man becomes a super ape, an accident of bio-chemistry, and on the basis of such theory communism expands its trade routes to the youthful hearts and minds.

For, if man is super ape his value and his functions are easily defined and charted: to serve the herd, the group, the State. And thus the two walk hand in hand across the fabled Constitution: super ape and super state.

Choose You This Day

A reconstructed faith for the reconstructed man. That is the new offering, the new dialectic. From each according to his ability to each according to his need. Forget about the spirit, forget about the soul. It is the mind and the belly–that's what matters.

Let Big Brother be your shepherd. He will lead you beside new waters–he will prepare your table–he will care for you. Come dwell with him, his rod and his staff will comfort you.

Well, listen. Listen to what Whittaker Chambers had to say in *Witness.* Chambers knew communism, from the inside out. He was one. He crossed the line, but he made it back to warn us.[11]

> "Communism is what happens when, in the name of Mind, men free themselves from God."
>
> "Economics is not the central problem of this century. It is a relative problem which can be solved in relative ways. *Faith is the central problem of this age.*"
>
> "The crisis of the Western world exists to the degree in which it is indifferent to God."
>
> "Religion and freedom are indivisible. Without freedom the soul dies. Without the soul there is no justification for freedom."
>
> *"Faith in God, or Faith in Man? That is the challenge."*

That is, indeed, the challenge facing our nation: faith in God, or faith in man? "He that is not with Me is against Me; and he that gathereth not with Me, scattereth abroad."[12]

"Choose you this day whom you will serve."[13]

CHAPTER THREE

God's Bed-Rock Laws For Freedom

There are those who see freedom as that state, or situation, in which the individual is released from all restraints; free of compunction or moral standard.

To them, freedom is a no-holds-barred opportunity for the big rip-off and the easy ride. No obligations, no discipline–just freedom to do their thing and let the other fellow take the hindmost.

Such persons are not libertarians; they are libertines, the product of their error is licentiousness.

The Apostle Peter makes it clear that we are not to use our freedom "as a pretext for wickedness but rather to be servants of God."[1]

Paul tells us that *"where the Spirit of the Lord is, there is liberty."*[2] But Paul also cautions us that we are *"not to use our freedom to satisfy the flesh but rather, through love, to serve one another."*[3]

Freedom, as Christians know it, is one of our precious gifts from God. *"The God who gave us life, gave us liberty."*[4] As with everything God bestows on us, we are to use His gift of freedom wisely and in harmony with His laws.

Spiritual and Physical

There are, essentially, two forms of freedom: spiritual freedom and physical freedom.

Spiritual freedom is that personal, inner state of being that comes through the Spirit of The Lord. It is that internal strength of peace that breaks the bonds of appetite and greed; *that makes us servants of God rather than slaves of self or other men.* It is the Faith that sustains, even in the meanest bondage–as it did the imprisoned Apostle Paul and as it did so many of our fighting men who were held captive long months and years in enemy jails.

"The spirit of liberty remembers that not even a sparrow falls to earth unheeded. The spirit of liberty is the spirit of Him who, nearly 2,000 years ago, taught mankind that lesson it has never learned, but never has quite forgotten; that there is a kingdom where the least shall be heard and considered side by side with the greatest." [5]

Physical freedom is that outer state of the individual, that external condition that is "the absence of force, the absence of coercion, the absence of restraint and constraint".[6] "Sociologically", freedom is "man not playing God, either individually or collectively." [7]

"To every man the right to live, to work, to be himself, and to become whatever thing his manhood and his vision can combine to make him . . .".[8] *In other words, physical freedom is that situation in which individuals live in harmonious cooperation and do not seek dominion over each other.*

The Nature of Freedom

The nature of freedom is personal, private–*individual.* It is the individual who is free; not the group, not society. The term "free society" is a misnomer, and a dangerous one; given full application, a free society can result in glorification of the State and diminution of the individual.

Freedom is also uniqueness–it means something different to each individual. It means each individual is free to be different–to be himself, to be unique. If one is free simply to be like others, or to do as others, or to conform to a predetermined pattern, one is obviously not free.

And freedom must, by its very nature, be available to all—equally. There can be no true freedom where there is inequity, no freedom where there is special favor or false barrier. Thus it follows that freedom can make no distinction, can practice no discrimination, other than its adherence to God's laws and Christ's teachings.

"Liberty and Tyranny"

It is important to think long and deep on the nature and properties of freedom for, as Abraham Lincoln wrote; "The world has never had a good definition of the word liberty, and the American people, just now, are much in want of one.

"We all declare for liberty, but in using the same word we do not all mean the same thing. With some the word liberty may mean for each man to do as he pleases with himself, and the product of his labor; while with others the same word may mean for some men to do as they please with other men, and the product of other men's labor. Here are two, not only different but incompatible things, called by the same name—liberty.

"And it follows that each of the things is, by the respective parties, called by two different and incompatible names—*liberty and tyranny.*"

Freedom and Atheism

Maximum individual freedom is most generally found within those nations where the laws of men are most in harmony with the laws of God.

That is not to say that an atheist cannot subscribe to the concept of personal freedom or the practice of liberty; many do.

As Leonard Read has written:

"Yes, you can be an atheist and, at the same time, believe in freedom. But, a society of active militant atheists will not be a free society."[9]

There are many atheists today who, while denying God, adhere to (the letter of) the laws God has set forth. But consider this: only those who truly comprehend the source of freedom can understand its parameters and recognize it for what it is—*in sum, an opportunity for man, through Christ, to regain that eternal life lost by Adam in Eden.*

The Most Exacting Form of All

Freedom is the most exacting form of civil government—it is, in fact, the most demanding state of all for man.

That is because freedom demands—depends upon—self-discipline from both the governed and the governing. *The foundation of freedom is self-government and the foundation of self-government is self-control.*

The very essence of practical Christianity is self-discipline, as taught by Jesus Christ. Christ does not force faith, or obedience, or good works upon us; that must be a personal decision and an internal regimen. And, "those who can thus govern themselves have little need for managerial government."[10]

No other form of civil government demands so much from each individual because in no other form of government is the individual so important. In other forms of government, the State is the central force; in the nation where freedom prevails, the individual is the central figure.

As Christian historian Verna Hall has pointed out, "Each religion has a form of government, and Christianity astonished the world by establishing self-government. With the landing of the Pilgrims in 1620, Christian self-government became the foundation stone of the United States of America."[11]

Rights and Responsibilities

We think of freedom and most often we think of "rights". But, freedom is not simply a matter of rights, it is also a matter of responsibilities. In fact, true freedom is a dynamic balance (self-imposed) of rights and responsibilities; for each right there is generally a corresponding and co-equal responsibility. *When this is understood it becomes clear that under freedom each individual really counts–and is accountable!*

Other forms of government are often motivated by appetite (either the personal appetite of the despot or the centralized appetite of the State, or the collective appetite of the mob). A government of freemen, if it is to survive, must operate on the basis of *self-restraint;* it cannot permit appetite to rule conscience or greed to violate equity.

In other societies–those fashioned by monarchs, or tyrants, or despotic councils–the individual can duck responsibility for the errors and the evils and the excesses of government. *But not freemen!* In self-government the individual is responsible for the acts of the State–no matter who holds office or who exercises the authority. For the citizen to think otherwise is to abdicate his powers. (For a development of this point, read Chapter Four, *Coercion–By Proxy.*)

Civil Laws

Freedom has certain laws.

Such laws are not simply–and sometimes not even–the statutes, codes, ordinances and regulations of "social control through law". Those are *civil laws,* extensions of the State carried down mainly from the Roman system. They are laws that now, as then, attempt to "spell out every detail and cover every situation".[12] These laws are evident in our lengthy Civil Codes governing almost every area of our lives–the laws (and supplementary administrative regulations*) that give life to the thousands of regulatory bodies, such as the municipal codes dealing with construction, sanitation, traffic, recreation, etc.

---

* Many of these administrative regulations have the force and effect of law.

Civil laws, in proper degree and application, are important in the maintenance of domestic tranquility. But, such laws are also dangerous; *their danger is that they can be proliferated, misused, misinterpreted, distorted and perverted.* These laws can get out of whack and out of bounds, requiring still more laws to set them straight and clear the air. Civil laws can be–and upon occasion have been–employed to restrict those freedoms they originally proposed to uphold. And in those instances, they magnify not liberty but license; they expand the sovereignty of the State rather than the primacy of the individual.

"The Laws of Nature"

There is another kind of law. It is called *Common Law.* It has its origins in the "Laws of Nature". These are the laws our founding fathers called upon when, in 1776, they made their Declaration of Independence to assume "the separate and equal station to which the Laws of Nature and Nature's God entitled them".

Webster's 1828 Dictionary defines the Law of Nature as

> "a rule of conduct arising out of the natural relations of human beings established by the Creator, and existing prior to any positive precept".

Webster's now defines natural law as

> "designating law discernible by reason as distinguished from law laid down in codes by state, church, etc."

Thus is Nature's God denied and man's reason glorified!

In essence, Common Law had its genesis in the internal, or Judaic-Christian, laws. Civil, or Roman, law is that external law or control that originated in the world's great pagan nation.[13]

"Organized Justice"

If we are to be free–truly free–the spirit of our laws must be in harmony with the Spirit of the Lord, and the letter of the law must be consistent with "the laws of nature and nature's God".

If they are not, they will violate us, our lives, our liberty and the various extensions of our selves–our possessions, our pursuit of happiness, etc.

The laws of freemen are established to preserve a system of "organized justice"; *their proper purpose and function is to protect the individual against injustice.*[14] Most basic laws spell out what man must *not* do to his fellow men, and what government must *not* do to the governed. Thus, these laws are "negative" in that they are not aggressive or tyrannical. Consider, for example, the Constitution of the United States (and the constitutions of most of the states):

"Congress shall make *no* laws . . . The right of the people shall *not* be abridged . . . or denied . . . or disparaged . . .".*

Toward the same end of freedom, most of our basic laws do not tell the individual what he or she must do–that is left to individual decision within the dictum that the exercise of such freedom must not interfere with the equal freedom of others.

Fundamental Laws of Freedom

Consider these basic, bed-rock, laws of nature and nature's God; the fundamental laws of freedom:

"Thou shalt love The Lord thy God with all thy heart and with all thy mind and with all thy soul."[15] That is the great commandment. *God first, last and always.*

"In all thy ways acknowledge Him and He will direct thy paths."[16]

"Thou shalt have no other gods before Me." No graven images, no false idols, no golden calves, no strange shepherds.

"For the kingdom is The Lord's and He is the governor among the nations."[17] Good government is necessary and is an extension of God's laws but when you exchange God for Caesar, you're bound to be short-changed, and long-chained.

Those are laws concerning the Fatherhood–and the Sovereignty–of God.

---

* See reference to R. J. Rushdoony, page 4-5, Chapter Four.

And, these are the laws concerning the brotherhood of man, in Christ:

"Thou shalt love thy neighbor as thyself."[18] There is no cop out there; no rip off, no easy ride.

"Do unto others as you would that they would do unto you."[19] There it is, the balance of rights and responsibilities.

Those are the laws that make men free. The laws that put man and his laws in harmony with God and God's laws. *"The man who looks into the perfect law of liberty, and continues therein, this man shall be blessed in his deed."*[20]

If you love God, if you love others as yourself, you will not covet, you will not steal their possessions, you will not bear false witness, you will not injure their person. No murders, no assaults, no undue interference in the lives of others; no violations of their rights, no trespassing on their freedom.

Freedom is in the Spirit of The Lord—not just "is" but lives, and moves, and thrives. And, what are the fruits of the Spirit?

Love, joy, peace, long-suffering, gentleness, goodness, faith, meekness, self-control.[21]

Seek first the Kingdom of God and all these things shall be added unto you. So it is with individuals. And so it is with nations. *"Blessed is the nation whose God is The Lord!"*[22]

Freedom and Christian Economics

There are certain basics—certain immutables—that should govern freedom-seeking Christians in their economic activities. These are the laws—*the source laws*—founded on God's laws and Christ's teachings. They provide for the application of the Christian ethic that gives free enterprise its purpose and its bounds.

It is certainly true that man is not meant to live by bread alone. Yet, as F. A. Harper wrote:

> *"It seems correct to say that economic liberty pervades the entire problem of liberty."*[23]

Thus, it is important that Christians examine some of the basics of Christian economics.* These basics should be practiced in concert with God's instructions and Christ's examples on love and charity (economic activity is what generally makes possible the material expression of love through charity). It is vital to keep in mind that all things come from The Lord and that we are His stewards.

Our practice of Christian economics is one manifestation of our stewardship to Him.

Some Christian "Laws" of Economics

1. THE LAW OF DYNAMIC BALANCE (The Law of Harmony)

When God created the heavens and the earth–and man, He put everything into perfect balance. Not some static, stagnant limbo but a dynamic balance. There was harmony, life, growth and abundance.

Our lives, our economic relationships with our fellow humans, are meant to have that same type of dynamic balance.

Consider the dynamism and the perfect balance of the Golden Rule. If we obey Christ's instruction, we achieve a dynamic balance between our rights and our responsibilities. There is harmony in the "give" and "take" of our work-a-day world.

It is the dynamic balance of the Golden Rule that gives free enterprise the thrust and equilibrium to create, to produce and to achieve yet keeps free enterprise from becoming an unrestricted "hunting license". Properly maintained, that balance enables the competitive enterprise of freemen to out-produce other systems while avoiding the excesses of greed, control and coercion–whether by cartel, centralized government, or labor monopoly.

It is a dynamic balance that assures the workman a "fair" (proper) wage, the entrepreneur a "fair" profit, and the investor a "fair" return on his capital. When that balance is upset, when one factor

---

* For additional consideration of the economic principles of freemen, see the *Ten Pillars of Economic Wisdom* in the book *How We Live* by Fred Clark and Richard Rimanoczy. For a more definitive and scholarly examination of these principles and Biblical references, read the Chalcedon Study, *An Introduction To Christian Economics* by Dr. Gary North.

of the relationship is given (or takes) more than it should, dynamism ceases and stagnation takes over; cooperation devolves into dissension, harmony breaks down into discord, decay replaces growth, loss wipes out profit and job security fades into unemployment.

The opposite of dynamic balance is distortion–the distortion of greed, ruthlessness, monopoly and coercion (violence). The headstrong, self-centered desire to seize special privilege at the cost to others has deprived the human race of untold treasures because of uncreated wealth.

Extreme distortion in our economic relationships often takes the form of exploitation, strikes, or wars; these oppress countless individuals and depress man's material welfare.

Consider a stereo. When it is in proper adjustment, there is a perfect–a dynamic–balance between the speakers. The result is brilliant harmony and beautiful music. But, turn the controls so that one set of speakers blanks out the others. What happens? The balance and the dynamism is gone. One speaker prevails to the detriment of the others and the whole. Harmony is destroyed and the totality of the music is lost.

It is much the same with our economic affairs. Let one party "take" more than it "gives" and there is distortion. The dynamic balance is gone; the totality of harmonious production is destroyed and negative forces prevail. Everyone involved is the loser.

2. *THE LAW OF PRODUCTIVITY*

The law of productivity is always at work, whether *we* apply it or not. If we work, and produce, we have; if we do not work, we do not produce and we go without, or take from others who do.* If no one works, if no one produces, there is nothing for anyone. If we produce at a marginal level–because of undue interference or controls, or work restrictions, or lack of capital and tools–productivity diminishes and there is less to go around.

Everything man produces involves three basic elements: natural resources, human energies, and tools. The fundamental formula for man's productive capacity is MMW = NR + HE × T; *Man's*

---

*"The man who is slothful in his work is brother to him who is a great waster." Prov. 18:9

Material Welfare equals Natural Resources plus Human Energies multiplied by Tools.

The Law of Productivity functions best (provides more goods and services for the greatest number of persons at the lowest possible price) in societies where men and women are free to use their talents and their energies to create, to increase their skills and replenish their tools, and to convert natural resources into useful products.

Natural resources are God's gift; they are God's creation. There is much we can do to conserve natural resources but we cannot create them; thus, natural resources are limited. As God's stewards it is our responsibility to use these resources wisely.

Human energy is also one of God's gifts; one of the attributes of God with which He endowed us. Each individual is blessed with certain mental and muscular energies. As good and faithful stewards, we should develop these to their maximum. But, human energies are also limited.

Tools are man's creation, extensions of himself that enable him to increase his potential (wheels and wings are extensions of man's limbs; computers are an extension of man's mind; hammers, cameras, telephones, surgical instruments, drill presses, these are extensions of his hands and fingers, and senses—his sight, hearing, feel, speech, etc.). Tools enable man to do more and to produce more.

Tools are made possible through the savings and investments of individuals. Such savings and investments occur most readily when law (government) protects the individual's right to control his own property and his right to use that property as he chooses.

The more widely held the ownership of tools (the means of production) the greater the total production and the greater the choice of products. When the State controls (confiscates) investment capital and also controls the means of production, total productivity declines and free choice disappears.

3. THE LAW OF DISTRIBUTION

We cannot distribute more than we produce; we cannot give what we do not have; we have no right to distribute (give away) what we do not own—that is the law of distribution.

Translated into the vernacular that reads: before we can sell we must create, before we can give we must earn, before we can teach we must learn.

It is possible to produce enough to meet man's needs. This can best be achieved, the records demonstrate, through the efforts of freemen in a free economy acting as God's good and faithful stewards.

It is virtually impossible to produce more than man wants. What we term overproduction *(surplus)* is actually unbalanced production; too much of one commodity. What we call underproduction *(shortage)* is also a sign of unbalanced production. If the dynamics of supply and demand are allowed to prevail, overproduction will be adjusted and the surplus will be consumed or converted. In the same manner, underproduction will be corrected and the shortage will be alleviated.

Such decisions of production and distribution are best made in the market place, by the consumer. Permitting the consumers to determine the law of distribution is an extension of individual freedom. Permitting government to make such decisions through centralized controls is a diminution of freedom and leads to shortages, surpluses, waste, inefficiency, increased costs and unmet demands.

When quantities of goods remain undistributed *(unsold)* it is not necessarily due to a lack of money. The production of goods always generates a commensurate purchasing power; the money paid for production (in salaries and wages and fees for services and materials purchased) is enough to buy what has been produced. The lack of sales indicates that what has been produced is not satisfactory (not wanted by the consumer) because of price, quality or need.

There are two ways to "move" unsold goods. The natural way is to lower the price until the customer cannot resist the "bargain". The unnatural way is to freeze the price (and the wages and other costs involved in the production) and to pump unearned "money" into people's pockets thus prodding them into the purchase (the impression of "cheap money" encourages the purchase of "uncheap" merchandise). This is a controlled–and ersatz–economy. The consumer pays more in the long run–through inflation, taxation, and loss of control of the market place.

4. THE LAW OF COMPENSATION

This is the law of returns–of sowing and reaping. *"Whatever a man sows, that and that only will he reap"* (Gal. 6:7).

We are instructed to "sow in righteousness and reap in mercy". We can testify to God's infinite generosity. *"Give and it shall be given unto you; good measure, pressed down, and shaken together, and running over. . . . with the same measure you use, it shall be measured to you in return"* (Luke 6:38). Give–meaning not only acts of love and charity but also give, meaning a full day's work for a full day's pay and full value for dollars received for the products or services we sell.

What is the basis for deciding what share of the total production those involved in the production of goods or the performance of services shall receive? There are two answers to that question: the first is the answer of free market economics and the second is the answer of Christian stewardship; they are completely compatible.

First the answer in economic terms.

In a regimented society (a controlled or managed market), the decision of who gets what is made by the State or a sub-State. The master of the unfree people decides their lot. Government is not an impartial (defensive) agent, it is the controller. In such a society the individual exists between a floor and ceiling impressed by the State. There is little, if any, room to grow; no latitude for bargaining, no freedom to accept or reject or withdraw.

In a society of freemen, the laws of nature prevail to see that each party receives a proper (fair) share. What is the proper share for each? The impartial and equitable laws of the free market will determine that–if allowed to operate from the top to the bottom. That means:

- *no restrictions that prevent the employe and the employer from deciding between themselves on an equitable wage and an acceptable working environment*
- *no restrictions that prevent the employe and the employer from deciding between themselves on an equitable wage and an acceptable working environment*
- *no restrictions that prevent the employer from designing and producing and pricing his goods or services, and*
- *no restrictions that restrain or constrain the consumer in his free choice of purchases (the expenditure of his personal funds).*

All of that is essential to the workings and justice of the free market—the best answer to economic justice man can reach. Those who deny the efficacy of any or all of those parts imply that all employes are stupid, or weak-kneed; that all employers are stupid, or greedy, and that all consumers are stupid, or defenseless. The day-to-day record of the dynamics of the free market disprove their insinuations.

Now, the answer of the "fair" (proper) share in terms of the Christian ethic:

- *observe the equilibrium implicit in the implementation of the Golden Rule*
- *act according to the amplification of that rule in employe-employer relations as set forth and applied in Colossians 3:23-4:1.*

"Whatever may be your task, work at it heartily as something done for The Lord and not for men, knowing with all certainty that you will receive the inheritance that is your real reward. *The one you are actually serving is Christ, The Lord.* He who deals wrongly will reap the fruit of his folly and be punished for his wrongdoing. With God there is no partiality, no matter what a person's position may be (employe or employer).

"Employers, for your part, deal with your workman justly and fairly, knowing you also have a Master in heaven."

- and, remember this: *"There are many members, yet one body. The eye cannot say to the hand, I have no need of you; nor again the head to the feet, I have no need of you. When one member suffers, all members suffer with the body."*

Thus, God's laws of harmony and dynamic balance can bring peace and well-being.

5. THE LAW OF PRIVATE PROPERTY

Implicit in God's commandments (Exodus 20:15,17) is the right of the individual to have private property. To have and hold and use it for himself and his own purposes as long as he does not infringe upon the equal rights of his fellow man.

And Paul, in Acts 5:4, underscores that right:

"(Ananias) Before you sold the property it belonged to you, and after you sold it the money was yours." Ananias' sin was not in owning and controlling the use of his property, it was in lying

to God.

Hannah, the mother of the Prophet Samuel, reminds us that God is the source of all wealth, that it is He who decides how it will be distributed and who will hold what measure of wealth as His steward. Who is Caesar, then, to second-guess God and overrule His decision?

Christ had the opportunity to play socialist–to take property from one and give to another. Remember? Luke tells about it in 12:13-14.

One of the group Jesus was with came up to Him and asked, "Master, speak to my brother. Tell him to divide with me the property our father left as an inheritance." But Jesus rejected the suggestion. "Man, who made Me a judge, or a divider over you?" And He turned to the crowd and warned, "Take heed. Beware of covetousness . . ."

The legal recognition and protection of each individual's right to acquire and hold property is an essential of law and order; it is one of the necessities of freedom. Property, in an earthly sense, is an extension of self. To destroy or control a man's right to own and use his property is to diminish the individual.

In diminishing the individual, we diminish freedom and we injure society. When the individual is not free to expand to his maximum potential society is not able to grow and improve to its maximum. Thus, both the individual and society (both the private and public sectors) suffer.

Consider how society has benefitted because men were free to search, to discover God's laws of science, to harness those laws, to earn and own and invest. Look at the by-products of such freedom! Electricity for heat and light and power, automobiles, antibiotics, frozen foods, dried foods, canned foods, petrochemicals, radio, television, telephones–and on and on. The list is endless, as are the numbers of jobs and the benefits and the support of public services (taxes) that have flowed through the release of such private ingenuity and the acquisition and use of such private property.

Laws that confiscate, restrict, or aggressively control–or permit others to infringe upon or control–the free use, exchange, sale, purchase or development of private property (including abilities, talents and tools) violate the individual and destroy untold benefits and opportunities for countless individuals in God's world.

6. THE LAW OF UNIQUENESS

This is sometimes called the "law of (infinite) variation." Whatever the term, it underscores the wonders of God's world.

Each and every inividual is equal in the sight of God, the Creator. Just so, each and every individual is (or should be) equal in the eyes of man's law.

But, no two persons are "equal" in all respects. There is an enormous difference in the talents, desires, abilities, motivations, and physical characteristics of each individual. And, Praise The Lord! What a dull place this would be if we were all stamped from the same mold!

The magic of the society of freemen is that it permits each individual to be different and provides each individual the opportunity to develop his uniqueness.

The United States, because of its Christian origins, was the first nation in history to put this magic to work . . . by releasing it; by defending and protecting the right of each and every individual to "fly as high as his vision and his abilities can take him". That is the promise and the secret of America, under God.

When God made man in His image, He endowed him with a free will and set him forth as a free agent. Thus, we know that we are in harmony with God's laws when we defend and protect man's freedom to be what he wants to be; his accountability is, in the final analysis, to God. Glory to God for His wisdom: this freedom of uniqueness provides us with such a range of choice and decision, such an infinite variety of products and opportunities–not to covet or to worship but to use to be "fruitful, to subdue and to have dominion" as His stewards.

There is also a scientific explanation (another one of God's laws of science) for the superior economic progress of freemen. It is called the "results of divergent phenomena"; the progress that is generated when two or more things are combined without any prior knowledge of what will happen. This has been termed "the alchemy of cooperative individuals". It is a synergistic relationship in which each distinct and independent part contributes to the whole and the sum total is greater than the combined contributions of those involved.

Essential to the recognition of individual uniqueness is the recognition of the proper role of incentive and reward. He who works harder, and achieves more, and contributes more, is entitled to receive more. What he does with what he receives is up to him.

Some would weaken, or repeal, the law of uniqueness–in effect if not in fact; they would enforce *equality* of reward *for inequality* of work. This is counterproductive; it leads to equal performance, at the *lowest* level. When that happens, everyone suffers. The first attempts at "communal living" by the early Christians and Pilgrims and the utter failure and general misery that resulted are cases in point.

7. THE LAW OF PREDICTABLE MONEY

Money is a medium of exchange.

We receive money as a receipt when we sell something (services or products). We spend that receipt at a later time when we purchase someone else's products or services.

That money is "best" that does not lose its value between the time we receive it and the time we spend it. Money that depreciates in value diminishes the worth of the individual, his abilities and his energies. Such money–that depreciates in that manner–steals from the worker, the consumer, the investor. Thus, it is an immoral commodity; it plunders the fruits of the individual's labors and/or savings.

The monetary system that comes closest to achieving the ideal of predictable money is the **"gold standard".** Under that system, gold is given a fixed value and the amount of money issued is tied directly to the amount of gold in hand or in circulation. Under the gold standard, the holder of money (receipts backed by gold) knows that his holdings have a constant (predictable) value and that no one will steal part of his earnings between the time he is paid and the time he spends his money.

Most politicians do not like the gold standard. That is because it enforces a monetary discipline that curbs their appetites and clips their wings. But, it protects the freeman from monetary exploitation–the swindle of inflation.

Inflation is the cruelest tax of all; it is deceptive. It confiscates the value of your money while leaving the money in your pocket. Thus, the actual value (the purchasing power) of your money is no longer predictable; your worth (the worth of your labors and talents) is subject to the whims of those who rewrite those receipts (money) you received for the sales of your goods and services. Inflation is not possible when the value of money is protected and assured. Conversely, it is impossible to have predictable money when inflation occurs.

Rising prices and wages and costs are not the cause of inflation; they are the consequences. Only government can cause inflation. **Inflation is an increase in the money supply (currency and credit).**

Government policies that permit (encourage) the money supply to increase faster than the productivity of the nation–that is the cause of inflation. Government causes inflation

- *when it prints money that has not been earned ("fake" money that has no backing), and*
- *when it permits banks and lending institutions to "create" money by loaning that which they do not have on deposit.*

This "created" (fake) money reduces the purchasing power of all money; that loss in purchasing power is one way to measure the tax of inflation.

Inflation is an economic cancer; it is deadly. Scientists are searching for a cure for cancer of the human body. We already have the cure for cancer of the economic body–*remove the cause:*

> Halt the increase in the supply of ersatz currency and credit, reduce government spending and balance the federal budget–and prohibit deficit spending. (For a more substantive study of the cause and consequences of inflation see Chapter Eleven, *Inflation Is Killing America.*)

CHAPTER FOUR

Coercion–By Proxy

Christians, especially, should know that the use of force or violence is a *no-no* . . . something to be condoned or employed only as a last-resort effort to protect themselves, their families, and sometimes their property.

Christ commands us to love one another.[1] Paul instructs us that love is the fulfilling of the law.[2] Not some maudlin, squishy, of-the-moment and needle-pointed passion but honest, deep-down love that moves us to do unto others as we would have them do unto us (or, *not* do unto others what we would *not* want them to do unto us).*

* The very finest definition of love–in all of its dimensions and the full spectrum of its beauty–is found in 1 Cor. 13: 1-13. An excellent dissertation on that passage of Scripture is Henry Drummond's *The Greatest Thing in The World.*

How is it, then, that every day we engage in coercion?
That every day we force others to act against their will and violate their lives and liberty?

Sic Semper—By Proxy!

You say you do not do such things? That you do not resort to coercion or violence against your fellow-men? Well, take a look at what you are doing, every day. Consider these acts of coercion:

—millions of Americans are forced each day to subsidize government-financed abortions even though that violates their religious beliefs and moral convictions;

—millions upon millions of Americans are coerced into paying for public school materials (books, films, reading aids) that offend their sense of decency and their religion and their patriotism;

—millions upon millions of American working people are forced to join labor unions in order to acquire or keep their jobs;

—hundreds upon thousands of employers have lost the right to hire and fire their own employes, or set their own standards, and many employers have lost the right to go out of business when they choose to;

—young people are kept out of jobs and many are prevented from earning the money for their education because minimum wage laws shut them out of the job market, and

—businessmen, in every state and every community, are daily coerced into serving, without fee or free will, as our governmental bookkeepers, accountants and file clerks.

There's more:

—in the name of "art and culture", taxpayers are coerced into subsidizing theaters, painters, orchestras and dance groups.*

---

*It is not a matter of being low-brow, or anti-art, or anti-music; it is a matter of being *for* the right of each individual to decide, for himself or herself, whether to support such cultural activities. Let those who love the arts support the arts to whatever extent they are able; let those who feel otherwise be free to support their personal avocation—whether it be bowling, or basket-weaving . . . or doing nothing at all.

–in the name of equality and "balance" millions of youngsters of all colors and creeds and family background are coerced into wayward buses that haul them to schools outside their local neighborhoods;

–in the name of "providing public service" hundreds of thousands of our elderly are driven from their homes by arbitrary and ever-rising assessments and taxes on their property;

–in the name of "spread-the-work", millions of Americans, thousands of employers, and hundreds of thousands of unemployed, are coerced into subsidizing featherbedding, dead-heading and other wasteful make-work practices, and

–in the name of "fair trade", citizens are forced to forego the benefits and energies of the free and open market.

How Does This Come To Pass?

You may object to such coercion. You may insist that you gave government no such proxy for interferences into the lives of other individuals, let alone your own. You may even stoutly proclaim your belief that each and every individual should be free to "do his thing"–as long as he does not interfere with any other individual's right to do his thing.

Well, then, if citizens never voted their proxies for such governmental excesses, how do these things come to pass?

They come to pass when citizens refuse to consider all the consequences of their proxied actions;

they come to pass when appetite is larger than conscience;

when apathy is stronger than conviction;

when convenience, or comfort, overrides "Thou shalt not covet" and ignores "Thou shalt not steal",

they come to pass when government is mis-used to cater to pressure groups and special interest blocs rather than to defend the rights of all the people, and

they come to pass because we fail to get out and support candidates who are committed to the cause of freedom.

Liberty vs. Coercion

There are always some who will be quick to justify collectivized coercion. They can find one thousand and one excuses to defend such use of force. Yet not all of their arguments equal the one reason to oppose such coercion: *the violation of individual liberty.*

Generally, but not always, the defenders of coercion are those who benefit from it; the recipient of the subsidy, the beneficiary of the taxpayer's funds, the person who is pushed to the front of the line. And, when their spoils are challenged, they are quick to respond:

"You just don't want government to do anything. You must be against any kind of government, period!"

That is an unwarranted accusation. It is as specious as suggesting that one is against religion because he is opposed to state religion. Or, that he is against medicine because he is opposed to government control of physicians.

Government is necessary and need not be evil. As F. A. Harper wrote: "For liberty to be at its maximum, there must be some government. . . ."[3]

For Mutual Protection

We, the people, perpetuate government and "loan" it certain powers to provide for the common defense, to insure domestic tranquility and to achieve a general well-being (a society of law and order). Such "loans" are voluntary actions on our part—freely taken in an effort to secure the blessings of liberty. Since the powers reside in government by the consent of the governed, in return for certain specific services, there is no coercion involved. We act in concert for mutual and equal benefit; government is our servant.

The Apostle Paul assures us that "civil government is not a terror to people of good conduct but to those of bad behavior."[4] The Apostle Peter advises us that the proper function of government is "to punish those who do wrong and to encourage those who do well".[5] In other words, to protect the law-abiding from the law-breaker.

Christians are supportive of good government. We recognize our obligation to uphold the civil authorities and to pray they will exercise wisdom and equity in their duties. At the same time, government has an obligation to us: it must stay within the bounds we have established and it must not abuse the powers we have "loaned" it.

The Constitution makes some 80 grants of power to the federal government and establishes 115 prohibitions ("thou shalt nots") against it. It gives the Congress 20 grants of power and places it under 70 restraints.[6] And, "the powers not specifically delegated to the United States, nor specifically prohibited to it by the States, are reserved to the States respectively, *or to the people.*"[7]

To Protect and Defend

Thanks to our God-directed founding fathers, the powers and functions of government are (or were, at least) severely restricted and essentially *defensive:*

To protect and defend the individual–his life, liberty and property–from those who might engage in violence . . . including government, itself.

In 1850, in his pamphlet, *The Law,* French economist and statesman Frederic Bastiat wrote:

"Life, faculties, production–in other words, individuality, liberty, property . . . in spite of the cunning of artful political leaders, these three gifts from God precede all human legislation and are superior to it.

"Life, liberty, and property, do not exist because men have made laws. On the contrary, it is the fact that life, liberty, and property, existed beforehand that caused men to make laws in the first place.

"What, then, is law (government)? It is the collective organization of the individual (God-given) right to lawful defense."[8]

Consider the essence of Bastiat's contention:

–each person has (from God) the right to defend his person, his liberty, and his property; it therefore follows that men have the right to organize and support a common force (government) to defend those rights in equal measure for all men.

Limited Government

Leonard Read, in his *Meditations on Freedom,* distinguishes between the good and the evil in government:

"Governments—assuming a proper limitation of their activities—are necessary and not evil. Their evil begins when they step out of bounds. The necessity is that their evil actions be discontinued." [9]

When does government "step out of bounds"? When does government cease to be good and practice evil? Well, to paraphrase Bastiat:

—since no man has the right to force his will upon another man (or act aggressively against his life, his liberty, or property) then no group of men (or government) can lawfully employ such coercion against other men.

These are the "bounds"—the fences—that contain government in a society of free individuals. Let's go over them again:

By mutual consent we can assign (or loan) government certain of the rights (powers) we possess. Thus, government becomes an extension of ourselves. But, we cannot give to other men, or government, rights we as individuals do not possess. Not even by common consent, not even by majority vote. To violate another individual's unalienable rights via the ballot is to legalize the law of the jungle. To endorse the violence implicit in the suggestion that "might is right" is to deny God's laws.

So, there is the evil:

—when government ceases to be a defensive instrument and becomes a coercive weapon

—when it engages in violence against the peaceful

—when it restricts the liberty of the law-abiding

—when it confiscates a citizen's property for its own or someone else's profit . . .

. . . then government is evil. Then it ceases to be in harmony with God's laws and judgements, and then "Thou shalt not covet" is set aside, "Thou shalt not steal" is ignored, and the Golden Rule is revised to read:

"Do unto others before they do unto to you—and get government to help you if you can."

The Roots of Coercion

Coercion most often finds its roots in greed and selfishness; in looking for those shortcuts to get what is wanted without working for it. Sometimes it takes the form of "getting a law" to give one industry an edge over its competition; what cannot be achieved through brains, initiative and energy is acquired by "using" the law. Sometimes such "legalized" coercion is employed to avoid the disciplines of the free market–for labor or product. When business or union demands such "rights" (which are not government's to give) they are no different than the individual who demands welfare payments as a "right".

But, legalized coercion is not always generated by greed or selfishness; sometimes it is motivated by good intentions; by a desire to protect the individual from his own stupidities (in such instances it is always "the other fellow" who is stupid).

Social Security is one example of good intentions. It was spawned on the argument that the average American does not have enough foresight, or self-discipline, to save for a rainy day or for retirement. Thus, legalized coercion was employed to implement the good intention of helping Joe Bagadonuts put something aside for his old age. Individual decision (voluntarism) was pushed aside in favor of compulsion–and all under the banner of good intentions.

Sometimes legalized coercion is generated by someone's desire to "improve our culture"–to bring us the "finer" things in life.

The millions upon millions of taxpayer dollars spent each year on the National Endowment of the Arts (and the millions more coerced through matching funds at the State level) is an example of this. It is assumed by the proponents of this "improvement society" that the average person of his own accord will not spend enough to keep the opera, or the ballet, or the art gallery, in business. Instead, he spends his earnings on such foolishness as fishing tackle, bowling balls and hotdogs at the stadium. Thus he must be coerced (via taxation) into supporting the arts and culture–because those finer things are "good" for society. *Art can, indeed, be uplifting but not at the cost of coercion.*

How To Recognize Coercion

If we were to witness one man physically (violently) forcing another individual to act against his will, we would recognize that as an obvious and direct use of coercion and we would know the act was illegal. The law-breaker would be held accountable, and punished.

"Legalized" coercion is not always so obvious—often because it is cloaked in the folds of the law. Yet the violence is there and the perpetrator is seldom held accountable, or punished. Usually, it is only when such "legalized" coercion is employed against us that we object and demand justice. None-the-less, "It is important to remember that government interference always means violent action or the threat of such action." [10]

How does one recognize the signs of "legalized" coercion? How does an individual who does not wish to have done to others in his name what he does not want done to himself detect the subtle compulsion of Caesar?

Try this yardstick for size:

—*any law or government action that forces an individual to act against his will, or his best and legitimate interests, is coercion.*
(Example: using wage and price controls to force a person to pay more—or less—than a product or service is worth.)

—*any law or government action that restricts an individual in his peaceful pursuits and free choice is coercion.*
(Example: forcing an individual to join—or not join—a union or association or group to gain employment or practice his skill, profession or trade.)

—*any law that takes from one individual what belongs to him (i.e. confiscates his belongings) and gives that to someone else to whom it does not belong, is coercion.*
(Example: welfare laws that forced a 59-year-old father in Sacramento, Calif., to support an able-bodied 31-year-old son who was receiving public assistance and refused a $600-a-month job at a service station because it was beneath his dignity.)

—*any law or governmental action that does for an individual, or a group, that which he does not have the right to do on his own or for himself is coercion–legalized but still coercion.* (Example: forcing citizens in Montgomery, Ala., or Cutbank, Mont., to pay part of the costs of installing a new sewer plant in Loomis, Calif.)

"Legalized Plunder"

There are basically two ways an individual can earn a living:

1. *by applying himself* (his energies, his talents, his capital) to provide services to others or to change the form, condition and location of a natural resource into a product of value to himself or others. Thus he acquires property–either goods or a medium of exchange (money).
2. *by seizing (stealing) that which belongs to another individual.*

Ever since Adam disobeyed God and was booted out of the Garden of Eden, man has been forced to earn his bread by the sweat of his brow. And ever since then, most men have been looking for shortcuts–ways to get what they need or want with a minimum of work.

Some men have harnessed the energies of nature (the sun, winds, water) to expand their own energies and thus ease their work. Others have discovered or invented or purchased machines and systems to amplify their efforts and multiply their producive capacities.

And, some men steal–rob, confiscate, plunder. Plunder is most often the purpose of coercion.

There are two types of plunder: illegal, and "legalized".

It is not difficult to recognize illegal plunder.

Suppose a crook breaks into a store and robs the till. Or, suppose he robs a bank. That is illegal plunder, punishable by law.

Suppose a gang of crooks busts into a town meeting and robs everyone in the room. Makes them turn over their valuables. That is plunder on a mass scale, and that is also illegal.

But, suppose someone knocks on your door, or walks into your place of business, and compels you to hand over a certain sum of money by threat of force (fine or imprisonment). Perhaps this individual walks into your store and forces you to give him all or part of the money you were planning to use to buy more merchandise, or new equipment, or to build an addition so that you could enlarge your trade. That is plunder, but it's legal . . . at least, it's "legalized".

By Proxy—Again

How come it's legalized? *Because the fellow is an agent of government.* He is acting for we, the people—by proxy. You and your friends and neighbors—or your elected representatives or unelected public officials—have empowered that agent to confiscate the citizens' property. *It's called taxation.*

Or, take another example of legalized plunder; one more difficult to detect. Suppose you manage to save some money over a period of time. Let's say you save $1,000 to buy something the family needs or you want. You go down to the store ready to make the purchase and the clerk informs you that what you want no longer costs $1,000—the price is now $1,500. You are $500 short. Why? Because your dollars are not worth what they were. While you were saving, government was spending; it spent about one-half of the value of your dollars. *That is inflation*—and that is legalized plunder, too.

Mis-use of "The Law"

Such "legalized" plunder is not always recognized and is often promoted:

tariffs, subsidies, progressive taxation, minimum wages, guaranteed jobs, guaranteed profits and wages, wage and price controls, the "right" to welfare (at various income levels)—*these are just a few examples of such legalized plunder.*

They are not prohibited by law, they are practiced within the cloak of the law—ones we enacted, by proxy. The perpetrators of such plunder are not punished; they are protected and usually elected and re-elected to office. Thus, the law ceases to defend justice; it becomes a system for organized injustice.

Not All Taxes Are Plunder

Are all taxes "legalized" plunder? No!

We are instructed to "render unto Caesar that which is Caesars". The money needed to enable government to perform certain necessary and legitimate functions (as established by the governed) is not plunder; it is a voluntary assessment–a willing commitment of a certain percentage of our property to support the proper and defensive activities of the law (government).

The plunder begins when government takes unto itself powers and functions never given by the people; when it acts without the consent of the governed; when it takes from one individual and gives to another.

That is stealing; that is mis-use of the power to tax, and that is "legalized" plundering.

"Predatory Practices"

"The Chinese scholar, Chang Hsin-hai, in his *The Moral Basis of World Peace,* asserts that this disease of our society stems from a double standard of morals. He says that the root of our troubles, both national and international, lies in the acceptance of moral standards in government totally different from those accepted and demonstrated as necessary for a good society so far as individual conduct is concerned." [11]

"At the root of the double standard of moral conduct, to which Chang Hsin-hai refers, is the accepted belief that many forms of *predatory practices,* when conducted under the name of government, are honorable acts. On that premise has been built a progressive encroachment on the liberty of individuals, which passes as 'progressive' in politics." [12]

Which Choice?

As Frederic Bastiat suggests, we should settle the matter of legalized plunder once and for all and, he wrote, there are three ways we can go about it. We can decide, by law, that:

1. a few may plunder the many.
2. everybody can plunder anybody.
3. no one may plunder anybody.

Deciding on the *first choice* would be to maintain many aspects of our so-called democratic system under which we are now governed. The problem with this—it's nothing more than "nascent socialism"—is that such an arrangement cannot remain static; in such a "thieves market" those who want *more* plunder will always have license to barter with those who want *some* plunder—and those who want *power.* Thus the cancer breeds and grows until it becomes choice number two.

The *second choice* we know as communism: the State takes all and gives all. In such a society the State becomes a god and competes with God in the workings of mankind.

The *third choice* is liberty. It is the way things should be in a society where man wishes to be free; a system wherein the law (government) is truly an instrument of organized justice upholding the rights of all men.

Which choice is ours?

In which nations, under which system and through what use of the law, have individuals prospered most in terms of personal liberty and material welfare? Where are *the most peaceful, the most moral, and the happiest people?*

"Those people are found in the countries where the law least interferes with private affairs; where government is least felt; where the individual has the greatest scope and free opinion the greatest influence; where administrative powers are fewest and simplest; where taxes are lightest and most nearly equal . . .

". . . *where individuals and groups most actively assume their responsibilities and, consequently, where the morals of admittedly imperfect human beings are constantly improving . . . (and) where the inventions of men are most nearly in harmony with the laws of God;*

"in short, the happiest, most moral and most peaceful people are those who most nearly follow this principle:

"Although mankind is not perfect, still, all hope rests upon the free and voluntary actions of persons within the limits of right; law or force is to be used for nothing except the administration of universal justice."

In other words, "try liberty; for liberty is an acknowledgement of faith in God and His works." [13]

CHAPTER FIVE

GOD'S "SUPER" STRUCTURE: THE FAMILY

"There are few statements today about the opportunity and the obligation of a Christian home in a republic. Yet, there is no single element in America which contributes more significantly to the success of Christian Constitutional government.

"It is in the home where the foundations of Christian character are laid. It is in the home where Christian self-government is learned and practised." [1]

The family is God's "super" structure.

It is his basic unit in society.

Through the family God established His line of authority* so that His people could live in peace, and harmony and righteousness.

Love is the mortar that bonds the home into a unit; home is

---

* From The Heavenly Father to the earthly father as head of the household and from him to the wife and mother and thence to the children, ranked by age.

the building block and the very foundation of the nation. If that foundation is strong, the society will endure; if the family unit weakens—or is destroyed—society will decline, and fall.

Super states may be built by governments, by tyrants and politburos. But, truly great nations—God-based, God-centered societies that free men's souls and send their spirits soaring—are built by righteous people.

"Where the Spirit of The Lord is, there is liberty!" [2]

And righteous people come from righteous homes.

"Train up a child in the way he should go and when he is old he will not depart from it." [3]

From Generation to Generation

The influence of the home and family life preserves the "current of life from one generation to another".[4]

Like father, like mother, like son and like daughter.

"The sterling worth of George Washington is a testimony to the formative power of paternal instruction. John Quincy Adams, even when his eloquence thundered through our legislative halls and caused a nation to startle from her slumber, bent his aged form before God and repeated the prayer of his childhood." [5]

When there is a Sarah in the home, there is generally an Isaac in the cradle. When there is a Eunice teaching a Timothy from the Scriptures, there will usually be a Timothy teaching the Gospel to mankind.[6]

Napoleon knew the power of the home:

"What France wants is good mothers, and you may be sure then that France will have good sons."

What America needs is more Christian husbands and wives, more Christian fathers and mothers—and you may be sure then that America will have Christian sons and daughters.

Strong Homes, Strong Nation

If we are to rebuild our nation we must first strengthen our homes and make sure they are Christ-centered. Husbands and wives must assume the full responsibilities of Christian parents so that children may walk in the ways of The Lord.

Husbands, love your wives.[7]

As Christ loved the church and gave His life for it.

Love your wives as you love your own bodies.

"For this reason, a man will leave his father and mother, and unite with his wife, and the two will become one."

Wives, be obedient unto your husbands.[8]

Submit yourselves to him as to The Lord.

And be his helpmeet.

And love him as he loves you. For the two of you are one.

Children, obey your parents.[9]

That is the Christian thing to do.

Honor thy father and thy mother . . .

. . . so that all may be well with you and you may live a long time in the land.

Parents, raise your children with Christian discipline and instruction.

Do not irritate them. Teach them with love.

Lest they be discouraged.

Finally—husbands and wives, parents and children—build up your strength in union with The Lord and by means of His mighty power. Put on the whole armor of God. You will need it to withstand the Devil's tricks and snares.[10]

Be persistent in prayer. And Praise The Lord.

Family Functions

In *The Christian in Society,* Earle E. Cairns emphasizes that the family is "an institution coming from the hand of God Himself for the good of man". Cairns outlines three major functions associated with the origin of the family:[11]

1. The moral and spiritual function

To develop love, forbearance and harmony between husband and wife, and to mold the character of both into the image of Christ.

> The fruits of the Spirit are these. Love. Joy. Peace. Patience. Gentleness. Goodness. Faith. Meekness. Temperance. Of such is the Christian home.

2. *Procreation*

Procreation for the perpetuation of God's children is the result of a deep and holy mutual love.

> And God blessed them and said unto them, Be fruitful, and multiply and replenish the earth, and subdue it.

"This view is vastly different from the present sensualizing of love as the basis for marriage." [12]

3. *The education of the children*

The major share of this assignment is given to the father.

> "Hearken unto thy father who caused your birth." [13]

Too many fathers have neglected this God-given chore and it has become a task left to the mother.

Included in the responsibility of educating God's children who are in our trust should be training in self-governance and individual accountability. The child who is not taught to obey authority and to govern himself–his appetites as well as his actions–is not being made ready for life. He will be sent into the world without the full armor of God because the parents failed in his training.

The Christian Home

This is not meant to be a chapter on Christian family relations or a guide to family counselling. There are many outstanding Christian books on the subject and several fine Christ-centered institutes and seminars in this field.

The purpose here is

> *to emphasize the importance of the Christian home and family life as the foundation of good government. The family is the nation in microcosm; the nation is the family in macrocosm. God has given us a clear blueprint for structure and behavior at both levels. If that blueprint is followed at the family level, it will be more likely to be followed at the national level.*

Within that context, there are certain properties–certain

duties–of the Christian home that should be stressed.*

STEWARDSHIP IN THE HOME

Parents are God's stewards. Our children are The Lord's, in trust to us. We are charged with their care and up-bringing; for preparing them for the life here on earth and for eternity. The greatest trust committed to parents is the soul of the child. Thus, the greatest responsibility is to attend to their salvation. *(Luke 12:42; Titus 1:7-9)*

RESPONSIBILITIES OF THE HOME

God holds us accountable for what we do with what He has given us. This Gospel principle is certainly applicable to the home, to the family, and to the children. It is the parents' responsibility to help children grow in the knowledge and love of The Lord; to mold their habits, direct their pursuits, lift their hearts, educate their minds, and train them in the ways of God's plan for civil government. *(Gal. 6:6-10)*

TEACHING BY EXAMPLE

Children are quick to discern any discrepancy between the parent's words (admonitions) and the parent's deed (actions). If parents wish to bring up their children in the ways of The Lord, they must conduct themselves accordingly–with Christian deportment. Christ, our Master, was the great example of living as well as teaching; parents should follow His leadership. *(1 Peter 2:21,22; 1 Cor. 11:1)*

HOME-GOVERNMENT

The Christian home is a commonwealth to be jointly governed

---

* Based on the 1861 writings of Reverend S. Phillips, "The Christian Home as it is in the Sphere of Nature and the Church–Showing the Mission, Duties, Influences, Habits and Responsibilities . . ." as reproduced in *Teaching and Learning America's Christian History.*

by the parents. When parents exercise loving authority, and require obedience, they are training the child for a future role in society and potential leadership in civil government. In the Christian home the child learns love, harmony, self-control, respect and order—all based on the Word of God. (*Eph. 6:1-17; Col. 3:20,21*)

FAMILY WORSHIP

The Christian home is sustained by Faith and thrives on worshipping together . . . parental Bible instruction, family prayer, and religious education. Too many parents excuse themselves from this; they claim lack of ability, or lack of time. This is a responsibility they should not duck. God will provide them with the ability if they will make the time. (*Deut. 6:6-7*)

Christians should be especially faithful in this regard, maintaining their guidance and fulfilling their responsibilities. There was a time when public education was the primary responsibility of the church. That has gone the way of the humanists and the statists and God is no longer welcome in the school. Thus, the home must be a bulwark—a reservoir—for Christ-centered education of the young.

FAMILY PRAYER

Every Christian home should have a family prayer time, every day. This will make it possible for all members of the family to gather as a unit, with one mind and one heart, one faith and one hope. This should be in addition to asking the Blessing at mealtimes, and it is essential to the well-being of the Christian home. We are instructed to be faithful in our prayers. Parents are the priests of the home; they should make talking with God—prayer and praise—a prominent feature of the home. *(James 5:13-16; Rev. 1:6)*

FAMILY BIBLE READING

The Bible is the book for the family; it is the book of the Christian home. It should be the textbook of home education, read and studied each day. (John 20:31)

"By wisdom is a house builded; and by understanding it is

established: And by knowledge shall the chambers be filled with all precious and pleasant things of value."

HOME INFLUENCE

Finally, if all of our Christian responsibilities in the home are attended to, it can have a growing influence in ever-widening circles. Bringing others to Christ and strengthening the community and the nation.

"The Christian home has its influence also upon the state. It forms the citizen, lays the foundation for civil and political character, prepares the social element and taste, and determines our national prosperity or adversity." *

The brilliant philosopher Jose Ortega y Gasset, in *The Revolt of the Masses,* observes:[14]

> "Public life is not solely political, but equally, and even primarily, intellectual, moral, economic, religious; it comprises all our collective habits, including our fashions both of dress and amusement."

And the genesis—the basis—for all of these individual habits, all of these values, is in the home.

How important it is that our Christian homes be diligent, holding fast to the Word of God, guiding our children:

For as the twig is bent, so the branch will grow.

Walking in His Light

In such times as these—as in the early days of Christ's church—the Christian home should be a holy refuge. A place of peace. An enclave of loving authority and Godly guidance, and truth.

The Christian home should be a "nursery for the soul".[15]

Its mission is the spiritual growth of each and every member of the family so that all become one with God, through Christ Jesus. That means keeping hearts and minds on Jesus. Being Christ-centered. Seeking first the Kingdom. Practicing the Christian

---

* Selected works of Rev. S. Phillips, 1861

virtues. Walking in His light.

Building a Christian core, a nucleus of Christian love within the home–and reaching out from there to others.

Society could have no greater foundation than this! No finer training ground for those, now young, who will someday go forth to lead and to rebuild this nation; to restore it to God, and to His blessings.

II.

He was born in the back room of a run-down restaurant. The illegitimate son of a waitress who gave him to a childless couple.

Even in his ghetto-world he managed to get an education. Somewhere in the depths of his soul and the corners of his mind he developed a compelling fascination for microbes, molecules and the agents of disease.

After he had worked his way through his formal education, he got a job in a medical research laboratory. It was there that he discovered the first link in what became a ten-year chain of discovery that led to the cure for cancer.

Today, thousands live because of that one life.

But, it never happened.

Because his was a life that never was–at least, not for very long.

He was aborted. Terminated in the 20th week.

A therapeutic abortion approved by the state and sanctioned by the courts and the medical profession. Not because of rape, or incest; not to save the life of the mother–but simply to satisfy the desires of a would-not-be mother.

What is outlawed by switchblade, or gun, or club, is condoned with syringe or curette.

When Does Life Begin?

Many–if not most–Christians oppose abortions.

They regard abortion as murder. The taking of a human life. A violation of God's commandment.[16]

Some argue that abortion is not murder if it is performed before the fetal heartbeat starts—at approximately the twenty-fourth week of pregnancy. Some posit that abortions should be permitted until the twenty-eighth week, when the fetal brain begins to show signs of "self awareness". And others insist that abortion at virtually any time during pregnancy is permissible—that life does not begin until the infant leaves the mother's womb.

Thus, a central issue in the controversy is this:

When does life begin?

There are two sources of information to be considered: God's Word, and worldly knowledge; the Scriptures, and science.

First things first: God's word. What does The Living Bible say?

The Scriptures make it clear to most Christians that life begins at conception. That God, and God's divine spark of life, is there at the beginning.

Speaking to the prophet Jeremiah, The Lord said:

> *"Before I formed you in the womb, I knew you; and before you came forth from the womb, I sanctified you, and I ordained you . . ."* [17]

Isaiah reiterates that conviction:

> *"And now, says The Lord Who formed me from the womb to be His servant . . ."* [18]

David, the writer of the Psalms, is even more explicit:

> *"I will praise You, for I am fearfully and wonderfully made. Marvelous are Your works and that my soul knows right well! My substance was not hidden from You when I was made in secret and intricately wrought . . . Your eyes did see my substance, yet being unformed; and in Your book all my members (parts) were written, which in continuance were fashioned, when as yet there was none of them."* [19]

What a vivid and detailed description of procreation and the beginning of life from the beginning, from the conception.

> The unformed substance. The sperm and the egg fusing to make the zygote. Containing all the genes, the chromosomes; the genesis of all his parts—the organs, the limbs, the mind and muscles. Fashioned in continuance, even before they took form and shape.

"Thus says The Lord, Your redeemer, and He Who formed you

from the womb: I am The Lord Who maketh all things." [20]

If God created the first man, and He did, then surely His hand and His breath is in the life of Adam's offspring–every one. And they are.

Who is man to destroy the handiwork of The Lord? At one week, twenty weeks, or twenty years?

At The Fusion of Egg and Sperm

Medical research confirms The Scriptures. It is always thus when science progresses far enough–it validates The Bible. Scientific studies reveal that life begins at the formation of the zygote (that single cell formed by the fusion of the egg and sperm).

Dr. Thomas L. Johnson, professor of biology and embryology at the University of Virginia, is one who is quite definite about the beginning of the infant's life.

> *"This individual organism (the zygote) cannot be a part of the mother . . . It has an entirely different set of chromosomes . . . it is a separate and unique life."* [21]

To those who suggest that life begins as the infant leaves the mother's womb, Dr. Johnson asks:

> *"Is it possible that by some magic, at the time of birth, this alleged potential being is somehow, within a matter of minutes, transformed into an actual human being? To rational individuals the answer is incontrovertible. Both the unborn child and the newly-born child is an actual human being and at the time of birth the child is merely moving from one required environment (aquatic) to a newly-required environment (gaseous) so that it can continue to develop into the succeeding stages of life."* [22]

Thus medical science now knows what David knew thousands of years ago; that life begins at conception and continues–through the zygote to the embryo to the fetus to the infant, to the child, the teenager, the adult. From the very special and divine moment when the egg and sperm are joined, it is life–one life "in continuance".

Yet some continue to argue that prior to certain biological or physiological indicators of "viability" the fetus is some form of animal life; that it does not become human life until it is delivered. Animals beget animals. Humans beget humans. Each reproduces after its own kind. The fruit of the seed is in the seed itself.[23]

Abortion on Demand

In 1974, according to Planned Parenthood, there were more than 900,000 abortions in the United States:[24]

75,000 each and every month
17,320 each week
2,470 each day
103 every hour
. . . *every 1.7 minutes, a tiny life is being taken.*

Yet, no one stands convicted before men.

In this nihilistic, humanistic age of situational ethics and convenient decrees and flexible laws, those murders were "legal".

They are called therapeutic abortions. The purposeful, clinical termination of human life. Justified by "science" and absolved by "legalisms".

Today, abortions can be had virtually on demand.

Not just abortions necessitated by rape or incest.

Those account for only *about three percent* of the total.

Not just abortions performed because the mother's very life is in peril.

Those account for about *three percent* of the total.

Approximately ninety-five percent of all abortions performed in this nation are performed for the convenience of the would-not-be mother–so that she can escape the consequences of her indiscretion.

"What Is Truth?"

During recent years, state after state has enacted "liberalized" abortion laws.–some approving abortions through the twenty-fourth week of pregnancy. As these laws were enacted, the rate of abortions began to climb.

On January 22, 1973, the United States Supreme Court handed down a key decision on the abortion issue. That decision is virtually more controlling than state law in that the court established certain guide lines those laws must follow.

Justice Harry Blackmun wrote the decision for the seven-man majority. Decreed the Justice, at any point during the first trimester (the first twelve weeks) of pregnancy, a woman has the right to end her baby's life. The state, said he, has no right to invade the privacy of the relationship between the woman and her physician. He ignored the question as to whether the state had a duty to protect the life of the unborn child (under the Fourteenth Amendment).

The court set the twenty-four to twenty-eight week period as the outer limit for abortions but held that states had the right to establish certain controls and restrictions to cover the second and third trimesters of pregnancy. Mostly, those restrictions deal with the mother's health–including the escape hatch of *mental health* that provides a wide latitude of interpretation and implementation.

The court's decision was more concerned with matters of health than it was with the right to life. Justice Blackmun observed that there is a strong difference of belief as to when life begins. But, asked the Justice, how can the Court be expected to know the truth in that debate? Thus he washed his hands of the central issue.

Is there not a similarity between such evasion and the act of Pontius Pilate?

You remember Pilate, the Roman governor. It was before him that Christ was tried. Pilate could find no fault with Jesus, but he had no desire to get caught in the middle–so, he let the mob decide.

And he washed his hands of the whole affair.[25]

Hands cannot be so easily washed in such decisions.

God will not hold guiltless those who take His seed in vain.

The Death Toll Mounts

As a result of the Supreme Court's decision and the liberalized laws, abortions continue virtually uncontrolled and the death toll continues to climb.[26]

In 1972, the national total was 586,000.*

In 1973, it was 745,000.

In 1974, it was 900,000 and officials predict the peak has yet to be reached.

Therapeutic abortion is now the second most common surgical procedure in the nation. Tonsilectomies are first.[27]

In 1972, the latest year for which comparable data are available, only cardiovascular disease outpaced abortion as a cause of death. There were more than half again as many deaths by abortion than there were due to cancer . . . and five times as many deaths by abortion as by accidents.[28]

Abortion has become a multi-million dollar business with approximately seventy to seventy-five percent of the procedures being performed in out-patient clinics.

"There is no business in the world other than the oil business that produces more financial return per square inch than abortion."[29]

That is the way Dr. Barnett M. Rhett describes the business side of the abortion issue. He claims that he has performed more than 25,000 abortions since 1947.

Not all physicians take this matter of life and death so easily. Dr. Frederick Hoffmeister, president of the American College of Obstretricians and Gynecologists, reports that the 17,000 physicians who are members of the college are "split right down the middle" with a slight majority refusing to perform abortions on demand.[30]

Dr. Hoffmeister said the college is working to establish a doctor's right to refuse to do certain abortions.

This Murder Is Subsidized!

Almost one-third–270,000–of the abortions performed in 1974 were financed by government, through Medicaid.[31]

The bill for those subsidized abortions came to $40 million.[32]

Thus does Caesar force millions of Americans to be a party to the violation of their conscience and their convictions. A large part

* This covers only "legal" and reported abortions. There is no count available for "illegal" abortions.

of those Medicaid funds come from taxpayers who are strongly opposed to abortions on religious and moral grounds. When tax money is arbitrarily used to violate the firmly-held religious beliefs of those who paid those taxes, Caesar goes too far.

Where does he get off forcing God's faithful to be a party to violating God's handiwork?

Abortion and Welfare

Some politicians boast a strange benefit from abortions on demand. They see it as a method of relieving the swollen welfare roll.

"It is cheaper to abort than support." That's their slogan.

What a price to pay! How cheaply life is valued by such mentality.

What if their "justification" were extended to other areas of our lives and our society. Would it not do away with due process, with the constitutional guarantee of trial by jury? With presumed innocence? Think of the money that could be saved by doing away with the courts. And the prisons.

Or, take their thinking even further.

If life is held so cheaply, and termination in the twentieth week is condoned as a way to save on welfare, how long would it be before such mentality would suggest that it would also be less expensive to do away with those over seventy, or sixty-five, or sixty years of age?

The answer to the soaring costs of welfare is to clean up the system—end the clerical and bureaucratic errors that are costing millions of dollars, remove the greedy that prey on the needy and the taxpayers. That is the answer: to clean up the welfare system, not to subsidize the abortion clinics.

Further, their boast does not hold water. Records indicate that the typical abortion patient is white, unmarried, between the ages of twenty and thirty, has a high school education, and comes from a middle income family. Welfare recipients are in the minority among those who seek abortions. By far the greatest number of those who obtain abortions are not the poor but the promiscuous.

Freedom To Control

The most militant supporters of unlimited abortion are the women's liberation groups.

Their major argument is that a woman should be free to control her body and her reproductive processes.

That is a valid argument.

Women should have the right to control their own lives.

And, in a word they do. That word is "No". That's all it takes. Less than three percent of abortions are performed because of rape or incest.

Further, there can be no question about a woman having the right to do what is essential to protect and sustain her life. If it can be medically determined that carrying a child to term might result in the mother's death, then she must make a decision. Certainly, she has the right of "self defense." Her decision and it must be respected.

But, no woman has the right to destroy a life—any life—to serve her own convenience, or appetite, or to escape the consequences of her own actions. Any more than she has the right to murder an individual who is standing in her way or caught her in an improper act.

The right to life is a basic right. *The basic right.* From it stems all other human rights. When that right is set aside, when it can be decided by whim or by vote that life at one particular stage of development is of no value, then the value of life at any stage is endangered.

Anti-Abortion Laws

Christians cannot condone those laws that permit abortion on demand. Such laws mock God's laws and God will not be mocked.

Thus, Christians should join together to endorse and work for legislation that prohibits abortion on demand.

There are several such measures now before Congress.

Senator James Buckley (NY) and Senator Jesse Helms (NC) have constitutional amendments pending before Congress. Both proposals would guarantee the protection of the Fourteenth Amendment (equal protection under the law) to the unborn. In essence both amendments, simply different approaches to constitutional law, would prohibit abortions except in cases of rape, incest and necessity to protect the mother's life.

Senator Dewey Bartlett (Okla.) has also introduced a measure that would outlaw the use of taxpayer (federal) funds for abortion services except in cases where the mother's life is imperiled.

The forces opposing these proposals are strong, and militant. Christians who are concerned about the growing wave of anti-life in America today should prayerfully consider what they can do to support these pro-life efforts.

"Dear God . . ."

Commenting on the apparent ease with which some can write off human life, Dr. Thomas Johnson wrote:

". . . in the dark cavity of the womb, out of sight, older humans find it possible to pretend these younger humans are not living or are not human.

"If the growth of the child were to be observed by the mother, the issue of abortion would most likely never have become a matter of worldwide concern. For, what psychologically healthy mother, seeing the unborn child within herself, would choose to destroy it?" [33]

But, destroyed they are. More than 900,000 in 1974.

As the attending nurse cried when the doctors aborted a perfectly developed 20-week-old fetus and dropped it into a surgical bucket:

"Dear God! What have we done?"

III.

A coalition of women's liberation groups and liberal forces is now pushing militantly for the ratification the so-called Equal Rights Amendment. As of now, thirty-four states have ratified the ERA which would be the twenty-seventh add-on to the U.S. Constitution.

The amendment would create federal guarantees of the "equal rights" for women.

In their passion to be "equal" the liberationists forge their own chains.

Ask any male chauvinist: women are not equal, most of them are superior; to be treated with deference (when they are ladies) and to be protected (when they are in need).

But, the ERA would bring them down a peg or two.

Down to equality.

If that is what they want, it's already on the books.

The Fourteenth Amendment (equal protection under the law).

The Civil Rights Act of 1964.

The Equal Employment Opportunity Act of 1972.

They are all there. Bound and binding.

Each and all of those laws can be applied anytime the women feel they are not being treated fairly and squarely. Whether it be that they want to belly up to a men's bar in Manhattan or drive a garbage truck in Los Angeles.

On top of all that, and the rules and regulations those laws have promulgated, most states already have their own laws on women's equal rights.

And, if those are not enough, the lotharios in the state legislators would no doubt fall all over themselves to please the gals and pass more laws.

That, of course, would not serve the liberationists' purpose. They use the ERA as a banner to rally their forces nationwide. A drive to free themselves from the home, the family, the responsibilities of wifedom and motherhood. Most would be free to be gay, to be loose, to be libertines.

Thus, the liberationists may speak for their kind–*but not their sex.* Not the ladies who rock the cradle and wipe the freckled noses and fry the chicken and nurse the wounds of their men who return from daily battle.

Equal Smarts, Equal Pay

There is little quarrel with equality in the work-a-day world—whether it be business, entertainment or recreation; trade or profession. If a woman does the same work as a man, she should receive the same pay. If she is qualified–mentally and physically–she should have the same opportunity as the next guy in her particular skill or occupation. Equal smarts, equal muscles, equal pay.

But, those who push the ERA do not stop there. They want equal everything and that could be demeaning.

The ERA could turn out to be more equal obligation than equal rights. Among other things, it could

–make women subject to conscription into the armed services and

–force them to pay alimony and child support.

It could even require that women share non-segregated living quarters in prisons and other public institutions. The courts have decreed that separate is not equal and the pro-ERA groups demand equality. No exceptions, right?

More Centralism

But, that is not the major flaw in the ERA.

What is of real concern, and cause for legitimate opposition, is this:

if the Equal Rights Amendment becomes federal law, it will invalidate, pre-empt, and throw into the trash can another chunk of state's rights.

Automatically, all state laws dealing with women's rights and protections would be blanked out by Caesar's statutes. And, on one more parade ground we would be forced to march to his beat.

It says so, right there in the ERA:

"The Congress shall have the power . . ."

And, when Congress is given such power, the federal government moves in–and takes over.

That is centralism. Whether you wrap it in striped pants, coveralls or miniskirts.

Centralism is the antithesis of freedom. It is the slide away from the Republic. Another snag in our checks and balances. An anathema to free individuals.

It is hard to believe that legislators in thirty-four states would be so quick to give Caesar's palace even more power. If they keep on giving away their store, we will soon be spelling it *"states' r-i-t-e-s"*.

And, the liberationists? They should take care.

A doctor over in London, England, reports that women who assume the role of male lose their femininity. Something to do with neuro-hormonal consequences. Says the Doc, such women often go bald!

Lonely, Desperate Wives

Not all of the women involved in the fringes of the women's liberation movement are wild-eyed radicals. Not all of them seek freedom from responsibility or restraint. Some are there out of sheer frustration, desperation, or anger.

They are the victims of today's world. Women who prefer to be housewives and helpmeets and mothers but whose husbands are so enmeshed in the things of the world that they spend little time at home . . . far too little time with their wives and children.

Thus the wife and mother is too often and too long alone. Without her mate, and without the needed help and guidance in the rearing of their young.

Too often, in today's high-pressure world, business keeps husbands apart from wives and parents apart from children. But where is the profit if a man gain the world, or win the promotion, and lose his wife, or his children?

The family is, indeed, God's basic unit; it is the first responsibility of the parent. *Both parents.* The father's hand is as important as the mother's heart. Too many children suffer from a lack of masculine authority and presence in the home.

It is not fair, it is not wise, for the mother to carry the burdens of the home and family on her own and by herself. Raising a family is a joint-venture. The Christian home is a commonwealth, remember? To be governed jointly by father and mother.

Too Great A Price

The way things too often work these days is not God's plan;

it is man's system. It weakens the family, destroys marriages and sacrifices children—all in the name of success, prosperity and a higher standard of living.

Small wonder more and more families are seeking other means of earning a living so that they can be together as a unit, in love if not luxury.

Let's get one thing straight:

> There is nothing wrong with a Christian—man or woman—being successful in his or her chosen vocation or profession . . . so long as it does not come at the cost of weakening the family, destroying the home, or alienating the children.

That is too great a price to pay.

A few years ago a survey of corporate wives found that most of them were lonely, lost and unhappy. With few exceptions they agreed they would rather have their husbands home with them, even if it meant a smaller income and a lower standard of living.

Another survey, this one among young people, found absentee fathers to be one of their major gripes. The repeated complaint was that their parents—mostly the father—"never had enough time to spend with me". In lieu of his presence, he gave presents; instead of his time, he gave money.

That is no way to build a home!

Love Your Wives

The Scriptures spell it out.[34]

> *"Husbands, love your wives."*
>
> *"Therefore shall a man leave his father and his mother, and shall unite with his wife, and they shall be one."*

How can two be one when one is seldom home? Parting can be more than sorrow, it can be devastating.

Love is being with each other.

Love is being patient and kind:

> not jealous, not conceited, not proud;
> not ill-mannered, not self-centered, not irritable
> and never unfaithful.

Love is giving, love is constant, love is always.

Love is loving as Christ loved us.
As men love their own bodies so they should love their wives for, are they not one through Christ?
Husbands, love your wives as Jesus loved His church.
Care for her.
Be with her.
And the two of you be with your family.

Wives, Love Your Husbands

And, what of wives? [35]
Wives, love your husbands and respect them, and obey them. For that is God's Word.
Knowing that love fashions love in its own loom and weaves its pattern from respect.
In the Christian home, obedience becomes the joy of fulfilling the wishes of a loved and loving husband. There is no greater joy, no greater fulfillment, for the complete Christian woman than to love and serve her Christian mate–the man who loves and cherishes her.

Christian wives: make the home a haven. A refuge. A place of God's peace and warmth and love. An island of serenity and support and understanding in a hectic, plastic, often avaricious world. A Christian oasis far from the maddening throng and godless currents and pressures.

Blessed by the homemakers, for they shall help their husbands raise their children in the love and light of God!

CHAPTER SIX

Must Public Education Ruin Our Children?

Consider the tribulation of Barbara Jacquelyn Hoag.[1]

Mrs. Hoag got into deep trouble with the law. Her crime? *Trying to do what was right by her children.*

Her two daughters, Sasha and Jamie, were students in the public schools of Sacramento, Calif., and Mrs. Hoag was mightily upset by some of the goings on in those schools and on those schoolyards.

Finally, she could take it no more. Mrs. Hoag stopped sending her daughters to school.

"Schools are not a fit place for kids to be.

"There is a clear and present danger to all children attending public schools. That danger is widespread drug usage and addiction. Added to that is the danger of pre-adolescent sexual promiscuity and experimentation.

"As a parent, it is my duty and my obligation to protect my children from such dangerous environs."

Mrs. Hoag advised the school authorities that unless the situation were cleaned up at the assigned school, or her children were transferred to an acceptable school, she would keep them at home. That put her in violation of the compulsory education laws: kids will attend school until age sixteen, or else.

The school officials would not transfer the Hoag girls to another facility. The principal, the school board, and the district attorney's office warned Mrs. Hoag to get her kids back in school–public or private, *and post haste.*

Her limited income would not permit Mrs. Hoag to send her daughters to a private school. But, don't equate income with moral values or courage of conviction. Mrs. Hoag stood firm; a self-educated black lady determined to hold her ground.

She was not out to change the world; she was out to protect her children. The Hoag girls did not return to school.

"Sending my girls to that public school is synonymous with sending them out to play in 'Sunset Strip' or any city's redlight district. With one exception: if I permitted my children to play in a redlight district I would be charged with neglect and with corrupting the morals of a minor."

It was not that Mrs. Hoag was anti-education. Her first husband had earned his PhD at Harvard. Her second husband was graduated from Sacramento State University with a degree in education. On her own she had already taught her four-year-old son to read and spell at the second grade level.

"I'm all for education. That is another reason I took them out; I saw what those schools were doing to my children. They were stifling their creativity. I intend to teach my children at home as long as the public schools remain the way they are."

The school board and the district attorney's office advised her that would be unacceptable, and against the law. She was not "credentialled" to teach her own children. In this day and time one must be credentialled–approved by the state–before one can teach one's own children in the prescribed courses.

Mrs. Hoag fought back.

One of the women in her neighborhood, who had been credentialled a teacher by the State, offered to tutor the Hoag children at home. The officials said, "no"

Mrs. Hoag took her case to court, *and lost.*

That was, really, to be expected. As R. J. Rushdoony writes in his *Messianic Character of American Education:* [2]

> "Early in the history of the United States, the courts had no doubt that education was a function of the parents and no more a function of the state than is the begetting of children. Education was seen as an aspect of child-rearing. With the birth and development of state schools, however, the courts steadily invaded the area of parental authority, and the school came to be seen, not as an aspect of parental authority, but of civil government."

Thus it was the judge ordered Mrs. Hoag to get her children back into the public school. Otherwise, her children would be placed in a foster home and she would go to jail!

And so the State had its victory–of sorts. Mrs. Hoag departed Sacramento. It was the only way she could keep her children and avoid sending them back to what she termed "a cesspool of drugs and sex".

Whose Children Are These?

Mrs. Hoag's story may be disturbing–but it is not unique. Many parents wrestle Caesar for the control of their children.

On any given schoolday, drive past a school and contemplate the children. Or better yet, look across the table at your own and ask yourself this question:

Whose children are these?

Are they yours, of God?

Or, are they of the State?

Surely all parents, and certainly all Christian parents, will answer:

These are our children! Parents are not incubators for the State!

A few may answer differently, but if it is true that children are of their parents and of God, then follows this inquiry:

Whose responsibility are these children?

The parents'?

Or, the State's?

Most parents, and surely all Christians, will reply:

Children are the parents' responsibility!

> "Train up a child in the way he should go and when he is old, he will not depart therefrom." [3]

God did not issue that injunction to the State. He gave it to parents. He instructs us to educate our children. As His stewards.

Obviously, Christians are not anti-education. Far from it. The first schools in this land were founded and operated by Christians, in voluntary effort through the local churches. The first institutions of higher learning (Harvard, for example) were founded by Christians so that students "be plainly instructed, and earnestly pressed to consider well, the maine end of his life and studies is, to know God and Jesus Christ which is eternall life, John 17:3, and therefore to lay Christ at the bottome, as the only foundation of all found knowledge and Learning. . . ." [4]

Today Christians are just as concerned with the affairs of education, even though the State has pressed hard to pre-empt the field. Christians realize that the teaching of the child is their God-given assignment; a personal responsibility with personal accountability attached.

By What Measure? By What Morals?

How, then, can we best educate our children concerning the things and the workings of the world? How do we train them up so that they can be in the world, and function in the world, but not be of the world or of its predilictions?

Few modern-day parents are completely qualified to teach their children at home, or on their own. The complexities of the present, and the challenges of the future, demand a wide range of knowledge. Ours is a highly interdependent society. And, at any rate, such at-home, at the parent's knee, learning is now prohibited by civil law.

Not all Christians can afford to send their children to private, church-supported or God-centered schools; though more and more are doing just that. Thus, the majority must send their children to those public schools their taxes finance. They must depend upon Caesar to provide a major part of the formal education of their offspring.

So it is Christians come face-to-face with the deepening conflict:

By what measure shall the child be trained?

In the nurture and admonitions of The Lord?

Or, by the dictates of the State?

Do we stand fast in Christ?

Or, do we submit to Caesar?

God First or After Hours?

Those who worship God believe that "the fear of The Lord is the beginning of wisdom."

He must come first—in education as in all else.

The State says, "No"—the State comes first. God can come later—after hours or in released time. Or, in "objective" studies of philosophy, along with competing theories.

But, what if the studies of the schoolday undermine the teaching of those off-hours? What if they negate the worship of that released time? What if they become a divisive instrument to separate the child from faith, and from his parents?

And then there is the question of morality.

Those who hold fast to their faith maintain religion is the only sound and constant basis for morality. And, that morality must be maintained at the highest possible level if the nation is to survive. Look, they demand, look what is happening to the morals of our nation.

As Dr. Billy Graham told a joint session of the California State Legislature:

"Morals are sinking lower with every passing hour, and if they sink much lower . . . we will head straight into the arms of a dictatorship in this country because America cannot survive without strong moral values."[5]

Even so, the State contends—not just contends but in fact insists—the measure of morality will be that which the State prescribes. And since in a democracy that level of morality must be acceptable to most, morals must seek the lowest common denominator.

There is a rule of economics called "Gresham's Law". Simply

stated it is this: bad money (money lacking in value) drives good money from the market. Observation will confirm that there is a similar law governing moral values: *in society, bad morals (morals lacking in value) drive out good morals.* Is that not what is happening in this land today?

And So The Battle Forms

Finally, many parents will protest that the school is (or should be) an extension of themselves and their responsibilities. Thus, they should have the final say in standards and they should set the proscribed directions of the institution.

Not so! say those who run the system. The schools are of the State; they are an extension of the State. What suits the State is that which shall be taught. Caesar will monitor the values and the morals.

> "Statist education increasingly assumes that (1) the child is the child of the state or the property of the state, which can therefore interfere extensively with parental authority. (2) The state 'priesthood' of educators is best able to rear the child and prepare him for life . . . (3) Statist education is alone 'objective' and hence true, the state having the impartiality and transcendance of a god." [6]

But, insist the parents, these are our children!

And so the battle forms. In Maryland. In West Virginia. In California. In Wisconsin. In New England, the South, the West . . . and all across the nation, there are those who challenge Caesar.

The Weight of The Institution

And what of those who wrestle Caesar? How do they fare? Some have lost their battle but a few have won.

Jonas Yoder won. He bested Caesar.[7]

Brother Yoder is a member of the Amish sect, those quiet, gentle folk who farm their farms and raise their families in an isolated serenity of worship free from crime, or juvenile delinquency. The Amish reject formal education beyond the eighth grade. From that point on, their religion calls for the child to be educated through life in the Amish community–farming, carpentry, animal husbandry, the various and daily affairs of faith and enterprise.

When Jonas Yoder's children completed their eight years of state education, he refused to send them on to the public high school. He defied Wisconsin's compulsory education laws and the state brought suit against him.

Wisconsin claimed first call upon the Yoder children.

Mr. Yoder insisted parental rights and religious convictions came first.

What was involved was this:

> Does the State have a right to force children to receive their education at Caesar's knee? Does the State, or the parent, have the right to direct the upbringing of the child–especially when religious convictions are involved?

The Wisconsin courts found against Brother Yoder. But he persisted. Finally, the United States Supreme Court found for him. His children were, in fact, his own. The method of their education was his to decide.

But, lest you consider that decision an across-the-board victory for freedom, dwell on this: The Court went on to say that Mr. Yoder's rights–and the rights of the Amish–*do not apply to all.* Unto all others the laws of the State prevail. For them, "Caesar's will" will be done. Thus, in fact, the Court established a religious test: to be free as Mr. Yoder was freed, one must be Amish!

Whoever gave the State the power to enforce its stale orthodoxy on each and every child? *When the weight of the institution crushes the individual, is it not time to re-examine the institution?*

Do not the droppings of the State–in cases such as Mrs. Hoag's and in such gratuitous asides as in the courts' decree in the Yoder case–reveal once more the arrogance of officialdom? Do not such actions smack of coercion? Are they not immoral?

Thus, would it not be proper to say this about the general attitude of the State in matters of public education?

> *The machine has been built. The apparatus stands and grows. It must be fed and its rules respected.*

Does it not follow, then, that the machine is more important than the child?

Suffer, little children. Come unto the State; it will be your new religion.

Whatever Fits

Situational ethics. That's the big thing in many schools today.

Whatever fits is right, baby. Whatever turns you on. Morality is a rubber yardstick. Stretch it as you will. Any ends justify any means.

School administrators–and boards–too often lack the courage, or the wisdom, to set specific moral standards before their students. And, in many instances, when they do set such standards, they lack the courage to enforce their application. It is easier, and popular, to hold that students should be free to seek their own way, to set their own standards and to reach their own conclusions.

Commenting on the rise and worship of situational ethics in the public school, Gene Ragle, a member of the California State Board of Education, protested:

"Students are led to the conclusion that there are always two or more sides to every question; that the 'right' answer is whatever works best for the individual–and with which the individual feels most comfortable.

"That definition of rectitude, carried to the ultimate, could earn eventual sainthoods for Adolph Hitler, Josef Stalin and Al Capone. The decisions they made worked well . . . for them.

"It might be mentioned that The Lord gave Moses the Ten Commandments as Divine Imperatives, not elective topics for group discussion, modification or rejection. Jesus Christ delivered The Sermon on The Mount in exactly the same way–as divine rules for human conduct." [8]

Mr. Ragle walked a lonely road. He spoke for the people but he could not communicate with the majority of his fellow board members or the professional educators and hirelings who advised them. It was not that they were necessarily immoral. It was that, by-and-large, they were amoral and irreligious. After all, if God is dead–or at least downgraded in the classroom–what's all this reference to Moses and Jesus Christ? How can such religious history be relevant to classroom ethics?

The Sliding Scale

When God is counted dead and when religion is thus belittled, morals have no moorings. They become fastened to the meanderings of humanism, to the sliding scale of situational ethics. They bob and drift with the tides of appetite and the currents of desire. And, in such a situation they seek the lowest common denominator. *Collectivism seldom lifts the inner man.* As Jose Ortega y Gasset warned, such levellings change a nation's perspective "from aspirations and ideals into appetites and unconscious assumptions." [9]

Further, such rubberized rules and cop-outs do students a grave disservice. Life is not so lenient; there is always an ultimate consequence; the individual pays for his actions. The sooner the child understands this fact, the more likely he is to avoid disaster.

There is a hue and cry these days about the garbage that infests our cities and the refuse that fouls our countryside. We are concerned about the smog and smoke that contaminates our air. These are critical problems to which we must attend. But, there is a problem far more crucial:

> *the garbage that is being pushed into the mind and the smut that is polluting so many of our schools.*

History attests that when morals decline and obscenity is glorified, nations are soon buried in their own debris.

"Anti-God and Anti-American"

Late in 1974, and through the early months of 1975, the people of Kanawha County, W. Va., rose up to protest some of the textbooks and reading materials used in their public schools. Mostly they were upset about some of the assigned reading in so-called language art programs.

The parents, including many miners and their wives, protested that the materials were harmful to their minors. They complained that the books were full of filthy language, that they were far too explicit about sex, and that many of the writings were "anti-God, anti-American and anti-family".[10]

It was not the first time that the folks in Charlestown and the surrounding West Virginia countryside had expressed their opposition to those books. Earlier in 1974, when the county school board had first considered the purchase of the controversial texts and reading materials, the parents had urged its members to reject the books. The school board went ahead and purchased about $500,000 worth of the volumes, mostly "stream of consciousness" writing, much of it straight out of the gutter and the ghetto.

That is when the Kanawha parents took to picket signs and demonstrations.

"We don't teach that kind of stuff at home and we don't want it taught in our schools." That is the way Charlestonian Joe Tuemler put it.[11]

Tuemler and thousands of other parents formed parents committees. They were joined by others and together they paraded and picketed. At one point they succeeded in closing every public school in Kanawha County. Some of the demonstrators were jailed, including Rev. Ezra Graley of Nitro, W. Va., who was one of the leaders of Concerned Citizens Protesting Text Books. Rev. Graley warned the members of his congregation that by taking on the educational establishment they were biting off quite a chunk, but that they must stand fast.

"We must be prepared to go to jail, if necessary, to stop the use of these objectionable books in the public classroom." [12]

He was one of the first to go.

"Secular, Humanist Philosophy"

Kanawha County, W. Va., is no island unto itself. More and more parents throughout the nation are rising to protest what they consider to be "dirty, disruptive, subversive, irreligious, immoral, or racist and sexist books" in the classroom.[13]

In Carroll and Bedford counties, in southwest Virginia, parents reviewed the *Responding* reading series (books used in the seventh through twelfth grades) and found them "anti-Christian, profane and pornographic". The school board subsequently banned the series.[14]

"It's not just a few dirty books we're objecting to," said Mrs. Mary Bowen, information director of Montgomery County, Md., CURE (Citizens United for Responsible Education). "It's the secular humanist philosophy that pervades the curricula; the concentration on what you think and what you feel, rather than academic skills and basics." [15]

During CURE's protest, parents circulated handbills condemning some of the books on the public school reading list. The editor of the local newspaper described their actions in that regard as "garbage". When the parents challenged the editor to publish verbatim excerpts from the books, he pleaded that it would be improper to print such material in his "family" newspaper.[16]

Frank Fox can hardly be described as a "disinterested observer" in the furor over classroom reading materials. He is president of D.C. Heath Co., publishers of some of the controversial textbooks. But, Fox cut to the core of the conflict when he assessed the gathering storm of parental protest:

"The real gut issue is—who controls the schools?" [17]

All That's Fit To Print

Mr. Fox was correct: who controls the schools is, indeed, one of the "gut" issues. Thus, it is not surprising that many pseudo-intellectuals have attempted to write off parental protests of books laced with "prostitution, dope addiction, racism and sex and four-letter words" as dangerous throwbacks "straight out of the McCarthy era".

The New York Times pooh-poohed the West Virginia parents' opposition as something to be expected "in the heart of the Appalachian coal fields where the airwaves are full of emotive radio preachers' fire and brimstone." [18] *The Times,* however, did not consider excerpts from the books as suitable for publication under its trademark, "All The News That's Fit To Print".

The late Dr. Benjamin Fine, once a major domo in the ivory

towers of the educational establishment and a columnist for North America Newspaper Alliance, described the textbook furor as "the greatest wave of book burning and teacher fear since the McCarthy era".[19]

When the US Commissioner of Education, Terrel Bell, urged textbook publishers to edit their material so as not to "insult the values of most parents", Dr. Fine found such a suggestion "incredible and astounding". He insisted that it would "set back education a century or more".[20] Obviously, that which was fine for Dr. Fine is not acceptable with most parents.

The writhings of *The New York Times,* and the fulminations of Dr. Fine, may be revealing of their philosophy, but they are not really relevant. There are no records at the county court house to indicate that the citizens of Kanawha elected *The Times* the keeper of their morals.

Why is it that academic freedom is so often equated with the gutter–with the irreligious, the immoral and the seamy? Where is the academic freedom in the public classroom to rise above the wallows of the past to seek the horizons of tomorrow? Must parents obtain special dispensation to have their children study those materials that lift the mind and set the spirit soaring?

Textbook on Sex

Not all controversial material comes in sordid paperbacks or lurid novels. Sometimes it bears the indicia of the State.

Consider, for example, a textbook on sex education approved by the California State Board of Education.

Human Sexuality, A Course for Young Adults. It was recommended to the Board by the State Commission on Curriculum. The "young adults" for whom the book was intended were *children aged twelve to fourteen in the seventh and eighth grades.*

Human Sexuality was explicit, in word and picture. It began by warning the young students that home was the worst place to learn about sex. Parents, the children were advised, are too ignorant, too old-fashioned and too narrow-minded to be satisfactory sources of information.

"The best place for objective sex instruction is the school." [21]

So much for dear old mom and dad. So much for the home, the church, or that quiet discussion with the family physician. Turn sex over to the school; let the State plot the course. The run-away rise in venereal disease and the soaring increase in teenage abortions can be counted as part of the fruits of such impersonal and humanistic indoctrination.

Perversion, advised the book, is like obscenity; it's all in the eyes of the beholder. The "young adults" were assured that "unusual sexual behavior should not be considered a perversion simply because it is out of the ordinary". *Whatever turns you on.*

As for *premarital sex,* the early teenagers were informed that America's "strong disapproval of premarital sexual activity is not shared by the majority of the world's cultures. One study of 158 societies throughout the world showed 70% of them do not condemn premarital intercourse". *So much for Judaic-Christian teachings; so much for those fuddy-duddy, narrow-minded Americans.*

It was much the same regarding *extra-marital sex.* Casual transgressions were condoned "unless he (the husband) becomes involved in a lengthy affair and falls in love with the other woman". *So much for fidelity.*

A reading of some of the other section headings in *Human Sexuality* will give you an idea of its contents:

Homosexuality	Masturbation
Incest	Nymphomania
Masochism	Sadism

Answer this question: what need does a twelve-year-old have for such detailed information? Why should he, or she, be burdened with such matters at such an early age?

Too Much for Television

To quote at length from that state-approved textbook would no doubt offend many adults. One California television commentator proposed reviewing the contents of *Human Sexuality* for his viewers;

he thought parents had the right to know what their children were going to be taught. His efforts were censored by the program's producer. Why? because the material would be beyond the limits of acceptability for a family show.[22]

"What you are saying to me," the commentator pointed out, "is that this material is too rough for our adult audience even though it will be compulsory reading in the seventh and eighth grades."

The section on *incest* advised the students that science was attempting to determine if there were any measurable effects or defects involved in incest . . . *"without regard to the biases of ancient and contemporary societies". Incest, in other words, is not a matter of morality, it is strictly a question of physiological consequences.*

Some of our "liberal" friends are alert to the connection between violence on television and crime in the streets. Why is it they fail to comprehend, or acknowledge, the link between such sex education in the public classroom and the degradation of sex in the back alley? The record is clear:

the more permissive the society, the more promiscuous its children.

Take A Stand!

There was a glimmer of rectitude in the book, a preview of things to come. The author commented:

"Often, after a relaxation of sexual attitudes, a wave of sexual conservatism follows. Some people say that this conservative trend has already begun."

That "conservative trend" caught up with *Human Sexuality.*

Alert parents in many school districts made it clear to their local school authorities that they did not want the book used in the classroom–not with their "young adults". The result: the number of orders from districts throughout the state was so minimal the publisher withdrew the volume.

That serves to make two points:

1. if the State had the power to arbitrarily mandate textbooks, as some now recommend, the parents would have had little

opportunity to exclude the book from their district schools, and

2. if parents will take a stand, if they will keep informed and speak out, and elect good men and women to their school boards, they can affect school policy in the local district. But, they must be willing to stand up, speak out, and work their precincts.

Christian parents should not only be willing to take a stand in regard to such matters, *they must also assume their full parental responsibilities and train up their children in the facts of life and faith in God.* In that way sex will find its proper role and its true beauty—an expression of deepest love between husband and wife whom God has joined together.

Modern Ape in Modern Schools

According to the Holy Scriptures . . .

Genesis 1:26-27 . . .

God created man. In His image created He him, and her.

But, according to the State, this is the gospel . . .

"Man is the result of a purposeless and materialistic process that did not have him in mind. He was not planned. He is a state of matter, a form of life . . . a sort of animal. . . ." [23]

That is the word, according to Caesar. And, thus it is that millions of Americans of different creeds and faiths are forced to violate their personal spiritual convictions by subsidizing the cult of evolution in the classroom.

Those who see in man a higher origin, a Divine conception, a part of the Master plan, cannot abide the materialistic and Godless teachings of the State.

Creationism is central to the Christian. Christ is in Genesis; at the creation He was, and all things were made by Him. God did not send His only begotten Son to save some super ape or "state of matter". Christ came and died and rose again to reclaim God's fallen handiwork. *If there were no creation, there would have been no Calvary!*

Yet the State persists in giving franchise to the theory of

evolution. Thus many who believe the Genesis account present their school authorities with this proposal:

—either drop the theory of evolution from the classroom, or
—give the story of creation equal time and equal weight.

Aside from whatever personal religious convictions may be involved, fair is fair.

When such equity is proposed, the National Academy of Science is usually one of the groups to rise in objection. In resolutions aimed at school boards considering the demand for such equal time, the Academy has stated that creationism is "an appeal to the supernatural causes . . . a concept not susceptible to validation by objective criteria".[24] Contends the Academy, the story of creation does not belong in the classroom; at least not the science classroom.

Vernon Gross, BS, MS, vice president of the Tustin (Calif.) Institute of Technology and a member of the National Academy of Science, does not go along with his colleagues. Mr. Gross suggests that the Academy, through its "all or nothing" demands for evolution hoists itself on its own petard.

"By the Academy's definition of scientific attitudes and methodology, the evolution theory is not an observable fact. Thus, by its own standards, evolution should be excluded from textbooks and classrooms."[25]

The Academy insists it opposes giving creationism equal classroom time because "it could affect the study of science for a generation". If, by that, the Academy members are saying they would be forced to recognize *the harmony of science and The Scriptures,* such an effect would be salutary; it could do much to improve mankind's existence in this tired world. But, if they mean they choose to be bothered by competing thought, then they indict themselves. In such closed minds there is no search for truth, there is only the design of indoctrination.

A Form of Worship

Mr. Gross believes the members of the Academy, in their fervor, come close to raising evolution to a form of worship. They do, indeed. Scratch an evolutionist and see!

Henry M. Morris, PhD, former chairman of the Department of Civil Engineering at the Virginia Polytechnic Institute and now of the Institute for Creation Research, expresses the same contention in a more scholarly yet just as pointed terms:

> *"Creation can be shown to be a more effective scientific model of origins than evolution, and evolution can be shown to require a higher degree of credulous faith than creation."* . . . *"In fact, the exclusive teaching of evolution is not constitutional, legal or proper, since belief in evolution requires at least as much faith as belief in creation and is therefore a religious belief."* [26]

There! There you have it. Evolution is, in following if not in fact, a form of worship. It cannot be validated by objective scientific criteria. There is ample evidence that the fossils put forth by evolutionists to support their theories "are invariably either of apes or men, with no true and unquestioned intermediaries between men and apes." [27]

Evolution is a chain of missing links. Yet, in many states it has virtually exclusive franchise in the public classroom!

Creationism in The Classroom

Can the creation story be taught in public schools without violating the separation of church and state–the First Amendment? It can, indeed. Several states are now following the equal time procedure. Tennessee is one state; Oregon is another. The Tennessee statute on "The specific statement of creation of man in biology textbooks" includes this sentence:

> "Any textbook so used in the public education system which expresses an opinion or relates to a theory or theories shall give in the same text book and under the same subject commensurate attention to, and an equal amount of emphasis on, the origins and creation of man and his world as the same is recorded in other theories, *including, but not limited to, the Genesis account in the Bible.*" [28] (Italics added)

In *Introducing Creationism Into The Public Schools,* Dr. Morris writes:

"Evolutionary philosophy is the foundation of atheism and humanism, which are nothing less than non-theistic religions. Exclusive teaching of evolution has the effect of establishing religious systems of this sort as state-endorsed and state-supported religions.

"The political reservation (about teaching creationism) is, therefore, not only invalid but actually applies in reverse. That is the very reason there is so much concern about this question around the country."

Thus the issue is joined, even on a secular basis:

> Is not religion to be separate from the State? Does not that dictum apply to all? Or, are some to be favored while others are excluded? Why does the State compel the parent to subsidize the Darwinian dogma to the exclusion of Creation?

Why does it?

Well, consider this:

> *The child who knows that he is bought with a price and is God's own is not likely to accept the role of slave to any man or any State. But, those who are taught that man is just "a sort of animal"—an evolutionary way station in some biological philandering—will be more likely, when they are grown, to accept the State as shepherd.*

Does that not make sense?

It does to Caesar . . .

. . . and, to those who hold in common the humanistic, pagan view that man is born to be a servant of the State, a unit of the mass.

II.

It is not as if the taxpayers had short-changed public education.

Since the end of World War II we have more than doubled the percentage of the Gross National Product spent on schools and learning: [29]

In 1950—3.4% of GNP

In 1974—7.3% of GNP.

In this year, 1975, we will spend more on education than we

shelled out for the entire federal budget in 1960!

In 1972* almost 40 percent of the total expenditures by state and local governments went for public education–elementary and high schools and institutions of higher learning.

In just the past ten years, education's share of the GNP increased twenty-five percent–even though enrollment has been declining during recent years.[30]

Between 1960 and 1974, expenditures for public education (kindergarten through high school–K-12) increased *more than six times* the rate of increase in enrollment (even allowing for rising costs due to inflation). In 1960, taxpayers spent an average of $430 per student (K-12). By 1974, that had increased 166 percent–to $1,145. The rise in expenditure per student in taxpayer-supported higher education was almost as hefty; in 1960, it averaged $1,000; by 1974, it had risen to $2,387.

Wasted Funds, Wasted Minds

Americans have seldom been stingy when it comes to the education of their young. The reason for taxpayer revolts in school tax and bond elections is basically two-fold:

–taxpayers are not convinced that the money already available is being spent wisely or efficiently, and

–school finance elections (taxes and bond issues) are often the only direct opportunity the taxpayer has to vote "No" to taxes in general.

Often it is not the outlay of money for education that bothers the taxpayer as much as it is

the way the money is raised (primarily through the property tax) and the waste involved.

Not simply the wasted funds

but also the wasted minds.

When taxpayers read about drugs and drunkenness, and riots and rebellion, at public schools

–when they read about some of the obscene literature that

---

*Latest available data.

passes as assigned reading
–when they read about pornography disguised as "sex education"
–when they hear about high school classes in basket-weaving and pottery-making or fly-tying . . .

. . . they tend to turn against the schools.

Not against education, but the system, and those in charge.

Can anyone truthfully say that on the whole Johnny is more capable of reading or writing or computing than his older brothers and cousins were–ten to twenty years ago?

Can anyone honestly claim that the levels of moral values and ethical standards in public education are higher now than they were a decade ago?

Or that the general caliber and expertise of the "new" teachers compares with the calibre and dedication of the older teachers, or has kept pace with the increase in costs?

On the contrary.

In the minds of concerned parents and irate taxpayers, moral standards as well as academic requirements and the teaching of basic skills seem to have declined as rapidly as the amount of money spent on public education has risen.

Accountability

Certainly the number of "functional illiterates" being turned out by our public schools seems to have increased.

Several years ago the executive vice president of a manufacturers association was asked by government officials what the public schools could do to prepare students for jobs in industry. His reply was curt, and to the point:

"Send us young people who can read and write and do simple math."

All of this came to a head, sometime ago, in San Francisco. A young high school graduate and his mother sued the city school board for one million dollars.[31] They complained that even though the boy had spent four years in the city's high school system, he could not read or write or compute well enough to qualify for a job or job-training. At the time of the lawsuit, he was carrying baggage for a rock music group.

In her statement, the mother asserted that time after time she had been assured by the school authorities that her son was doing passing work; that he was at the average level for his class, and that no remedial work was needed to bring his abilities up to par. The mother told inquiring newsmen that one of the purposes of her suit was to force the school board and the school system to get *"oriented toward the end product"*–young people who can read, and write, and do simple arithmetic.

What the mother was saying was this: Schools should be held accountable for their performance. *Accountability.* The same type of accountability we demand in other areas of life.

If we buy a car, we expect it to run properly. If we buy a dozen eggs, we expect them to be fresh. If we buy a piece of furniture, we expect it to hold together. We get what we pay for or we hold the merchant accountable. All too often, in the public education system, the parent pays his taxes and sends his children to school and takes his chances–hoping "their" school is one of the "good" ones; hoping their education will have some substance.

Virtually Impervious

The cost of the failure of many public schools to get "oriented toward the end product" must be calculated in far more than lost dollars and cents. It must be counted in terms of personal tragedy, personal misery and public distress. What we pay for, and seldom get, in public education we pay for again and again in the rising costs of public welfare, the soaring cost of crime in the streets, the courts, and the prisons–and those wasted minds and wasted bodies.

There are many reasons for such poor performance in so many of our public school systems–weak and faulty administration, student anarchy spawned by permissiveness, antiquated techniques of teaching in a space age, shallow subjects that turn students off, lazy teachers, sloppy teaching, indoctrination rather than education, lack of student motivation, lack of parental concern or guidance, schools that are "placebos for the short cuts of political activism" . . . the list goes on.

There are many fine teachers—and administrators—who struggle against the tide; men and women who labor against the odds; who do their best to educate, inspire and motivate. Mostly, they swim upstream; they push against the academic crowd.

As long as the educational establishment holds a public monopoly and elects "its" people to the local school boards, the conscientious teacher and the desperate parent find it almost impossible to fight the system. The twins of coercion—*compulsory attendance and monopoly*—make the establishment virtually impervious to overhaul and improvement.

Voucher Plan

There must be some way to let the fresh air of accountability, competition and innovation into the public education system. There is.

It is called "the voucher plan".

It would introduce the dynamics of the free market—the energies of customer-producer relationships—to public education. Accountability would become the rule rather than the exception.

Under the voucher plan, now being tested in school districts in several states, taxpayers would "subsidize" the student rather than the educational establishment. The parents of the school child would receive a voucher from government worth a pre-determined amount of dollars, depending upon the child's grade level. Generally, the higher the grade, the larger the dollar-value of the voucher, since it costs more to educate a high school student than a first-grader. In one test, the value of the vouchers ranged from $680 for elementary school to $970 for junior high grades.[32]

Parents "spend" their voucher at a public school of their choice,* usually within the district in which they reside. If one school is delivering a better "product"—doing a better overall job of teaching

*This aspect of the voucher plan is similar to the G.I. Bill for veterans' education.

the students—that is where the parents would probably opt to send their children. Other parents might choose another school that was stronger on vocational education, or science, or discipline, etc.

If such a plan were implemented on a general basis, those schools doing the poorest job (as "rated" by parent selection) would quickly experience a drop-off in students, revenues and job opportunities for teachers and administrators. Faced with such a direct impact of the give-and-take of the free (open) market, school boards, administrators and teachers would be forced to work harder and deliver a better product—or suffer the consequences of their sub-standard performance.

The voucher plan would throw open the now-closed doors of the public education establishment and let in the fresh air of competition, accountability, imagination and innovation—attributes currently stifled by the monopoly inherent in the system.

Consider the voucher plan in this light:

When you want a physician, you search for the best one available. When you want an auto mechanic, you look for the best one—the man who has been doing the most satisfactory work. It's the same with attorneys, accountants, engineers, or whatever.

Should not the same opportunities apply when it comes to seeking the best school and the best teachers for your child?

Points of Controversy

The voucher plan is controversial.

Its most passionate opponents are some of the largest teachers' organizations. That is understandable. Their empire is threatened.

That fact, of course, is not their stated public reason for opposing the voucher plan. Generally, their opposition comes on two fronts:

—they charge it would violate the First Amendment, and

—they claim it is a device to perpetuate segregation.

Both arguments are without merit or foundation.

As to the first, the voucher plan would not and should not be used to subsidize student attendance at private (parochial) schools. *In fact, any private school willing to participate in the voucher plan would be sticking its head in a noose.* With public funds go public control

–control of the curriculum
–control of basic operational standards, and
–control of budgets, tuition, and on and on.

For parochial schools to participate in the voucher plan, or any type of program of public funding, could mean the end of those schools as private institutions. The purpose of the voucher plan is not to devolve the private school into a public facility; the purpose of the voucher plan is to improve the public school system–to make it more responsive, more accountable, to the parents and taxpayers and to break the chains which now make that system, in effect, a closed shop.

As to the second charge–that the voucher plan is a device to perpetuate segregation in the public schools–that is neither the design nor the intent of the proposal.

The in-grade allowance ("purchasing power" of the educational voucher) within the state or district would be the same for each child regardless of his residence or the location of the school. Thus, the plan would work to equalize educational expenditures and opportunity. Implementation of the voucher plan could, and should, be coupled to a requirement that *no child would be excluded from or compelled to attend any school on the basis of color, creed, or ethnic background.*

As a matter of practical fact, the voucher plan could unlock the door of opportunity for many so-called minority children. It would provide them, and their parents, an option they do not now have: the opportunity to depart schools that do not offer solid educational foundations. Busing, within the voucher plan, would be strictly a voluntary affair; a matter of individual choice–*not compulsory.* And, that is the way it should be: Caesar is out-of-bounds when he forces children to get a large part of their education on a wayward bus, or in a school far from the child's family home and neighborhood.

Tax-Credit Plan

There is another plan that would also help to curb the monopoly of the state school system: *the tax-credit plan.*

Through such a plan, parents could take as a tax credit (could subtract from their federal income taxes) the amount they paid to send their child to private school. Enactment of the proposal would provide a measure of equity for those parents who do not use the state school facilities but are being taxed to fund them.

The per student costs in public elementary and high schools averages between $600 and $900. If the 4.5 million students now attending those grades in private schools were suddenly dumped on the public school system, *it would add between $3 billion and $4 billion a year to the costs and tax take of that system.* And, that would not cover the capital outlay needed for additional classrooms and other facilities.

Thus, while the parents of private school children are relieving the state system (and the taxpayers) of billions of dollars in expense, they get no assistance in return. That is not fair; it is not just. It amounts to a kind of compulsory double levy for the right to exercise free choice.

Those who oppose the tax-credit plan argue that the state should not help finance parochial schools. The tax-credit plan does not propose such subsidy. It simply states that those parents who support private and religious schools should not be compelled to subsidize the state schools.

Those who oppose the tax-credit plan also argue that parents who wish to send their children to private schools should be willing to pay the extra costs—over-and-above the tax for state schools. What that adds up to is this:

> *only the wealthy are entitled to free choice. Caesar's tax take leaves most middle and lower income bracket families no option. They must send their children to state-controlled schools.*

What Neutrality?

There must be a strong and permanent separation of church and state. Government should practice strict neutrality when it comes to religious affairs. And, that is exactly where existing tax laws (and court decisions regarding such laws) do violence to religious freedom:

> *Where is the neutrality when Caesar erects extra hurdles and enforces double burdens on those who wish to send their children to non-state schools?*

What is at stake is not the issue of church and state. What is at stake is the matter of equity—equity and free choice. The law now operates as an economic sanction against millions of Americans. Some can afford to pay the tax on free choice; most must submit the care and mental-feeding of their children to Caesar.

The tax-credit plan would help to put a stop to such inequity.

State Controls

In addition to injecting the open market drive for excellence into the state school system, there is another reason for the implementation of the voucher and/or the tax-credit plan:

—*recent court decisions (such as Serrano vs. Priest) require that every child within a state be given equal educational opportunities in terms of public expenditures—meaning that no matter where a child may live, and no matter what the relative wealth (tax base) of the school district, the same amount of tax money must be spent for each child's education in the public system.*

The court's decision carries with it some frightening specters for those who believe in keeping the administration of public education close to home. These are the grim potentials:

—*the end of local control of public schools*
—*the end of pluralism and diversity* (or, what little remains)
—*the accelerated onslaught of uniformity,* and
—*a levelling down to mediocrity.*

Many states now wrestle with these problems; other states will face them soon.

One solution that keeps popping to the top is advocacy of a *statewide property tax.* That would be a horrendous solution. It would be a giant leap backward—for education and for the taxpayer.

To shift property taxes to the state would be to transfer complete control of public schools to the state level and destroy what little local control that now remains. If parents think wrestling with the local school board, or the district office, is rough–wait until they tackle the state bureaucracy! *And, that is just what would happen!*

When the state starts doling out the money for salaries and books and supplies, the state will also start dictating what textbooks will be used, what courses will be taught and how, what teachers will be employed, and what rules of conduct will prevail.

Furthermore, once the state moves into the area of property taxation, any control homeowners might have over assessments and rates would vanish. Property owners would be like plums on a tree, ready for the picking; plucked at the whim and ways of the taxers and spenders at the state capital–far from the county seat or the city hall.

Federal Controls

There is another specter raised by the courts' decisions on "equal educational opportunity". That is the distinct possibility of federal control of public education.

Already, there are those who take this line:

> if the courts' decisions for "equality" and "uniformity" make sense at the state level, they make even more sense at the federal level. Why, they argue, should not the child living in one state receive the same education as the children living in every other state? Thus, according to their gospel the federal government should take over public education.

Those who seek ever-higher levels of control in their quest for "equality" and "uniformity" should know by now that the higher the level of control, the more the individual shrinks–in size, importance, uniqueness, and opportunity. At the local level, the individual may be a giant; at the state level he is a digit, and in Washington, he is a speck.

Big government always comes at a tremendous cost to the little people.

The Root Evil

It would take at least a volume, of and in itself, to consider all those issues surrounding public education that concern most parents.*

All are pressing problems that demand attention and solution. But, those problems—each in its own way—stem from a central cancer, a root evil:

compulsory education.

As Leonard Read suggests, *"All the furor now going on against our schools, if carefully diagnosed, would be found to stem from this one evil."* [33]

If we are to solve the crises in our schools and our public school system, we must have the courage and the intelligence to face this root issue head-on.

Just when was it Caesar grabbed so much power over the lives of our young? It did not start with the founding fathers. They knew better. They feared God. And, they respected the individual and the family unit. They did not make the State the keeper of the child, or of his mind. That was reserved for the parents—and Almighty God.

The coercion came when the State replaced God as lord and parent as mentor (Ref. Chapter Two, *False Gods, Strange Prophets*). It came through subtle salesmen who saw Humanism as the shepherd and the State as man's instrument of salvation.

They proclaimed that education is good. *And, it is.*

They proposed that therefore compulsory education, under the wing of the State, would be even better. *And, it wasn't.* Coercion never is. One compulsion leads to another.

But, in its laudable vision that each and every individual would

---

*To name a few: the failure to teach effectively basic subjects and academic skills; increasing smut and sex in the classroom and on the school grounds; the tide of drugs and drunkenness; the cult of evolution and humanism; compulsory busing and the decline of neighborhood schools; increasing intervention from state and federal agencies; the push for "early education" starting at age three years, nine months; the lowering of standards for teacher credentialling; the rising costs of public education in face of declining enrollment and deteriorating quality, etc.

have the maximum opportunity for self-improvement and for growth, America went along. It bought the short-cut of coercion. The goal of educational opportunity was commendable; it was the short-cut that was deadly. Coercion does not propagate freedom or perpetuate faith. Each brings forth its kind and only freedom germinates freedom.

It all came together eventually; the belittling of God, the glorification of Caesar, the revival of the pagan view that man was born to serve the State, the socialization of America—all part of the root evil.

> "I am as sure as I am of Christ's reign that a comprehensive and centralized system of national education, separated from religion, as is now commonly proposed, will prove the most appalling enginery for the propagation of anti-Christian and atheistic unbelief, and of anti-social nihilistic ethics, individual, social and political, which this sin-rent world has ever seen." [34]

Thus our children develop by the numbers. Hup-two-three-four. Out of the home, out of the church, into the computer. By the cipher, march. Another six-year-old devolves into a digit. Gradually individuality and diversity vanish and each is stamped with Caesar's mark.

Aggressive Force

"How a child, during the formative years of life, could spend a large portion of his waking hours in a socialistic institution and not emerge with socialistic ideas, defies imagination. Many persons who believe aggressive force to be evil, if called upon to name the one single behavior pattern more responsible than any other for such socialism as we now have in America, would no doubt name the aggressive elements in our education system." [35]

This is not to negate, in any way, the many good works achieved through education—or to suggest its demise. Or, is it to ignore or downgrade the dedicated efforts and accomplishments of the many fine administrators and educators in the system. But, as Leonard Read points out, "The good work being done in government education is in spite of, not because of, aggressive force (compulsory education)." [36]

Three-Pronged Coercion

The public (government) education system engages in coercion in three areas–on three levels:

–compulsory attendance
–compulsory curriculum, and
–compulsory financing (taxation).

As matters now stand, there are few avenues of escape from such coercion for the average citizen. They must endure the heavy hand of Caesar. Some, through wealth or sacrifice, can send their children to private institutions. But, the great number of American parents, and taxpayers, submit . . . and the necessity of the situation is too seldom faced squarely by most Americans:

> "The need to attack (the evils) by advocating the outright abolition of all statist schools as inimical to liberty." [37]

Union Control

Now we are faced with an additional emerging coercive force; the specter of additional control through the teachers' unions. Apart from demands on wages and working conditions, more and more teachers' unions are employing aggressive force against the parent and the child. They demand the right to veto such decisions as pertain to curriculum, class-content and lesson plans, and the governance of student activities. Such policy decisions do not belong to the teacher, or to the union; they belong to the citizen–the parent and the taxpayer–and to the administrators and boards to whom they have entrusted the governance of the schools.

There are now moves to lump school management-labor relations into one giant monolithic structure–elementary, secondary and higher education. Should that occur, labor monopoly would join government monopoly in the control of public education. Parents and students would be helpless—pawns in a power struggle that seldom, if ever, had their best interests in mind.*

Lest you think this to be exaggeration, ponder the words of Herrick Roth.[38] In 1973, the former head of Colorado's labor council told delegates to an American Federation of Teachers' convention that the labor movement would not reach its "ultimate" until Union Shop signs were posted in every classroom. He also advised the teacher-delegates that they must place their union obligations first—above their professional responsibilities and above the best interests of the students.

That is not academic freedom; it is not even education. It is coercion; it bespeaks indoctrination in the classroom. Consider the impact of such activities, and especially teacher strikes, on the minds of the students. The message—the "learning"—is clear:

> *get what you want any way you can get it, regardless of who is inconvenienced or injured.*

Instant Drop Outs?

Even in the face of all those evils, the individual who openly opposes compulsory government (statist) education is usually scored as an anti-social heretic, or a kook. In kinder terms, the person is belittled as being "anti-education".

Such defamatory remarks are baseless. If anything, those who have the courage to oppose government coercion are in fact pro-education in the finest and fullest sense of the word.

To charge that a person is opposed to education because he is

---

*"The *Congressional Quarterly* reported on the emphasis which the million-and-a-half teacher members of the National Education Association placed this year (1974) on electing people who are 'friendly to education'." Dr. John Howard, pres., Rockford (Ill.) College, in a speech before the Natl. Soft Drink Assn., 11/20/74. Dr. Howard also noted, "We have in higher education today a large and very powerful segment of society which seems to be locked into a dependence upon the federal government and, with the exception of a few maverick professors here and there, is heavily committed to the social philosophy we have been following since the 1930s."

opposed to compulsory government education is akin to insinuating that an individual is opposed to religion because he is against state selection of the clergy and compulsory attendance at a state church.

There are, for example, physicians who will raise their eyebrows at the thought of halting compulsory government education and permitting voluntarism to hold forth. Yet, these same physicians rail against state control of medicine. Are the healing arts any more important than education? Are they suggesting that the patient and the physician should be free of state control but that the student and the parent and the educator should be captives of that coercion?

And, what of the clergy who condone compulsory statist education? Are they saying that Caesar should hold sway in the classroom but not the chapel? Can training of the spirit truly succeed if the training of the mind is chained at an opposite—or antagonistic—pole?

The most prevalent rebuttal to the call for a halt to government coercion in education is this:

If there were no coercion, there would be no education.

How fatuous! Pursue that line for a moment. Ask yourself, or your neighbor, *"If compulsory education were to end tomorrow, would you remove your child from school?"*

The answer is, *"Of course not. But, others would."*

It's always "the other guy".

How does one presume to speak for him—or predict his actions, or prescribe his values. Perhaps "the other guy" would say the same about you: "I wouldn't, but he would."

If that is the reason for opposing a halt to compulsory government education, is this not implicit in it:

That you claim the right to compel him to act against his will? That, since you feel he does not know what is best for him, or for his children, you must force him to do what is correct?

Well, who gave you the right to play god—either directly or by proxy?

"If aggressive force is evil—and if the end pre-exists in the means—then it follows that compulsory education is evil. If education is good, then it cannot possibly be the product of aggression. These conclusions must be correct, or one or both of the assumptions must be proved incorrect.

"It appears that the assumptions and the conclusions are correct, for is not aggressive force evil? And, does not the end pre-exist in the means? And, all of us believe that education is good." [39]

Is it not strange that those who tout academic freedom do not understand this truth?

No Coercion, No Schools?

The other argument generally raised to defend coercive education is this:

> *If we do not compel people to support a public education system we would have no schools. Furthermore, children of those who could not afford private schools would be deprived of their right to education.*

That bucket, too, is full of holes. It has no bottom.

In 1974, Americans paid more than $80 billion in taxes to finance the public schools. In addition, millions of Americans paid $16 billion (on top of their taxes) to send their children to private schools and colleges. That was a total outlay of more than $96 billion.

Do you really believe that if those taxes—or a major portion of them—were cancelled Americans would simply pocket the funds, or fritter them away on what some might deem non-essentials.* *To make such a suggestion is to belittle the intelligence and demean the values and the aspirations of the average American.*

Most of the tax saving would—voluntarily—go back into education. It would be used to finance educational institutions—sectarian and secular. In addition to restoring freedom of choice and action, it would result in better education—accountable education—at less cost.

Let us suppose, for a moment, that compulsory education and coercive school financing were ended. This is a fairly realistic picture of what would transpire:

---

*It is risky to label someone else's purchases as non-essential. In a society of free individuals, each refrains from judging his neighbor's personal tastes ("to each his own").

- hundreds of thousands of churches, synagogues and other organizations would swing into action. They would establish—or enlarge—their own school facilities and teaching staffs. Thus there would be diversity and a wide-range of free choice. The institutions would be funded voluntarily by the members and by the parents of the children in attendance.
  (At present, about 10% of all the money going to elementary and secondary education in America is spent voluntarily to send 13% of all students in those grades to private schools. If the heavy hand of government coercion and confiscation were removed, those totals would mushroom.)
- the great majority of those schools would open their doors to children from low-income families—through scholarships, work-aid and earn-and-learn programs. Many private schools do that now.
- many individuals who already contribute to private schools would increase their contributions and many who do not now give would do so, since a reduction in taxes would enable them to give more.
- many companies and corporations and foundations, free of the burden of compulsory education taxes, would increase or institute programs of support to educational institutions, and
- given the open door of free enterprise, many educators, administrators and business firms throughout the nation would support joint ventures to offer vital, innovative and responsive education at the lowest possible price. Those new enterprises would attract the best of the teaching profession who would welcome the opportunity to be freed from Caesar's enervating apparatus.
  (Those who would question the validity of such potential should consider this: Suppose that fifty years ago government had taken over the development, manufacture and sales of such important commodities as automobiles, electricity, houses, or telephones or petroleum products. What would have happened? Look to the postal service for an answer. Or, to the state schools. Coercion and monopoly seldom result in excellence.)

Train Up a Child . . .

Even the very real potential of higher quality and lower costs are subsidiary to the central issue:

the issue of coercion and government control over the education of our young.

Does not the contention that coercion (the use of aggressive force) is necessary for the perpetuation of the system indict government education? Does it not lay bare its failures as well as its compulsion? Any apparatus that requires coercion to preserve its existence is immoral; it is also generally rife with mediocrity, if not outright failure.

If American parents truly desire to regain control over the formal training of their children they must have the courage to face the question of government education. Not just the courage, but the wisdom to pursue the matter to its proper solution.

"If the foundations are destroyed, what can the righteous do?"

Answer: *Rebuild the foundations!* And that includes working to elect God-centered men and women to the school boards, to the state legislature, and to the U. S. Congress.

CHAPTER SEVEN

STEWARDSHIP OR SOCIALISM?

"All that we have comes from God . . .".[1]

We are God's stewards.

The way we produce and the way we use what we earn—these are important measurements of our stewardship.

God wants us to prosper. As a loving and bountiful Father who holds the riches of the world in His hand, He wants to bless us . . . both spiritually and materially.

"The desire of the righteous shall be granted."[2]

The key word there is "righteous"; thus the promise is provisional, not automatic. The test is whether we are motivated by the things of The Spirit, or the things of the flesh. To put it bluntly, it is not wealth that is the root of all evil (wealth can be used to serve God); it is the *love* of wealth—putting it ahead of God—that is the root of evil.

"Blessed Is The Nation"

The Scriptures are full of God's promised blessings to His people—blessings both spiritual and material.

God assures us, through Moses, that "all these blessings shall come on thee and overtake thee, if thou shalt hearken unto the voice of the Lord thy God. Blessed shalt thou be in the city (in your profession or trade or industry), and blessed shalt thou be in the field." [3] "Blessed shall by thy basket and thy store." [4]

David tells us in Psalms 33:21, "Blessed is the nation whose God is The Lord and the people whom He has chosen for His own inheritance."

And the Apostle Paul reminds us that "God shall supply all your need according to His riches in glory by Christ Jesus." [5]

To be sure, these are first and foremost spiritual blessings; but they are also material blessings; God's blessing of our efforts so that we may be a blessing to others. How we apply ourselves and our talents is a measure of our *Christian stewardship.*[6] How we use God's bounty as a blessing to others in His name is a measure of our Christian *love.*[7]

(The subject of Christian love and sharing is developed in Chapter Nine, *The Greatest of These Is Love*).

"Economics"

When you get right down to it, all economic systems have the same components:

Natural Resources (God's earth and its riches)
Human Energy (man created in the image of God), and
Tools (the extensions of man's mind and body).

All economic systems are concerned with the same basic problem:

The production and distribution
of goods and services
to meet the needs and wants of people.

That is what economics is all about: The utilization of natural resources and human energy and tools to provide man's material well-being.

The fundamental diffe ... " stems from the value placed upon the ... dividual. In some systems the individual c ... al is simply counted.

Basically, Two Systems

There are, essentially, two basic economic systems in the world:

The Christian Idea (stewardship)–in which man is considered a divine creation, made in the image of God. Under this idea man is a free agent, accountable to God. Man should not be subservient to the State, or to the system. The individual is his own decision-maker, the manager of his own affairs. The State is his instrument, his protector. As God's steward, man should be free to use his energies, his talents, and his property (including his tools) as he chooses so long as he does not interfere with the equal right of other men to do the same.

The Pagan Idea (socialism)–in which man's value depends upon his worth to the State. The State is the master. It demands "divine rights"–whether it be for kings, dictators, or commissars. It controls man's energies; it controls the natural resources; it controls the ownership and use of tools, and it attempts to control man's mind.

We call the pagan idea *socialism.* We can see it in operation in the atheistic Soviet Union, in Red China and in other countries.

"Socialism is the antithesis of Christianity. It is urged by people who have lost faith in God and the power of their religion to motivate men, and who have resorted to government and coercive power of the state as a substitute."

That is the way Archbishop Fulton J. Sheen put it.[8]

We call the Christian idea of stewardship *free individual enterprise.* It is the system we use, in varying degrees, in the United States. There was a time when we applied it to a greater degree and reaped a fuller measure of its bounty.

Christian Economics

Spiritual freedom and economic freedom are two sides of the

same coin.

As Fred G. Clark and Richard S. Rimanoczy point out in *Christianity and Capitalism,* the great economic reforms—as well as the great political reforms—stemmed from the Christian faith. In terms of economics, Christianity is the foundation of the free individual enterprise system:

> *—the right to own and use property without government interference*
>
> "Private property is one of the expressions of spiritual freedom because it is one of the flowerings of the essential dignity of the individual ascribed to him by God."[9]
>
> *—the right of every man to consider his home his castle*
>
> *—the right of the individual, alone or in concert with other men, to own and control the use of the tools of production,* and
>
> *—the Christian concept of business ethics*
>
> . . . the idea of *fair competition*
> . . . of *true value*
> . . . of *full measure*
> . . . of *fair wages*
> . . . of *honest labor*
> . . . of *honest advertising and selling,* and
> . . . the idea of the *free market.*

Archbishop Sheen explains the fruits of Christian economics this way:

> *"Christianity would allow each man to have the use of all he earns. This encourages capital expansion, greater production, more jobs, less poverty and increased well-being."*[10]

And then the Archbishop adds:

> *"Christianity also teaches each man voluntarily to share the results of his success with those who are less fortunate."*[11]

Thus, part of the dynamics of Christian economics is God's *law of returns:* as you sow, so shall you reap.*

In other words, to complete the productive cycle in Christian economics, the "Christian love" with which we use the fruits of our personal property is just as essential as the "Christian ethic"

---

* "Give and it shall be given unto you; good measure, pressed down, and shaken together and running over . . ." *Luke 6:38*

of private property. The Golden Rule must be the *modus operandi* of free individual enterprise (Christian capitalism).*

"Every man's work shall be made manifest." I Cor. 3:13.

Look At The Record!

The economic by-products of God-centered individuals in free enterprise have outstripped the productivity of all other systems. That should be no surprise. When we walk in the light of The Lord, we prosper; when we stray from the way, things go sour. It was thus in the days of the Prophets; it is thus in these days of the followers.

Today, the United States–

with *six percent* of the world's population

5.4 percent of the world's labor force, and

seven percent of the world's land mass–

accounts for *more than thirty percent* of the world's total production.[12]

Working together–in labor, management and capital–the people of this nation produce [13]

–20% of the world's steel
–35% of the world's electric power
–20% of the world's crude oil
–46% of the corn
–73% of the soybeans
–25% of the coal
–38% of the synthetic fibers, and
–about 40% of all manufactured goods in the world.

As a result of their productivity, the people of the United States have [14]

–more than two-thirds of all the digital computers in the world
–45% of all the motor vehicles (cars, trucks and tractors)
–42% of all the telephones

---

*This can often be seen as the difference in the conduct of those who practice freedom for freedom's sake and those who practice freedom for Christ's sake.

—45% [illegible] os, and

—70% of all the television sets.

Our railroads carry about thirty percent of all the *rail freight* hauled in the world and our commercial airlines fly more than fifty percent of all the miles chalked up by *civil aviation* in all nations.

Freemen Produce Better

All of this is not brag. Not boast. Just fact.

Freemen try harder and produce better.

We have not achieved perfection. Utopia will not come until Christ returns to establish His kingdom. But, we have achieved more than others and in the meantime we strive to improve what we do and how we do it.

Forty years ago, almost ninety percent of our people lived below what is now called the "poverty level". Today, that figure is about ten percent and we are working to reduce that.

Forty years ago, two-thirds of our people lived in what would now be called sub-standard housing. Today, that figure is less than ten percent and if the dynamics of free enterprise are not completely stymied, we'll improve on that.

Twenty-five years ago, only thirty-three percent of our adult population had a *high school education.* Today, it is more than sixty percent. The number of *college degrees* granted each year has more than doubled since 1960. During that same period, the number of persons enrolled in *vocational schools and programs* has more than tripled.

During the decade, 1963-73, *median family income* increased at an average rate of 2.9 percent a year and per capita disposable income rose 3.5 percent a year (in 1974 constant dollars).

Even with the increasingly voracious appetite of government gnawing away at the nation's productivity, free enterprise has managed to outpace the rise in taxes and inflation until just recently. The average factory worker, who earns about $10,000 a year, must now work fifteen percent of his day to pay his federal income and Social Security taxes—state and local taxes are on top of that.

In 1939, he worked one percent of his day to pay those federal taxes.

Racial Solution

As freemen, Americans have faced up to the racial problem in a way no other nation has done before—*or yet.*

There is still much to be done before the ground at life's starting gate is as level as the ground at the foot of the Cross. But, let no one negate the spirit of America in this regard. Its people are working to solve the so-called "race problem" as rapidly as possible within the practicalities of reality and within the concept of building up rather than tearing down.

The record of the past ten years is a manifestation of that affirmation:

—during the past ten years [15]

. . . the number of black attorneys, accountants, college teachers and other professionals has almost doubled

. . . the employment of blacks in white collar jobs increased more than fifty percent

. . . the number of blacks being graduated from college each year has doubled

. . . the number of young black people being graduated from high school has increased by one hundred percent, and

. . . the number of blacks employed as skilled craftsmen and foremen has increased more than fifty percent.

Today, thirty percent of our black Americans hold jobs in the highest employment categories.

Between the years 1968 and 1973, the number of blacks earning $15,000 a year or more almost tripled; the number earning $12,000 and above more than doubled, and the number of black families with incomes of $10,000 or more was doubled.[16]

Between 1960 and 1973, the median income for black families increased sixty-three percent and the number of families with incomes of less than $3,000 a year was almost halved.

There are now some 3,000 elected black officials in the United

States; ten times the number in office just ten years ago. There are eighteen black congressmen, 278 state legislators and 120 mayors of towns and cities (including Los Angeles, Detroit, Atlanta and Cincinnati).[17]

Again, this is not brag, or boast, or smugness. Just fact.

Minimum Wage

One of the economic categories in which the blacks (and other non-whites) have made no progress–and, in fact, have lost ground–is the rate of unemployment among teenagers 16 to 19 years of age.

In 1954, the unemployment rate among white teenagers was 12.1 percent. The rate among non-white teenagers was 16.5 percent; a spread of 4.4 percent. In 1973, that spread had increased to 17.6 percent; it was 12.6 percent among white teenagers and 30.2 percent among non-white teenagers.

Why the drastic increase in unemployment among non-white teenagers? *By far the greatest cause has been the Federal minimum wage laws. Every time the minimum wage is raised, another door is slammed shut for those who are trying to grab the lower rungs of the economic ladder.**

Today the $2.10-an-hour minimum wage law keeps hundreds of thousands of young non-white teenagers out of the job market. It consigns them to welfare, or to the streets; it robs many of them of the opportunity to earn sufficient money to get additional education. And it prevents many of them from learning on the job so that they can begin the climb on the ladder of economic self-sufficiency.

Some first-time job seekers just do not have the education or the abilities to deliver $2.10-worth of work an hour. Any businessman who expects to stay in business cannot afford to pay for something that is not produced. As Henry Hazlitt points out:

---

* In 1956, the minimum wage was raised to $1.00 an hour; in 1968 to $1.60 an hour, and in 1973 it was set at $2.10 an hour.

> *"The law cannot make a worker worth a given amount by making it illegal for anyone to offer him less. It can merely make it unprofitable for employers to hire workers of low skills and therefore forces such workers into unemployment."* [18]

That is a fact of life. If it seems harsh, blame the consumer. To raise the hourly wage, the businessman must raise his prices. When prices get out of line, the consumers won't buy. Ask yourself, isn't that true?

And, consider this:

Is not the minimum wage law a violation of the unalienable rights of those young people? You bet it is. Who are we–and who is Caesar–to tell them they cannot pump gas, or sweep floors, or carry parcels for less than so much an hour? That is a matter between the employe and the employer. As long as their transaction is made voluntarily, that's their business–not some lawmakers' in Washington.

If we truly want to help the non-white teenagers, one of the most helpful things we could do would be to *repeal the minimum wage laws.* Get government out of the wage-setting business and let minimum wages seek their own level in the market place. Employers could then afford to employ the unskilled teenagers who are trying to get a start–and the young people could then begin to *earn while they learn.* What is involved in this area is not just economic factors but psychological and sociological factors as well.

Foreign Assistance

There are those who sneer at the United States and call it stingy and selfish. Yet, no nation has ever given so freely of its substance–its wealth, its production, and its resources.

- During World War Two, America sent *more than $42 billion* in lend-lease to sustain our Allies and help defeat tyranny abroad. We still pay the interest on that part of those gifts that was deficit-financed.
- Since the end of World War Two we have given *more than*

$170 billion in aid to other nations.* Add the interest we have paid for the resultant increase in our Federal debt and the total cost of that foreign aid now stands at more than *$264 billion.*

- Our gifts to Great Britain and France helped those nations climb back from the devastation of war.
- Our economic aid rescued West Germany from the brink of economic disaster.
- Our help gave Japan a new life and helped make them one of the great economic powers in the world today.
- Our economic and technical assistance has meant the difference to many emerging nations.
- From 1950 to 1953, we spent $54 billion and the lives of 54,000 of our men to help the Republic of Korea make its fight for freedom.
- All told, we spent more than $150 billion and 55,000 lives to try to help the South Vietnamese defend themselves from the tyranny and bloodbath of Communism.

Consider what all of this has meant and done for those nations that received our help.

Consider what those sacrifices have cost us.

Think about what we might have done with all those monies had we thought only of ourselves and spent the funds here at home while ignoring the agonies and needs of others.

Just the $170 billion reportedly spent on foreign aid from 1946 to 1974–just the principle without including the interest–could have provided the capital investment for

–*3,400,000 productive jobs* in industry (at an average capital investment of $50,000 per job for plant, machinery and equipment).

–*7 million private dwellings* (at an average cost of $25,000

* If the whole truth were known, the total costs of foreign aid would no doubt be even more startling. Robert S. Strother asserts that the actual annual amount spent can be as much as five times more than the total for the "mainline programs" established under the Foreign Assistance Act. In 1974, for example, the items openly tabbed as foreign aid totalled $2.4 billion–but the actual amount spent was close to $11 billion! [19]

per house).

–*34,000 miles of divided four-lane freeway* (at an average cost of $5 million per mile for right of way and construction).

–*17,000 hospitals* (at an average capital outlay of $10 million each for land, buildings and equipment).

–*6,800 college campuses* (at an average cost of $25 million for land, buildings and equipment), or

–*a $3,200 savings account for each and every family in the United States.*

All of that is just an indication of what Americans gave to other nations since 1946 . . .

. . . through our government *and over and above the voluntary gifts of individuals and private institutions* to support missions and medical, educational, relief and various self-help programs.

All of this is what we gave. And yet there are those who damn us for doing so little. What other nation has done so much? *Name one!*

What If There Were No United States?

Several years ago John Gorton, then Prime Minister of Australia, commented on the compassion and the generosity of the American people:

"I wonder if anybody has thought what the situation of comparatively small nations would be if there were not in existence a United States of America–with a heritage and a willingness to see that small nations who might otherwise not be able to protect themselves are given some shield. Imagine what the situation would be if there were not a great and giant country prepared to make such sacrifices!" [20]

This review of what Americans have done is not made to boast. It is made to make a point–to make two points:

–*We have shared God's blessings with others.*

–*We could not have helped as we did without first working and saving and investing to produce America's material wealth. Before we could share we had to produce; before we could give we had to earn. And the reason we could do so in such magnitude was due primarily to the free enterprise system that is a manifestation of the Christian Idea.*

II.

Socialists boast they will provide the most for the greatest number.

But it is free individual enterprise that produces the greatest good (and goods) for the largest number of people. While socialists are busy confiscating, free enterprisers are busy inventing, creating, producing—and spreading real wealth.

In *America's Needs and Resources,* Frederic Dewhurst whacks the spike on the head:

> "Of all the great nations the one that clings most tenaciously to private capitalism has come closest to the socialist goal of providing abundance for all in a classless society." [21]

Yet, there are still those who depreciate the achievements and the aspirations of this free America. Those who extoll the "virtues" of socialism. Those who urge that we change our system and "match" the accomplishments of collectivism—as in the Soviet Union.

Assuming they refer to the production of goods and services—to the creation of material welfare—rather than Russia's slave labor camps and purges and invasion of hapless captive nations, let's compare the achievements of the two systems.

Here is what we would have to do to "equal" the Soviet Union: [22]

—close down 20% of our petroleum production.
—scrap 40% of our electronic equipment
—junk 60% of our electric generators
—cancel 50% of our aluminum production
—shut down 50% of our hydro-electric plants, and
—slash our natural gas production by two-thirds.

Just to "keep up" with the U.S.S.R., we would have to

—rip out 18 of every 20 miles of paved highway
—tear out one of every three miles of railroad track

–junk 18 out of every 20 cars and trucks
–destroy 95 out of every 100 computers
–discard about 39.5 million television sets
–rip out nine of every ten telephones
–tear down seven of every ten private homes
–dump one-third of all our refrigerators, 90% of our radios and 80% of our vacuum cleaners, and
–reduce our standard of living by about 50%!

Our Daily Bread

In 1972, with a total population of about 250 million, the Soviet Union had an estimated gross national product of $545 billion. In that same year, with a population of 208 million, the United States turned out a gross national product of $1.1 trillion–more than double that of Russia.

On a per capita basis, Russia's GNP came to $2,280; the GNP of the United States averaged $5,375 per person.[23]

Translate that gap into some of the necessities of life.

In the United States, it takes the average working man about five minutes to "earn" a loaf of bread; in Russia it takes seventeen minutes.

In the U.S., it takes the average worker twelve minutes to earn one dozen eggs; in the U.S.S.R., it takes ninety-three minutes.

In Russia it takes Ivan about 160 hours to earn a man's suit and it takes Katrina about 42 hours to earn enough for a woman's dress. Here, Bill Bagadonuts can earn a suit in about 20 hours and Mrs. Bill can earn a dress in about six.

In the United States the average working Joe can earn the money for a new compact car in about six months; in Russia it would take Dimitri at least four years–if one were available.

Those are just a few of the material differences. *The spiritual gap–the chasm between individual freedom and socialism–is a Grand Canyon.* There are no Baptist ministers in the United States being sent to Siberia; no Jews being refused the right to emigrate to Israel. Some of our politicians may reject the presence of God in government but as yet they have not tried to tell our clergy what they must and must not preach to their congregations.

Down on the Farm

Nowhere is the failure of socialism more obvious than in Soviet agriculture.

The most obvious indication of that was Russia's recent forced importation of thirty million tons of grain to forestall bread shortages and calm the threat of worker protests. Soviet authorities blamed their wheat shortage on the weather. But farmers in other nations with similar climatic conditions–Canada, for one–cope with the weather and produce enough grain for both domestic and foreign sales.

The fact is "Russian agriculture under the Communist system has proved to be both costly and woefully inefficient." [24]

The plain truth is, freemen do produce better. One American farmer outproduces seven Soviet farm workers. It's not simply that there are more than four and one-half million farm tractors in the United States, as compared with only one and one-quarter million in the Soviet Union. It's that *plus* the fact that the American farmer owns his tractor–and his farm.

In *The Old Story,* radio commentator Earl Nightingale reported that workers on state-owned and collective-owned farms are allowed to have small plots of land and a few head of live-stock on their own. The produce from those private farms can be sold on the open market at open prices.*

"All together these tiny, scattered patches of ground total less than four percent of the cultivated land in Russia–but the communists' own statistics show that they produce about one-third of the total Russian food supply." [25]

To be more specific, that four percent of the land–worked by Russian peasants on their own and for themselves–produced more

---

* A gesture originally made by Joseph Stalin to appease the peasants and reduce sabotage on state-owned farms. The private mini-farms were legalized in 1962.

than sixty percent of Russia's potatoes, half the Russian milk supply, three-fourths of their eggs, and almost one-half of the Soviet's meat production!

Results of Regimentation

The Soviet Union has had complete–*complete*–control over the people of Russia for the past fifty-six years. Even with such total regimentation, it cannot make socialism work.

The Soviet Union has had, over the years, billions upon billions of help from American government and American industry–from $11 billion in lend-lease, to hydro-electric plants, automobile and truck factories, and the "liberated" tools and machinery from the factories of a defeated Germany. Even with such outside assistance, socialism continues to be a failure.

The gap between the achievements of socialism and free enterprise–in terms of gross national product and standard of living–is not closing; *it continues to get wider.* In recent years, even while carrying the increasing burden of governmental costs and governmental controls, America's free individual enterprise continues to outproduce the socialism of the U.S.S.R.

Analysts see no likelihood that the Soviet Union will match the economic achievements of the United States within any foreseeable span of years.[26]

Archbishop Fulton Sheen tells why:

> *"Socialism which seizes, divides, expends and dissipates wealth is anti-Christian. It always has produced poverty. It always will, for it discourages the man who is dispossessed. Few will work hard if they know they are to be dispossessed of the fruits of their labor. On the other hand, those who receive something for nothing learn to depend upon it. Their initiative, self-reliance and effort decline accordingly. These two factors combined are the reasons for poverty and suffering produced by socialism."* [27]

A Lesson for Us

Far from trying to "match" the Soviet Union. we should take

the lesson of its failure to heart.

Freemen produce more.

Free individual enterprise works.

Borrowing a phrase from our young people, "it's where the action is". The action–and the results.

But, there is nothing of survival inherent in freedom and there is no assurance that our government will limit its activities to preserving freedom while confining itself to its Constitutional responsibilities. In fact, recent years and recent events give us reason to fear that the Caesars of America become bolder by the day. They may not be lean and hungry–but they have that look, that arrogance of officialdom.

"A government that manipulates money and credit, that regulates and controls wages and prices and rents and profits, that owns or closely supervises numerous business activities, and that offers welfare programs from cradle to grave, is a government that threatens to tax the citizenry into serfdom." [28]

And a serf is a serf is a serf–is a slave . . .

. . . not a steward, a slave!

CHAPTER EIGHT

CONTROLLED PEOPLE AND UNCONTROLLED GOVERNMENT

It wasn't government spending, or government planning, or government controls that built this nation. It wasn't the red tape of the petticlerks, or the hot air of some politicians or the schemes of demigods that did it.

It was the minds and muscles and the tools and capital of America's producers—the working men and women of this nation: that's what built America!

Look at the tremendous record of the recent decades.[1]

- In 1946, the *gross national product* of the United States was $208 billion. By the close of 1973, it had increased six-fold—to $1.2 *trillion!* (Even in terms of constant 1958 dollars our GNP almost tripled in those 27 years.)
  - —That spectacular increase in GNP has meant *more for more people.* In 1947, 37.2 million families had a *median income* of $6,032; in 1973, the median income for America's *55 million families* was $11,120.*

---

* In 1973 dollars.

–During the years 1945-72, *per capita disposable income tripled,* from $1,074 to $3,595.

–In 1947, nineteen percent of the families in our nation had incomes of less than $3,000 a year. By 1973, only six percent of all families had incomes under $3,000. At the same time, the number of families with incomes of more than $10,000 more than tripled–from 13 percent to 49 percent.

Muscles, Minds and Money

These achievements of production and distribution of wealth did not come out of any council chamber or any legislative hall. They came in spite of most of the actions of government. They came from the productivity of free men and women working together–labor, management, and investor.

- Since 1946, American business and industry has invested *more than $1 trillion* in new plants, machinery and equipment.[2]

  –In 1947, the annual total business and industry *expenditure for new plants and equipment* was $20.6 billion. By 1972, those investments had increased to $90 billion a year.[3]

  –In 1959, the *average capital investment* per productive worker was $17,528.[4] By 1974, the average investment per worker–to provide the plants, the tools, and the equipment–came to more than $30,000.*
- In 1950, there were 59 million *workers employed in American business and industry.* By 1973, that had increased to more than 84 billion.[5]

  –Total wages and salaries and benefits paid to America's private sector workers increased more than five-fold during the years 1950-73.

  –During the past two years alone, employe benefits to

* In some industries (chemical and petroleum) per-worker investment can reach $200,000.

manufacturing workers increased twenty seven percent.[6]

- From 1950 to 1973, the nation's output per man-hour almost doubled and the average compensation per man-hour tripled. And, workers had more leisure time as more machines–and more sophisticated machinery–increased their productivity.
  –*Today, machines supply almost ninety-five percent of all the manufacturing work energy expended in America!*

A Sea of Red Ink

It is only this amazing, and unequalled, productivity of American business and industry that has kept this nation from floundering in the rising tide of government confiscation, regulation, spending and debt.

Even as the gross national product rose, government's take of that GNP rose *even more rapidly*. In 1947, it took eighteen percent; in 1974, thirty-five percent.

While the nation's number of employed rose twenty-eight percent from 1960 to 1974, the number of government employes increased *more than sixty percent.*

> In 1947, all governments (federal, state and local) employed 5.8 million persons; *by 1974 that had risen to 14.1 million.* And, the total monthly government payroll had zoomed from $1.2 billion to $11.1 billion–*more than $130 billion a year.* Government expenditures for goods and services went from $25 billion a year in 1947 to $309 billion in 1974–*a twelve-fold increase.*[7]

And what of the increased taxation and debt to pay for Caesar's insatiable appetite?

> –The annual total tax take for all government *increased more than eight times* during the years 1947-74 . . . from $55 billion to $455 billion.[8]
>
> –But, the annual expenditures of government increased *eleven-fold* during those same years and thus . . .
>
> . . . *the nation's total public debt was tripled*–from $237

billion to almost $700 billion at the close of 1974.

–And meanwhile *America's gold stock* (owned by the people of this nation and once used to back our dollar) has been cut in half–from $23 billion in 1947 to $11.6 billion at the beginning of 1975. Today we have one dollar in gold reserves for every six paper dollars in circulation.

By The Rules and By The Numbers!

What does it all mean?

Simply this.

The faster our economic heart pumps, the faster government drains our economic lifeblood. Government is bleeding the patient. It is gobbling up our increased productivity at a rate faster than we can manufacture it.

Not only that.

The Lilliputians of politics and bureaucracy are binding our productive Gulliver with more and more controls, laws, regulations, ruling and edicts.

It costs business and industry (and thus the consumer) almost $20 billion a year to handle the paper work involved with government regulations. It costs government (and thus the consumer) another $20 billion a year to pay for its printers and processors and papershufflers. *That's $40 billion a year for red tape, triplicate forms, filing cabinets, postage stamps and wastepaper baskets.* And most, if not all, of it is counterproductive.[9]

–It took 1,100 different permits and approvals before the construction of the Alaska pipeline could begin. When that project was first proposed, the estimated cost was $1 billion. After years of political demagoguery and governmental foot-dragging, the estimated costs now stand at more than $6 billion. Politicians and bureaucrats won't foot that increase; the consumer will, through higher prices.

- *The Interstate Commerce Commission,* established in 1887 to regulate railroads and prevent monopolies, has driven some railroads into bankruptcy, created monopolies of its own, and stifled competition in all areas of the nation's surface transportation.[10]

- Under the *Civil Aeronautics Board* controls and restrictions, interstate air carriers have been forced into a form of government-controlled cartel that destroys competition. CAB-imposed "excess fares" and "excess capacity" cost air passengers more than $100 million in 1969. Intrastate airlines (not under CAB's thumb) fly their passengers at fares that are generally forty percent lower than those enforced on interstate airlines by the CAB.[11]
- *Banks and thrift institutions* are probably the most highly-controlled industry in the nation. Virtually every aspect of the banking business is under government control–including the rate of interest such institutions can pay their depositors.
- *The Federal Power Commission* through its policies has deprived millions of consumers (private and industrial) of badly-needed natural gas. By arbitrarily holding the wellhead price of natural gas below profitable levels the FPC has destroyed incentive and diminished production. As a result, the FPC has been responsible for forcing the increased importation of petroleum and petroleum products–thus increasing the consumer's fuel bills while adding to our deficits in international trade.
- *Federal agricultural price supports* force the consumer to buy with his tax dollar what he would not or could not buy on his own. And, *Federal agricultural export subsidies* force the consumer to pay farmers to sell produce to foreign buyers at prices lower than than the consumer can buy them here at home.[12]
- *The Federal OSHA laws* (Occupational Safety and Health Act)–and the state OSHA laws (that must comply with Federal mandates)–are sending into the field a new army of bureaucrats, inspectors and spies. Under OSHA, these "safety engineers" have the authority to invade any business any time of the working day or night–without warning or permission. These legions of demiCaesars hold the power of life and death over the businessman. They can act as prosecutor, judge and jury. They can tell the entrepreneur

what he must and must not do, what type of equipment he can and cannot use, and set the penalties and levy the fines. Complaints against an employer can be made to OSHA representatives *in secret* and anyone found guilty of alerting an employer to an OSHA inspection can be fined $1,000. (Occupational safety is important and the vast majority of employers are fully conscientious about it–but police-state tactics, that is something else!)

Productivity Down, Prices Up

The list of government red tape and restrictions and counterproductive regulations goes on and on–the fair trade laws, the Robinson Patman Act (that prevents competition and subsidizes inefficient companies), etc. And for it all the consumer pays, and pays, and pays.

The *1975 Economic Report of The President* made this observation about the impact of government control and manipulation:

> *"Less efficient producers are protected, and in effect subsidized, by lower-cost producers who would expand their output in the absence of regulation and by consumers who end up paying higher prices and buying less."*

The report should have added . . .

> ". . . and by unemployed workers who would have been employed by those more efficient producers if government interference had not prevented expansion and production."

The record clearly demonstrates that as productivity increases, employment rises. Why? Because as productivity increases more consumers can afford to purchase more products; thus demand is increased and production (and jobs) rise to meet demand. Further, as more persons are employed in productive work, purchasing continues to increase and production continues to increase–thus the dynamics of free individual enterprise are unleashed to the benefit of all.

II.

During recent years Americans have gone through a succession of "crises" . . .

. . . the *dollar* crisis
. . . the *energy* crisis
. . . the *food* crisis
. . . the *fuel* crisis
. . . the *pollution* crisis
. . . the *stagflation* crisis (higher prices and rising unemployment).

In largest part, these crises have been engendered over the years by government interference in our productivity and by political manipulation of the free market. Yet, with each new crisis, as federal, state and local panaceas are unveiled, they turn out to be proposals for *even more government control* over more and more areas of our daily lives.

Add it all up, it comes to this:

controlled citizens and uncontrolled government.

The real crisis in this land—aside from the moral crisis—is the grinding growth of the costs and controls enforced by government.

Take the energy-fuel crisis as a case in point.

A Rigged Deal

Some folks think the energy-fuel crisis is a rigged deal. A stacked deck.

They may be right.

But, the rigging and the stacking was not done by the oil industry, or the energy producers. It was done by Federal bureaucrats, environmental extremists and certain expedient congressmen who were more concerned with personal power than electric power—or gas power, or nuclear power.

If these people were to have their way, there would come a day—and soon—when you would flip the switch and there would be no light; when you would adjust the thermostat and there would be no heat, no air conditioning. A day when you would go to the office, or the factory, and there would be no work–because there would be no energy to turn the wheels or power the lathes or run the computers.

This nation is already in the throes of a power shortage that can only worsen unless additional energy-generating facilities are constructed. Yet in the face of such a shortage the posey pluckers and the bug and bunny folks persist in battling every effort to build new power plants, every effort to construct new dams, every effort to explore and drill for offshore gas and oil, and every effort to expedite the surface mining of badly-needed coal and oil-bearing shale.

Look at the record.

First, in 1954, the Federal Power Commission slapped price controls on *natural gas.* A good deal? No, a bad deal. The controls stifled incentive and stymied production. As a result, by 1970 there was not enough natural gas to keep up with demand for heat, energy, fertilizer, plastics, etc. Thus, the FPC was party to the enforced reliance on high-priced imported crude oil for fuel.

At the same time, federal controls and environmentalists' demands just about finished off the *low-sulphur coal mining* industry. And, when the mines closed down or shut back, the railroad coal-hauling stock turned to disrepair and junk. Now, as coal production increases, the task of getting it where it is needed is ham-strung by a shortage of coal cars.

The ecology lobby, aided by politicians such as U.S. Senator Henry Jackson (D-Wash.) cooked up a little deal called an *"environmental impact" statement.* That little dilly was enacted in 1970 and look what it has done:

–For more than three years it stalled the construction of the *Alaska pipeline* (with its potential of 84 million gallons of oil a day).

–It has held up the development and construction of *nuclear power plants.*

–It has been used to delay the development of *shale-oil mining* and it has been employed to delay the construction of *new oil refineries.*

On top of all of that, the federal government prevented *off-shore exploration and drilling* for oil from 1969 until just recently. Those tidelands probably contain the greatest portion of this nation's oil reserves.

And finally, at a time when this nation is in an oil shortage and a dollar bind because of high-priced foreign imports, the Congress passes and the President signs a tax law that repeals the *depletion allowance* for petroleum producers. Thus, a major incentive to explore, drill and pump more oil is removed!

Wrap all those and other similar idiocies in a basic tax structure that makes it more profitable to produce oil in foreign fields–add the declining value of the U.S. dollar in foreign markets–and there's the oil crisis. It was bound to come. The problems in the Middle East simply hastened the day.

Now the left-wing talks about nationalizing the oil industry. Can you imagine the same outfit that masterminds the postal system being put in charge of the processing and delivery of petroleum products?

Conservation, Yes; Extremism, No!

As God's stewards, Christians should not waste the resources of our nation. We should husband the air, the earth, the waters and the gifts thereof. We should be judicious in our stewardship and considerate of generations yet to come as well as those here now.

Conservation and development of our natural resources is morally correct and economically sound. But, extremism in the pursuit of ecology is no virtue; it is a vice.

In an address before the National War College in Sept., 1974, Charles H. Smith, Jr., chairman of the board of the Chamber of Commerce of the U.S., described the calculated requirements to bring the discharge from one industrial plant up to U.S. Public Health standards for drinking water: [13]

> "To remove 4,000 tons of pollutants per year from the plant's discharge would require the following resources:
>
> –"Nineteen thousand tons of coal to produce steam, 9,000

tons of chemicals, and 1,500 kilowatt hours of electricity.
"In the course of the 'purification operation', the 3M plant would produce:

—"Nine thousand tons of chemical sludge . . .

—"Twelve hundred tons of fly ash . . .

—"One thousand tons of sulfur dioxide . . .

—"And 200 tons of nitrogen oxide.

"That's just at the plant. To that total must be added the environmental costs of producing the 9,000 tons of chemicals, the 1,500 kilowatt hours of electricity and the steel, concrete and other resources used in the pollution control facilities.

"What's the grand total? All together, to remove those 4,000 tons of pollutants would take 40,000 tons of natural resources per year and produce 19,000 tons of solid and gaseous waste material, for a net deficit to the environment of 15,000 tons of pollutants per year."

Ecology is indeed an important consideration in our society and no doubt the great majority of those concerned about our environment are sincere and well-intentioned. But, when they permit emotion to pre-empt reality and passion to ignore fact, they can cause more damage than good.

This Will Bug You

Take, as a case in extremism, the problem with the tussock moth.

The tussock moth is no big thing in your life. From stem to stern it measures only one and one-half inches, at the most. But, it can destroy giant fir trees. The great douglas fir, that nature may have taken fifty to sixty years to nourish, can be ravaged in one or two seasons by that pesky moth. It makes its home in the tips and the tops of those trees and is carelessly prolific with its eggs and larvae. Some of the larger trees can be salvaged after the moth has done its work, but smaller trees are lost forever.

There is only one chemical that can put an end to that pesky insect, and thus protect the trees—and that is DDT.

The Federal Environmental Protection Agency says the use of

DDT is a "no-no". It refuses to let the foresters employ the insecticide claiming that it might harm the environment. Thus, the trees die while the EPA "protects" the environment. Hundreds of millions of board feet of lumber are being destroyed in the name of ecology.

In one spectacular example of stupidity, the EPA permitted the use of 84,000 pounds of DDT to dust a dried pea crop but it refused to permit the use of the chemical on an adjacent stand of fir trees that was being infested with the tussock moth. The peas survived; the forest was wiped out.

This Will Kill You

And what did the EPA recommend as a substitute for DDT?

Methyl parathion!

On June 14, 1972, William Ruckelshaus, then administrator of the EPA, issued a directive that stated: [14]

"I am accordingly making this order (restricting the use of DDT) . . . the cancellation of any use of DDT is predicated on the availability of methyl parathion as a substitute. . . . It is abundantly clear that methyl parathion will be widely used."

What is methyl parathion? It is a highly toxic—*deadly*—organic phosphate. Check these items:

Item one: Years ago more than one dozen persons were killed in Tijuana, Mexico. The cause of death? Eating bread made from flour that had been accidentally contaminated with methyl parathion.[15]

Item two: "The tragic wave of parathion poisonings in the South, mostly of children, raises some extremely pressing questions for the federal government." (*New York Times,* Aug. 23, 1970)

Item three: "Methyl parathion is the hottest of organic phosphates. Five drops can kill a 150-pound man. It is infinitely more dangerous than DDT." (James Stearns, rancher, ex-crop duster pilot, and former California Secretary of Agriculture.)[16]

Parathion, the EPA's substitute for DDT, acts like mustard gas. It paralyzes the respiratory system.

Furthermore, it is not always effective. As a pesticide it may kill the insect but it has no effect on the insect's eggs. Farmers using the deadly chemical must spray or dust several times–after each batch of insect eggs is hatched. That not only multiplies the hazards, it increases the costs of production–and that price is paid by the consumer.

III.

The rising costs of government

–the continual counter-productive bungling of bureaucrats

–the political pandering to extremist groups . . .

. . . *these are working to wreck the productivity of America.*

The so-called "new" politics and "new" economics make it extremely difficult–impossible in some cases–for business and industry to save or secure sufficient investment capital to replace, or expand, or modernize their plant and equipment. Often what capital is available "costs" so much its use is unprofitable.

The two-digit inflation caused by the spend-in-debt policies of the liberal politicians and their bureaucratic colleagues blunts initiative by destroying incentive. In *The Hidden Injuries of Class,* economist Richard Sennett warns that inflation is feeding a hatred of work among the working class.

"The attitude is you work more and more and get less and less, so the work becomes a meaningless humiliation." [17]

Sennett sees the "why work?" infection spreading to the middle class. He suggests the high absentee rate among white collar workers is one manifestation.

The spend-free economists and politicians believe government can spend this nation into prosperity. They have made a fetish of growth at any price–not sound growth, just growth. Theirs is a "credit card" philosophy; spend now, inflate the balloon and pay later. Thus they have mortgaged this nation far beyond the anticipated fruits of future productivity. They have, indeed, decided how the wage-earners will spend a major portion of their incomes for years to come.

By eating our seed corn in this manner—even before it is raised and harvested—they relegate millions of lower income families to State dependency and invite millions more to hunker down at the public trough.

That is no way to sustain an expanding economy. It is no way to build a truly great society. It is the route to bankruptcy, disruption and despair.

Productivity

The years of strain under those spend-easy policies are beginning to take their toll. The cracks are beginning to appear.

During recent years, the rate of increase in output per man-hour in the United States has lagged behind that of the other free world nations.

The following table compares our growth in productivity with a number of other nations for the years 1960-72: [18]

Country	*Output per man-hour**
United States	3.2%
Belgium	6.5
Canada	4.2
France	5.9
Germany	5.9
Italy	6.2
Japan	10.4
Netherlands	7.1
Sweden	7.3
United Kingdom	4.0

* Average annual percent change

The gap was pretty much the same for the years 1970-72:

While our average increase in output per man-hour for those two years was 4.9 percent, it was 6.9 percent for France, 5.1

percent for West Germany, 7.7 percent for Japan, and 6.6 percent for the Netherlands and the United Kingdom.[19]

In 1974, according to the President's economic report, "the decline in output and the rise in prices were the greatest for any peacetime year since the early post-World War II period." The gross national product in 1974 increased eight percent but there was a two percent decline in output and a ten percent rise in prices.[20]

From the fourth quarter of 1973 to the fourth quarter of 1974, national productivity dropped five percent.[21]

What's the relation between productivity–output per man-hour–and gross national product? Well, here's the magical equation: [22]

a one-tenth of one percent increase (or decrease) in productivity equals a $1 billion increase (or decrease) in the gross national product.

A five percent drop in productivity can mean a loss of about $50 billion in the GNP.

Productivity is the key to prosperity.

When productivity increases, the standard of living rises. When it falls, the standard of living drops.

From 1973 to 1974, real disposable income fell 2.5 percent. That was the first time that happened in America in twenty-five years.[23]

Foreign Competition

The decline in output, and the increase in prices, is catching up with us not only at home but also in the world markets. Many American businesses are finding it increasingly difficult to compete with foreign companies.

Since 1970, the amount of goods we import has grown at a faster pace than the growth in our exports.[24]

Even before then, the shift began. During the period, 1965-70, while our exports were increasing at a rate of about ten percent a year, imports were increasing at the rate of fourteen percent per year. In 1974 our imports rose one-third more rapidly than the increase in our exports.[25]

And, in 1974—for the first time since the depressed years of 1935-40—imports exceeded exports.[26]

The impact of such a trade deficit may not seem crucial to many Americans, *but it hurts.* Every dollar in imports means dollars and jobs going to competing industries in competing nations instead of to companies here at home.

The goal is not to stop imports; the task is to rebuild our productivity. To restore our competitiveness to the point where we can maintain a strong and favorable balance of trade. The way to do that is not through embargoes or higher tariffs; the way to do it is to increase the production of America.

Working Together

It is time for Americans to get back on the ball.

Time for us to bite a few bullets instead of a few fingernails . . . or, the other fellow's backside.

Together, labor and management and capital built the prosperity of this nation. Together, they can get this nation moving again as it enters its third century. Together, they can make government the servant instead of the master.

What are some of the steps we must take to increase our productivity? To restore our vitality so that we can continue the war against poverty and win the battle against inflation?

Well, one thing is sure: we won't do it by looking to Caesar to be our shepherd. We won't win the battle through increased government spending or intervention.

"Those who think that it is up to the government to create growth overlook the fact that increased economic growth depends upon the intelligence, work and thrift of individuals and corporations.

"People—not government—create growth. All the government can do is to encourage people to save and invest." [27]

People—working people, saving people, investing people—create prosperity and promote well-being.

People, working in harmony, build great societies.

Savings, Investments and Tools

"There is only one way to achieve growth–that is by the increased savings and by increased investment in the tools of production. In this way there is a greater flow of goods resulting from every hour of human labor." [28]

Remember the magical formula?

$MMW = NR + HE \times T.$

Man's material well-being equals natural resources plus human energy multiplied by tools.

That's it!

The tools used by freemen are the key to productivity–and, productivity is the key to economic growth and well-being for the greatest number of people. James Watt, the man who invented the steam engine and pioneered the idea of replacing muscle power with tool power, did more to fight a war against poverty than all the kings and emperors and statesmen and politicians and bureaucrats combined–*before or since.*

And the fact that our free individual enterprise system enabled our people to save and invest and buy and own the tools of production has resulted in this nation being able to achieve the greatest material well-being for more people than ever before in the history of mankind. Thus it is obvious our material fruits had spiritual roots!

Freemen, under God, produce better.

Slowing Down

But of late we have been slowing down. For one thing, the rate of capital investment per man-hour has declined.

During the ten years, 1950-60, the average annual rate of increase in capital invested per man-hour was 3.1 percent. During the following ten years, 1960-70, it dropped by one third–to two percent.[29]

At the same time, capital investment in other nations outpaced us. From 1960-70, the United States had the lowest rate of capital investment in relation to output–and the lowest average annual increase in output per man-hour in manufacturing:

	*Output per man-hour**	*Capital Investment***
United States	3.1%	14.5%
Belgium	6.6	19.9
Canada	4.4	21.0
France	5.8	21.2
Germany	5.8	22.2
Italy	6.0	17.9
Japan	10.4	28.1
Netherlands	7.2	21.4
Sweden	7.1	18.8
United Kingdom	4.2	16.6

* Col. 1–Annual average percent change in output per man-hour in manufacturing, 1960-72

** Col. 2–Capital investment as percent of output, 1960-70.

Source: National Commission on Productivity

It is obvious that we must increase our capital investment in tools and equipment if we are to increase our productivity.

But, Caesar is chewing up our resources and competing for that which is available in the money market.

As Charles H. Smith, Jr., head of the US chambers of commerce, pointed out late in 1974:[30]

"An increase in productivity can help cure inflation caused by government borrowing, but government borrowing makes an increase in productivity more difficult to attain by disrupting capital markets and impeding the flow of investment funds, and therefore capital formation."

In other words, Caesar is eating our seed corn. And making it difficult–if not impossible–to get more. The Prophet Samuel warned us that would happen. Remember? *I Samuel 8:10-18!*

Capital Conservation

The savings and the capital of Americans is now being drained off by excessive government. It must be rescued. It should be conserved so that it can be invested in tools and equipment needed for productivity, rather than ingested by the non-productive and counterproductive toils of bureaucracy.

The conservation of private capital–one of the real resources of this nation–will not come to pass without some real reforms:

tax reforms, and
government reforms.

The problems of capital and savings confiscation–plus some suggestions for basic tax reform–are covered in Chapter Ten, *Taxes And The Power To Destroy.*

The problems of inflation–and what it is doing to stifle America and pauperize its people–plus some suggestions on how to halt inflation, are covered in Chapter Eleven, *Inflation Is Killing America.*

If we are to close these bleeding economic wounds that Caesar has opened in our national body, we–the people–must assume the role of attending physician. And, soon.

Control Government, Not Productivity

We must also remove the idiotic–counterproductive–governmental controls and regulations that stymie competition, reduce output and increase costs.

Government is not the only source of interference with the activities and productivity of freemen. Unrealistic strictures in the name of "the environment" are also dampening the output of the nation.

The desire for economic revival should not be an excuse to debauch our lands or foul our nests; yet it is reason to balance environmental considerations with concern for economic impact. What one person rejects as pollution hundreds of others may view as a sign that the factory is still running and their paychecks are still coming. Food on the table and clothes for the kids is just as important–and, in fact, more important–than an unobstructed view of a field of dandelions.*

Progress and conservation are not incompatible. It is the unrestricted extremes that cause the conflict.

Stop Featherbedding

Finally, we must remove all restrictions on output (productivity) that exist as a result of union monopoly.

Such work restrictions should be an anathema to freemen. It is immoral to prevent individuals from producing to their fullest and best capacities. At this time when the nation—and the world—needs increased productivity, that is not only a matter of principle, it is an economic essential.

Featherbedding on the nation's railways and highways costs consumers hundreds of millions of dollars each year.

Make-work rules in homebuilding and manufacturing are counterproductive; they are destructive. They cause waste and they raise costs—and prices.

Bricklayers once laid more than a thousand bricks a day; now they are not permitted to lay more than half that amount.

In some areas painters are not allowed to use brushes more than four inches wide and the use of sprayguns is prohibited.

In many industries workers are not permitted to produce at their full capacity. Machines that are capable of much higher output are restricted. Attempts to increase production to curb costs and compete with foreign enterprise often result in labor management disputes and costly strikes.

Some of these make-work (and/or slow-down) practices have already been outlawed. Yet many persist because of bureaucratic and judicial twistings of the law. This is an open flaunting of the intent of Congress, and should be stopped.

---

* "The current anti-pollution campaign has the following distinguishing marks. It is hysterical, it misjudges the nature of the environmental problem, and it is suffused with an animus against the free enterprise system." *Arthur A. Shenfield*, lecture at Rockford College, Rockford, Ill., 4/71.

Anti-Trust

Americans have traditionally been opposed to cartels, and trusts, that destroy competition and impose their demands and will by controlling huge segments of the market. Yet, we permit one monopoly to continue, year after year: the monopoly of organized labor—as separate and apart from the great mass of working men and women.

Labor unions should be brought under the anti-trust laws. This is essential to the protection of both the public and the working men and women of America.

At the same time, industry-wide bargaining should be outlawed. Too often such negotiations are permitted to run rough-shod over the rights of others and the interests of the consumer. Coastal and even nation-wide dock strikes are certainly a case in point: they have cost farmers not party to such strikes billions of dollars in both lost crops and lost markets and have resulted in increased prices to the food-buying public.

Freedom of Choice

There is no room for monopoly in a society of freemen. Monopoly kills freedom of choice. It breeds coercion and it promotes the use of force.

There is no room for such coercion in America—regardless of goal, regardless of source. Compulsion in general—and compulsory unionism in particular—should be an anathema to Americans; if not on the pure basis of principle, then at least on the basis of economics.

Freemen do produce better: [31]

—during the years 1950-73, per capita income rose faster in right to work states than it did in those states that permit compulsory unionism (the closed shop and the union shop).

—the rate of employment in voluntary union states during that period was higher than in those states with compulsory unionism.

–right to work states have had a greater industrial growth, have experienced a greater increase in job opportunities, and have benefitted from a higher rate of increase in capital investment than those states condoning compulsory union membership.

This is not to deny the right of individuals to join unions, or to engage in collective bargaining. The right of free association (the freedom of assembly) is an unalienable right. But, it must be just that–based on individual voluntarism and practiced without duress or retribution from any source.

The Measure of Wealth

A nation's wealth is not–and will not be–measured in terms of material prosperity alone. It will be measured more for its spiritual well-being. But, material wealth that is a by-product of spiritual growth is important. In addition to making it possible for us to care for our own, it enables us to

–feed the poor
–help heal the sick
–clothe the naked
–comfort the widows and the orphans
–care for those less fortunate, and to
–give tangible expression to our love for others in the name of Christ, our King.

It is how we gain our material wealth–through the application of our God-given talents and energies and resources rather than through plunder or coercion–

it is how we use that wealth–freely, as individuals, through love, compassion and concern . . .

that is the real reckoning of our riches.

The Meaning of Wealth

Thus material wealth–productivity–is a spiritual channel as well as a physical tool. It enables us to use the blessings of God's love and bounty to help not only ourselves but others. It enables us to give, as well as to receive.

By being productive–as individuals and as a nation–we can serve as God's pipeline. To be God's instruments and His blessing.

The Lord God Almighty could, with the sweep of His hand, transform this earth into an Eden. And, someday He will. But for now, and in this realm, He chooses to work through us, if we will let Him.

In the final analysis, that is what productivity is all about.

To produce, so that we can not only benefit but share . . . so that we can be ministers, and support His missions.

To earn, so that we can give.

To learn, so that we may lead others in the paths of righteousness.

To love–as He first loved us.

To be motivated–to be moved, impelled–through The Living God rather than to be controlled and compelled by the dead hand of Caesar.

Praise God! Thank The Lord! What a time for greatness this is!

CHAPTER NINE

The Greatest Of These Is Love!

Christians are under the law . . .
. . . not the law of the ancients
. . . *the law of love.*
"If you love Me, you will keep My commandments."
"This is the commandment I give you:
"That you love The Lord thy God with all thy heart and with all thy soul, and
"Love your neighbor as yourself."
Love is the fulfilling of the law.[1]
Now, there is faith and there is hope and there is love . . .
but the greatest of these is love.

Not the needle-pointed, maudlin, ersatz love of this plastic day. Not the chrome-and-glass computerized love of the Super State. The real, moving, deep-down love that lifts, that moves, that acts. That walks with God. And does His work and will.

The love that never fails.
This is the mark
—the stewardship
—the discipleship
—the more excellent way
of the Christian life.

Charity

Love is like faith: without works it is dead.

Charity is love in action. It is the act of loving. Without love, charity is diminished.

So, you bestow your goods upon the poor. So, you give your body to a cause. So, you climb the highest mountain for a goal . . .

. . . *without love, all that is as nothing.*
A tinkling cymbal. A sounding brass.
A play to the crowd. A bid for acclaim.
A boast of righteousness.
An empty gesture.

But, love is not puffed up. Love is not an empty gesture. Love is in secret—not for acclaim. Love is personal.

The saved for the Saviour.
Husband for wife.
Parent for child.
Christian for Christian.
Christian for stranger.
One for another.

Crowds do not love. Institutions do not love. They are lifeless. There is no love in inanimate objects. Caesar may act—but not through love.

Love, true love, abides no middleman.

Love by proxy is a sham. A brittle thing. Sparkle without warmth. Shine without soul.

Christ had no proxy. He came. He came Himself. He paid the ransom. There was no middleman at Calvary. That was love—*the real thing!*

Do Thou Likewise!

Love is an action word!

A doing. A giving. A blessing. One-to-one.

Consider the Good Samaritan. There on that dry and dusty road from Jerusalem to Jericho. There in the heat of the day.

After the goons had finished with the traveller, after they had stripped him of his belongings and his clothes, they left him for dead. A crumpled heap by the side of the road.

Several other travellers came along. A priest and a Levite. They kept right on going; they didn't want to get involved.

But the Good Samaritan, *he was something else.* He stopped. He knelt down in the dust. He gave of himself, of his oils and balms and bandages. He bound up the stranger's wounds and carried him to the village.

He didn't check to see if the fellow had Blue Cross. Or, whether he was eligible for Medicare. He didn't go running to the county hospital or the welfare office to say, "Hey, there's a guy back there by the side of the road." He carried the victim to the inn and cared for him.

That was love. Real love in action.

And the next morning he gave more. He paid the hotel bill and assured the innkeeper. "Care for him. Whatever it takes, do it. When I come again, I will repay thee."[2]

Remember that parable? Remember Jesus' concluding words?

"Go thou and do likewise."

There! There is the law of love.

The second part of the Great Commandment.[3]

Hail, Caesar!

There was a time when Christ's church was the center of charity. When the manifested glow of Christ's love radiated and gathered and loved and aided those in need.

One to another. Person-to-person.

Congregation to member and member's family.

Church to community . . .

as part of Christ's ministry.

There is still some of that, some of that love in action.

But, in many ways things are different.

Partly, we have let things slide.

Mostly, we have let Caesar take over. Sometimes we even invite him to do our chores. And now he does it without invitation. Coercion replaces compassion. Law pre-empts love; not Christ's law, man's.

Thus we follow politics instead of the steps of the Apostle Paul.

And so it is that Caesar is exaggerated and God denied.

Well, the welfare state is a lousy stand-in for Jesus and the computer is a poor substitute for love.

Milton Mayer wrote of this in his book, *What Can A Man Do?* In the chapter on love, "Caritas", Mayer recounts the days of Hitler's Germany to illustrate the point that there is not necessarily a relationship between love and the giving of bread to the poor.[4]

"The need for bread was great in Germany and the Nazis fed the poor, but they fed them without love, and in taking over the feeding they relieved the Germans of the necessity to love one another."

The State made possible the gift without the sacrifice. Without sacrifice there is no love.

What's that you say? One must sacrifice to pay Caesar! True. But there is a difference between willing sacrifice and the coercion of confiscation. The one builds, the other destroys; the one worships God, the other bows to Caesar.

As Mayer reminds us, Hitler's instrument for feeding the poor was the *Volkswohlfahrt* (the people's welfare program). That program was primarily intended to strengthen the Nazi regime and that was hardly a regime of love.

Personal Responsibility

Welfare today is seldom an act of love. It is more often than not a tool of the politician, an instrument of the State, employed to pacify pressure groups.

Things are out of whack . . . out of hand and without the Spirit.

Nowhere–nowhere in the Scriptures does Jesus teach the institutionalization of love or charity. Over and over He speaks of personal responsibility. Of loving one another, person-to-person. Jesus makes it clear we cannot use the law as an excuse to duck our personal responsibilities.

"There is no Christianity in the concept that pressure groups, desiring material benefits, have the right to use the power of the state to take property from some for the material gain of those who have the political power. That is plunder, and it is still plunder even if Robin Hood declares that he is robbing the rich to help the poor." [5]

Good intentions are not enough. Compassion, strained through the State, is not love; it's a cop out. Coercion that robs one to relieve another is not an act of love; it's a rip-off. Each individual is responsible. Accountable to God. In the final reckoning, Caesar's tally is for naught.

Yet, there are many modern-day Christians who have reached the stage where they are willing to permit—even seek—social control from Caesar to supplant Christian love and Christian action. How could they? There is nothing of Christian love in Caesar's controls!

"The proponents of social control by the state collide as directly with the teachings of Christ as would two trains running toward each other upon the same track." That's the way Rev. Russell Clinchy put it in his tract, *Charity, Biblical and Political.*[6]

And Rev. Clinchy, who was the pastor of the First Church of Christ in Hartford, Conn., when he wrote his timeless essay, went on to stress:

"Jesus was so uncompromising in His insistence that responsibility be placed upon the individual for both his personal life and his attitude toward others . . . Jesus never suggested an institution of any kind that could take the place of such individual responsibility. Nor did He ever mention an institution or a power to which an individual could transfer such responsibility, either by acquiescence, force or plunder." [7]

How Great Thou Art!

Why? Why did not Jesus seek the power of institutions to provide for others?

Because He knew the infinite power and the infinite bounty of His Father, our Lord God Almighty!

To put it in the vernacular, why fool around with a box kite when there is a Boeing 747 at your disposal?

Remember the time Jesus fed the multitude? With five loaves and two fishes He fed them–five thousand persons, *plus!*

There in the desert, away from the city, the crowds had gathered and Jesus ministered unto them. He healed the sick. He made the lame to walk. The blind to see. The dumb to speak, through the miracle of God's love.

At eventide the disciples suggested that He send the people home so that they could get some supper. But Jesus said, "No".

"There is no need for them to leave. Feed them here."

Feed them! With what? Five loaves of bread and two little fish? They asked this of Him to whom all power is given–in heaven and on earth.

Jesus took the loaves and the fish and He blessed them and gave them to His disciples to feed the multitude. And they ate. Every one of them, the whole five thousand–plus women and children. They ate until they were filled and even then there were twelve baskets of food left over.[8]

How great, how truly great, are the works of The Lord.

Oh, ye of little faith!

How is it we turn to Caesar for the answers to our problems?

"We Must Be Practical . . ."

Late in 1974, the ministerial association of Washington, D.C., conducted a survey to check on the needs of the poor within that city. That survey indicated that there were some pressing needs. Need for food, need for housing, need for clothing and medical assistance. This in a district that has a higher per capita income than any state in the union.

Spokesmen for the ministerial association called a press conference to announce their plan of action to relieve the needs revealed by the survey:

they would call upon government to provide the assistance required.

One cannot fault the clergymen for their concern. But, one can fault them for their course of action. Caesar was their answer. They belittled God.

In their impatience they adulterated their compassion with a call for coercion.

Every one of those clergymen represented a congregation. What were the members of those congregations doing to help? What of their personal Christian responsibilities? Were they praying? Seeking God's blessing? Doing His work?

Everyone in those congregations—pastors and members, alike—is the child of a rich and powerful Father. He holds the wealth of the world in His hands.

Ask and you shall receive.

Had they forgotten that? Or, did they not believe?

What Love Can DO!

How much more Christ-like are the works of Dr. Veronica Maz, also of Washington, D.C.

Here is a woman who translated her deep concern into action. A woman who put her faith to work.

Dr. Maz left her post as a professor at Georgetown University to love the destitute. She is the driving force *(and what a force love is!)* behind S.O.M.E. (So Others May Eat) and Shalom House.

S.O.M.E. came first. It is a home where men ravaged by alcohol, men without hope, can find a meal, some warm clothes, a bed—and a compassionate rehabilitation program. S.O.M.E. serves more than 5,000 meals a month and provides beds for those who would otherwise sleep in gutters or empty doorways.

The idea for Shalom House developed as Dr. Maz noticed the number of homeless, hopeless women who drifted into S.O.M.E. There was no other place for them—except the street and the savagery of the alley. Today, Shalom House provides for these women, as many as it can on its limited income and facilities.

What is the source of that income?

Not Caesar!

S.O.M.E. and Shalom House are supported by free-will love offerings. By the fund-raising programs and prayers of ladies' Bible classes in churches in nearby towns. By groceries given by supermarket chains. By unsold food donated by a drive-in restaurant chain. Surplus sandwiches and other foodstuffs from a catering company. And all the other avenues of giving God has opened.

This because one lady cared enough to love . . . and because others have responded to her example and her call.

That is Christian love. Love in action.

> *For as much as you have done these things unto the least of these, so you have done it unto Me.*

God bless Dr. Veronica Maz!

Their God Is Dead

Speaking before the Economic Club of Detroit some years ago, Dr. Alfred Haake, a Christian businessman and mayor of Park Ridge, Ill., recalled a situation that had occurred in Pittsburgh, Pa. There was some pressing needs in that city and in the face of them a prominent clergyman asserted:

"The improvement of mankind through religion is nice to think about; but, after all, we are dealing with sin. Religion has its place, to be sure, but we must be practical about these things."

Commented Dr. Haake, "In that little talk he set forth the idea which many other men have followed, that if God won't do His job, we will have to get Caesar to do the job for him. What in many cases appears to be a splendidly-motivated approach, an approach motivated by love for one's fellow men, motivated by a genuine desire for the good of men, is coupled with impatience with the speed with which God is working things out. We cannot wait for the visibleness, the availableness, of God–if you please.

"So," concluded Dr. Haake, "we set out to implement our aims in social and governmental devices. It means, in the last analysis, that whose who follow this course have lost faith in God." [9]

Dr. Haake is too kind. If he had been blunt he might have said:

"Their god is dead."

When a man is dead to God, it is just a skip and a jump to go along with the thought expressed by Reinhold Niebuhr, founder of the Fellowship of Socialist Christians:*

> "(The Marxian) analysis of the technical aspects of the problem of justice has not been successfully challenged. . . . The program of the Marxian will not create the millenium for which he hopes. It will merely provide the only possible property system compatible with the necessities of a technical age." [10]

In other words, we should use Marxist means to seek Christian ends. That was Mr. Niebuhr's invitation! Nothing could be farther from the Scriptures. Only God's means will meet God's ends. The delusions of false prophets will not do the job.

As Rev. Edmund A. Opitz observed, "In sober truth we are forced to recognize that many of our most articulate religious leaders are part of the problem, not part of the remedy. I have reference here primarily to denominational and super-denominational agencies, rather than to local churches and their ministers".[11]

In an address before the Maine Farm Bureau, Rev. Opitz referred to John C. Bennett, once dean of the world's wealthiest seminary and once a member of the Socialist Party. Dr. Bennett, praising what he termed "the awakening of the social conscience of the churches", asserted:

> "The leadership and many strategic centers, such as theological seminaries and church boards and periodicals, in most denominations are committed to the position that Christianity demands drastic changes in the structure of social life." [12]

Commented Rev. Opitz, "These 'drastic changes' spell out into something like Socialism or the Welfare State—'an economic order based upon the social ownership of the large sources of wealth and power.' "**

Christianity does, indeed, call for drastic changes.

---

* The term "Socialist Christian" is in itself a contradiction of both fact and purpose. Can a Christian be a Socialist? How? Socialism is paganism.

**As Rev. Opitz wrote: "I do not condemn these men for their opinions; I am merely trying to identify the point of view which prevails in important ecclesiastical circles."

The changes it calls for are in the hearts of men.

Seek ye first the Kingdom of God.

Christians know that it is the power of The Living God–and not the programs of Marx or the socialized reordering–that can change the world.

Change it for the better, that is.

II.

"What happens when government takes over? Charity gives way to politics. (And love gives way to force.) Funds coercively collected are dispensed to individuals according to group, class, or occupational category. This has no semblance of charity; it is the robbery of Paul to pay Peter. Further, when government constructs a feeding trough and fills it with fruits forcibly extorted from the citizenry, it creates new claimants and aggravates the problem it set out to solve." [13]

What manner of house of welfare has Caesar built?*

Let's take a quick "tour of inspection".

About Eight Percent of The People

Today, over-and-above voluntary giving to philanthropic causes,** social welfare takes almost eighteen percent of our gross national product and accounts for more than half of all our governmental expenditures.

Nationally, approximately eight percent of the people receive

---

* There are many writings available that deal with the incredible increases, the costs, the abuses and failures of the numerous social welfare programs. The purpose of this section is not to dwell on problems but to suggest solutions. However, it might be helpful to know where we are so that we can better see what we should do, and how to do it.

**See section III this chapter.

public assistance payments of one type or another (not including social security, unemployment compensation, etc., that are funded in whole or in part by private contributions). In some of our major metropolitan areas, more than ten percent of the population receives regular public assistance payments. And, in some cities–such as San Francisco, Baltimore, New York and St. Louis–the reported ratio is closer to one out of every seven.

Since 1950, the number of persons on welfare increased from 6,052,000 to almost 18,000,000 in 1974. The number of recipients has almost tripled in the past twenty four years.

Individual public assistance payments have also increased; thus, total expenditures for public assistance have increased at an even more spectacular rate:

PUBLIC ASSISTANCE PAYMENTS
(In millions)

Year	*Total Payments*	*Federal Funds*
1940	$ 1,124	$ 279
1950	2,488	1,096
1960	4,039	2,055
1970	14,434	7,594
1973	23,731	13,250

Source. U.S. Social Security Admin., Statistical Abstract, 1974, p. 274

The annual cost of public assistance payments in 1973 was *more than twenty times greater* than it was in 1940, and about ten times higher than in 1950.

Those soaring expenditures do not reflect the full picture. They do not include the increased cost for the rest of the social welfare apparatus–the offices and facilities, the vendor payments, the salaries and wages, and the other indirect payments. Here is what happened there:

SOCIAL WELFARE EXPENDITURES
(In millions)

Year	*Total Costs*	*Federal Funds*	*State & Local Funds*
1940	$ 8,795	$ 3,443	$ 5,351
1950	23,508	10,541	12,967
1960	52,293	24,957	27,337
1970	145,350	77,321	68,029
1973	215,228	122,331	92,897

Source: Statistical Abstract of the U.S., 1974

Total social welfare expenditures in 1973 were *more than twenty three times greater* than they were in 1940; more than nine times what they were in 1950.

In 1960 the federal government employed 72,747 persons in its various social welfare programs; by 1974 there were 158,904. And, in addition, in 1974 there were approximately 1,220,000 state and local social welfare workers being paid a combined annual salary of more than $1 billion a year.[14]

Absentee Fathers

By far the largest single welfare category is Aid to Families with Dependent Children (AFDC).

In 1973, 3,155,000 families with 7,813,000 children were receiving taxpayer funds through AFDC. Eighteen percent of those families had been on AFDC for five years or more; thirty-five percent had been receiving public assistance payments for three years or more.[15]

In only twelve percent of those more than three million AFDC families was the father deceased or incapacitated. In *eighty-three percent* of the homes, the father was "absent"–meaning that in most cases he had skipped out on the mother and children and left them and the taxpayers holding the bag.

The Need for Reform

In many welfare cases there is a real and sometimes desperate need. In some there is blatant evidence of the free ride–abusing the program and playing the taxpayers for suckers.

Several years ago Congresswoman Edith Green of Oregon did some probing to learn that a mother with four children could conceivably get public assistance grants and services worth more than $11,500 a year. A mother and eight children on welfare could conceivably have a total "welfare" income of more than $21,000 a year.

Such welfare "incomes" would, of course, be extreme. But flagrant violation of welfare assistance and the taxpayer is neither unusual nor difficult. Recent studies indicate that millions upon millions of dollars are wasted each year because of clerical errors and sloppy office procedures. There are literally hundreds of different federal welfare programs and new ones are spawned every year. The nearest thing to immortality on earth is a federal program; few ever pass away and most go on and on–*in perpetuity*.

Many states have made valiant efforts to curb welfare abuses–to help the needy but to catch the greedy. Millions of dollars have been saved as a result of such reforms.

Congressman John B. Conlan, Ariz., recently introduced a bill calling for major reforms in the multi-million dollar AFDC program.[16] Conlan's proposals would

- –permit AFDC benefits only to families with incomes of less than $5,076 a year
- –mandate tight identification of welfare recipients to eliminate fraud
- –require states to establish criminal sanctions for willful abuse of AFDC grants
- –allow states to require community work service in return for welfare, and provide incentives for welfare recipients to find employment, and
- –emphasize family responsibilities and strengthen child support requirements (from absentee fathers).

Such reforms are vitally needed to protect both the legitimate needy and the burdened taxpayer. But until the entire welfare program is *totally overhauled*–from basic principles to final implementations–it will continue to increase in numbers and in costs.

By 1980

The Tax Foundation predicts that if present trends and systems continue, by 1980 more than 21,200,000 persons will be receiving public assistance payments.[17]

Payments and total expenditures, predicts the Tax Foundation, could very well increase by at least forty-five percent by 1980.[18]

That would mean that in 1980, the annual public assistance payments would total more than $34 billion and total costs for the social welfare program (all governments) would be in the neighborhood of $312 billion a year!

That is no doubt one of the factors that prompted former federal budget director Roy Ash to warn President Ford that the day may not be too far away when government takes *two-thirds* of our gross national product! [19]

A Right? Or, A Responsibility?

Economist and author Henry Hazlitt has described the situation as "welfarism gone wild". He delineated the underlying causes:

"The causes of this accelerative increase are hardly mysterious. Once the premise has been accepted that 'the poor', as such, have a 'right' to share in somebody else's income–regardless of the reasons why they are poor or others are better off–there is no logical stopping place in distributing money and favors to them, short of the point where this brings equality of income for all." [20]

Continues Hazlitt:

"If I have a 'right' to a 'minimum income sufficient to live in decency' whether I am willing to work or not, why don't I also have a 'right' to just as much income as you have, regardless of whether you earn it and I don't? Once the premise is accepted that poverty is never the fault of the poor but the fault of 'society' (i.e., of the self-supporting), or of the 'capitalist system', then there is no definable limit to be set on relief . . . the politicians who want to be elected or re-elected will compete with each other in proposing new 'welfare' programs. . . ." [21]

Welfare is not a right.

It is a responsibility.

That responsibility starts with each individual: to take care of himself, and to take care of his family.

The Apostle Paul was quite blunt about this:

> "For even when we were with you, this we commanded you, that if any would not work, neither should he eat. For we hear that there are some which walk among you disorderly, working not at all, but are busybodies. Now them that are such we command and exhort by our Lord Jesus Christ, that with quietness they work, and eat their own bread." [22]

And concerning the responsibilities of the father to care for his family, Paul wrote this to Timothy:

> "But if any provide not for his own, and specifically for those of his own house, he hath denied the faith, and is worse than an infidel." [23]

Those who can—but will not—accept the responsibility of providing for their own welfare surely have no "right" to demand the fruits of another's labors. Nowhere—nowhere in the Scriptures does Jesus teach that any man has the "right" to coerce another man into giving—or, the "right" to steal or take another man's possessions for himself. There is a clear biblical distinction between those who cannot work and those who will not work.

Christians do have a responsibility to care for those in need. To minister to them physically as well as spiritually. And to do this with love and without any thought of receiving in return. To do it as unto The Lord, not as unto Caesar.

That is our responsibility. But, that is not the recipient's right. No man has a right to take from another—unless that which is taken has been voluntarily offered.

Any other type of transaction is coercion—a coercion that demeans the taker and violates the taken.

Not An Easy Road

Some may say all this talk about love and free-will is a cop out, a dodge to escape responsibility.

They have it backward.

The easy way is to pass a law. To force the gift. To coerce, to confiscate and redistribute.

Things are not so easy for the Christian. Love is demanding. It demands responsibility. It demands discipline. There is no cop out there. No easy road. No pushing, no prodding from the outside. Just the burning compulsion from within. From love.

What? Is it love to tell an individual who can work but won't that unless he works he will not eat? You bet it is. It would be much easier to throw him a buck, or a bundle, and stop your caring there. To shrug and say, "We already gave at Caesar's place."

*But if you love, if you really care, you take the time to help him get the lead out of his pants and some steel into his backbone. You try to help him learn a skill, earn his way, rebuild his life and his dignity. That is love.**

And, if you really love–you not only help the sick, the lonely, the hungry, you do it on your own and in concert with like-minded friends. You don't go running to Caesar or his cousins, or his bureaucrats. As the Good Samaritan did, you do.

Enough of Caesar!

There are those who preach a social action gospel. They are no doubt well-intentioned but all too often the gospel they really preach is the gospel of Caesar: governmental action.

There are times and circumstances when government action is required, and proper. But Caesar and his agencies are no substitute for Christian action.

Consider this:

> *Rather than trying to expand Caesar's welfare apparatus, Christians should be working to get Caesar out of the welfare business. If not all the way out, then reduced to those bare and temporary essentials that can be–and should be–handled at the local level.*

* As Booker T. Washington once wrote, "In bestowing charity, the main consideration should be to help those who will help themselves".

Heresy? Heartless? A pious protestation in the face of misery? Not at all!

An act of love.

The existing system is obscene.

Its obscenities can been seen in the way they violate the giver:

"The Welfare State replaces charity with the confiscation and redistribution of the wealth." [24]

Its obscenities can be seen in the way it demeans the recipient:

It dehumanizes. It treats all claimaints according to a fixed formula that fails to take account for individual differences.

Its obscenities can be seen in the way it wastes incredible amounts of money. The National Life Underwriters Assn. once offered this as a rule of thumb ratio between giving and receiving:

–*in person-to-person giving,* a dollar given is a dollar received.

–*in giving through voluntary organizations,* twenty-five cents goes for administrative costs and seventy-five cents reaches the needy.

–*through state government,* it costs one dollar to get another dollar to the beneficiary, and

–*through federal government,* it takes almost three dollars to deliver one dollar.

Caesar is a lousy steward!

Bring Charity Home!

If we Christians–as individuals, as families, as congregations and as volunteers and supporters of Christian charities–would truly fulfill our responsibilities as set forth by Jesus and the Apostles, we could put Caesar out of the welfare business and get him back where he belonged.

We could dismantle the leviathan of "public welfare" and bring charity back home–to the individual, to the churches and synagogues, to the neighborhoods at the local level where it belongs.

"To humanize the process of assisting those in need, the welfare system will cease to be a function of government. The problems of determining who genuinely are entitled to aid will become a function of those groups and associations who have most consistently concerned themselves with humane and charitable works.

"The churches, the synagogues and temples of the world have occupied this role for centuries, recognizing that

> " '. . . the poor shall never cease out of the land; therefore I command thee, saying, thou shalt open thine hand wide unto thy brother. . . .' "[25]

An impossible task? An idle dream?

Not so.

Not if we become God's hands and open them wide.

> *"The things which are impossible with men are possible with God."*[26]

III.

Americans, by-and-large, are a generous people.

In 1974, they voluntarily gave more than $25 billion to various charitable and religious organizations.[27] They did that on their own, and because of their willingness to give a hand to those in need.

All told, more than forty-three million Americans volunteered their time and effort to help raise that $25 billion.[28] And, in addition, countless millions of dollars were given on a person-to-person, neighbor-to-neighbor and congregation-to-needy-family basis. Such gifts were never reported, simply given in love.

Such an outpouring of time and money is not unusual in America. During the past eleven years, from 1964 through 1974, Americans gave some $200 billion to charities and religious efforts. That money came in dimes and dollars, in checks and pledges—and over-and-above the forty-three percent of the total personal income tax take by federal, state and local governments.

Americans have done much. And, when asked, will always do more. In fact, if permitted to—and encouraged—would do more.

In California, in 1969, floods ravaged several sections along the Pacific Coast. Winds and rains and high waters caused hundreds of millions of dollars of damage to homes, businesses and farms. Many families lost everything they had and few were covered by insurance.

The leaders of various volunteer groups—the Red Cross, the

Jaycees, the Salvation Army, the various service and civic organizations–were called to the state capitol to form an emergency Governor's Flood Relief Task Force. They responded with enthusiasm, eager to do what they could to help their fellow Californians.

During the course of the meeting, after the devastation had been inventoried and the needs assessed, the head of a state agency rose and addressed the group. The substance of his remarks were wrapped up in his concluded statement:

"We have developed a system to take care of these emergencies. *That system has obviated the need for individual assistance.*"

In other words, Caesar has taken over. There is no need for individuals getting involved!

It is a tribute to the volunteer groups that they went ahead, on their own, and brought millions of dollars worth of assistance to those families in need.

The system has not obviated the individual–it simply makes it more difficult to get involved.

Applied Christianity

If we are true to our calling, Christians must get involved. Not in so-called "social action" but in personal action. Being about His ministry both spiritually and materially.

It is estimated that there are today between forty and fifty million Bible-centered Christians in the United States.

Imagine the tremendous–the infinite–power available for good works if all of those millions of Christians would plug into God's circuit. Imagine what could be done to alleviate suffering, hunger, pain, deprivation. Imagine what could happen if we put God's multiplier-factor–His Blessings–to work helping others. Helping others here at home; helping our Christian brothers throughout the world.

What if those forty million Christians in the United States did these things and did them in the name of The Lord.

What if we prayed? Really prayed!

What if we gave? Really gave!

What if we worked? Really worked!

Can you imagine the power that would be generated–the Holy, Almighty power–if forty million Christians got down on their knees in prayer and praise to God for His direction and His help and His blessing in solving the problems of this world. In feeding the hungry, in caring for the needy, in healing the sick, in opening the avenues of progress and self-sufficiency to His children throughout the world?

Not just some *pro forma,* weak-kneed prayer but bold, positive, assured prayer because of Jesus' promise that whatsoever we ask in His name will be provided. Not just a now-and-then prayer, but prayer without ceasing.

Such faith and prayer could change the world!

Faith and prayer–and works. These are the transmission lines of power–God's power.

One Billion More Dollars

First. The faith.

Then, the faith and the prayer.

Then, the faith and the prayers and the giving.

"All that we have is The Lord's and we give it out of His hand." [29]

Consider again those forty million on-the-move Christians.

What would happen if–in concert with constant and Christ-centered prayer and faith–we gave? Gave more? Gave over-and-above what we give now?

What if each one of us, each one of the forty million–young and old, rich and poor–gave one more dollar each week? One extra dollar. On a planned and constant basis.

Each week that would be $40 million. Each month more than $160 million. Each year more than $2 billion!

Or, let's say that there are about ten million Christian families (households) in the United States. Ten million Christ-centered families. And, let's say each family gives two dollars a week–two dollars over-and-above what they now give to The Lord's work. That would be $20 million a week, more than $1 billion a year!

What's that? You say that sounds good, but . . .

Where's your faith? Where's your prayer? Where's your giving?
Ours is a Living God. Right? Right!
As our young people say, "You'd better believe it!"
And, what could one billion dollars a year do?
Well, consider this:

World Vision International workers in Southeast Asia can care for a child for about $12 a month.

Dr. Jesus Sigmani and his co-workers in South India can pull a family out of starvation for about $25 a month.

The volunteers for the *Dr. Thomas Dooley Foundation* can get doctors and nurses and nurses' aides and medicines and healing to a village in Laos for a few thousand dollars.

Here! Let Ted Engstrom, executive vice-president of *World Vision* tell you what one dollar can do:

> "Our own experience shows that one dollar of costs (i.e., all costs to get items overseas) will provide for $60 worth of medicines, $37 worth of vitamins, $6 worth of clothing, and $5.40 worth of food." [30]

Now can you better imagine what one billion a year—*more*—in Christian giving could do!

And how would that $1 billion be dispersed? In any number of ways, including these two suggestions:

—through any one of the some 600 missionary agencies now in the field and/or

—through the programs and decisions of the various congregations involved in the giving. Perhaps by congregations here at home "adopting" congregations in other lands. As the early Christian churches did—sharing God's love and blessings with their brothers and sisters in new-born congregations in other lands.

Four Opportunities for Stewards

Paris Reidhead, of the Christ-centered Institute for International Development, has suggested four opportunities to serve The Lord by helping Christians in the developing nations:

1. *Christian businessmen* can use part of their business funds in joint-ventures with Christian nationals overseas. This investment capital, which would be repaid, could help established job-generating projects and provide employment on a continuing, expanding basis. A large part of the poverty in foreign lands stems from the lack of job opportunities.
2. *Christian congregations* can set up "over-and-above" revolving funds (over-and-above present missions commitments). These funds could then be loaned to Christians overseas to start or expand projects that would be job-producing.

   Reidhead stressed that such "seed corn" funds are difficult to obtain in foreign lands and usually command exhorbitant interest rates. In Brazil, for example, interest can run as high as thirty-five percent. A $5,000 revolving fund established and used to help generate jobs for Christians overseas could work wonders.
3. *Christian families* saving for retirement can ear-mark fifteen percent of their investments to feed revolving funds established by their congregation. Such investments would be insured and would bear interest.

   And, most importantly, as in the parable of the talents *(Matt. 25)* they would be productive–helping other Christians become self-sufficient.
4. *Christians in many walks of life* could make their experience and expertise available to their Christian brethren in foreign lands. Farmers, food processors, civil and hydraulic engineers, carpenters, small businessmen–all have skills and talents that could be of tremendous help to their Christian counterparts–or would-be counterparts in other lands.

What Reidhead is advocating is that Christians in the United States can and should help Christians in other lands build material self-sufficiency for themselves and their co-workers. As Kuan-tzu's ancient Chinese proverb says:

If you give a man a fish,
he will have a single meal.
If you teach him how to fish,
he will eat all his life.

Our Godly Treasures

The world is much in need right now. In need of Christ and in need for material help, especially in the emerging nations.

Is there an answer to these problems? There is and Jim Underwood of Christian Financial Services sets it forth:

> *"Christians already have the material answers to the needs of the world. But, not just by giving it away. It's by constructively taking those assets and using them—working them—in a productive and on-going manner. If we believe that we are God's stewards, then what we have are Godly treasures. The irony of the situation is that we have sought the counsel of the ungodly in how to plan and use those Godly treasures."*

Jim Underwood's God is not dead. He is very much alive—and more than equal to any situation. Ours is, indeed, a Living God. He has the answers!

All we have to do is search His scriptures and seek His will.

World Hunger

God's answers and God's workers are sorely needed now to cope with the growing problem of hunger in many parts of the world.

World hunger is a complex problem comprising many elements: weather, population growth, diminishing food reserves in the large nations that have traditionally been a source of relief, increasing fuel and fertilizer prices, and rampant inflation.

Christians must be concerned about this serious problem and should do all they can as individuals and as members of Christian groups to help alleviate the suffering.

"Immediate needs are facing millions of people in drought-stricken west and central Africa, in parts of India and in northeast Brazil. Food shortages affect millions more in Bangladesh, parts of Central America and Southeast Asia." [31]

This calls for prayer, and giving, and works. In earnest.

Can anything be done? In its January, 1975, report *World Vision* says, "Yes".

"The world's hungry can probably be fed—by using more irrigation, high-yield seeds, improved farming methods and tools, multiple cropping, improved food distribution systems and policies, increased agricultural research, international food reserves, high-nutrition food supplements, more land under cultivation and other responses.

"One scientist has estimated that, with appropriate technology, fertilizer, irrigation, seeds and farm techniques, the earth's cultivable land could support 50 to 60 billion people on an adequate diet of 4000 to 5000 calories per person per day." [32]

Many Christian organizations are already hard at work—helping to meet both the immediate and the long-term needs. These efforts should be whole-heartedly supported with prayer and giving and works.

The immediate (crisis) needs call for immediate (crisis level) giving. The long-term needs call for helping the needy and underdeveloped nations build an economy and a productivity that will enable these countries to be self-sufficient in the future.

At the World Food Conference in Rome, in 1974, nation after nation—many of which have been recipients of American aid over the years—lambasted the United States for being a "have" nation. Their solution to the world food problems seemed to be that the U.S. should strip itself of its productivity and turn to sack cloth and ashes. This would solve nothing. It would, in fact, push the world over the brink of total chaos. Regardless of what some may claim, this nation has been the major source of help in a needy world.

The solution is not to tear this land down into the role of a "have not" nation; the solution is to help other lands build themselves up to become "have" nations.

At the same time, what is needed is to increase the productivity of the United States—increase the harvest of its fields, its factories, its skills and trade. The more we produce, the more we will have to share with others.

Unleash The Giant

The United States, through the enterprise of its free people and free capital, is the giant among the producing nations of the world. This did not happen by accident; it did not come about by robbing or depriving or exploiting other nations. It occurred because we employed a system of economics based on Christian principles.

Today, the giant is increasingly hamstrung, whipsawed and controlled by the Lilliputs of the "new" economics and the "new" politics.

Too often those who say this nation should give more to other countries are the very ones who work and vote to increase the restrictions on our giving-potential; they call for even greater government spending and control of our productive enterprises. That is not the way to increase our abilities to help others; it is the road to stagnation. Before we can give we must produce. There is nothing productive about government; Caesar produces little but redtape and paper forms. Those will not fill the bellies or stem the hunger—at home or abroad.

We cannot control the policies of other governments but surely we can control the policies of our own. And, the time is now to remove the controls and costs and restriction that hamper America's productive genius and capacities.

Let's Talk about Waste!

There are those who are "embarrassed" about America's abundance. Their emotions are misspent. They should praise The Lord that America has such bounty so that it can share with others.

If they really want to be embarrassed, let them consider the waste in this land.

There is no greater wastrel than big (and inferior) government. Consider, for example, the $30 billion a year that goes for the interest—just the interest—on the federal debt. Imagine what that could do if it were put into productive enterprise! Imagine what the fruits of such enterprise could do to help those in need. The waste of such funds is a sin.

The Scriptures warn us about the costs of indebtedness, and admonish us to refrain from debt. Caesar has us in debt up to our eyeballs.

And, consider this:

> A recent survey shows that the rate of productivity per man-hour in government is thirty-nine percent below the average productivity level of the private sector. *Thirty-nine percent!* [33]

Think of the waste involved there.

Caesar's annual payroll is now running at close to $130 billion a year for 14,100,000 employes. On the basis of that productivity survey, one can conservatively estimate that billions of dollars of the taxpayers' money is being wasted through inefficiency and padded payrolls.

When Caesar wastes the fruits of our labors in such a manner, we cannot share them with our brethren in other lands.

The lack of public support for foreign aid, as practised by Caesar, is not to be taken as an aversion toward helping others. Rather, it is a rejection of the waste, the inefficiency, and the improprieties, of many such government programs. It is the intuitive feeling, and the direct knowledge that, for every dollar spent through many of those foreign aid programs, three-to-five-or-ten times as much good could be done by a dollar voluntarily given to an independent, God-directed agency engaged in efforts to help persons in other lands.

Yes, we do have a responsibility to help others wherever they may be. But it is just good stewardship to insist that it be done wisely and well.

Render unto God . . .

Christian love, and Christian action, is not a cop-out.

It is not letting George–or Caesar–do it.

It is personal response and personal responsibility.

It is living and giving–as Christ lived and gave for us.

"Render unto Caesar that which is Caesar's; and unto God that which is God's"

Remember Christ's counsel?

Go back and read it now. Read it again:

> "Render unto Caesar that which is Caesar's . . .
>
> ". . . *and unto God that which is God's*"

Does that now take on a new light? A new dimension? A new direction?

What is God's?

We are. We all are. Each and every individual.

We are to love one another. We are to help one another. Help one another grow not only in grace but also in skill and self-sufficiency and as good stewards.

We do these things for Christ. Not Caesar.

Caesar has his own limited works to perform. And we render unto him to finance those works.

But we are not to render unto Caesar our fellow-man, our less fortunate. The care and feeding and keeping and loving of those less fortunate–that is ours to do. *In Christ's name.*

CHAPTER TEN

Taxes And The Power To Destroy

Those pharisees! Some of them were always ganging up on Jesus. They were constantly looking for ways to trick Him; anything to get Him in trouble with the civil authorities.

One day a group of them joined up with a bunch of politicians who were high on Herod. Together, they went down to see if they could talk Jesus into a box.

"Master." That's the way they started their little caper, "Master". They hadn't accepted Christ as their master; but you know these smooth-talking politicians!

"Master, we know that You are sincere and that You teach the word of God truthfully, regardless of the consequences, for You are afraid of no man.

"So, tell us: is it against God's law to pay taxes to Caesar?"

Jesus knew what they were up to; He was 'way ahead of them.

"Why do you come here trying to trap Me, you impostors? You hypocrites! Here, show Me the coin you use to pay the tax."

The pharisees handed Him a *denarius*—a coin similar to our

penny.

"Whose face and name is this on the coin?" Jesus asked. And they answered, "Why, Caesar's, of course."

"Then render unto Caesar the things that are due to Caesar, and render unto God the things that are Gods."

At that point, according to the Scriptures, the pharisees and their political buddies went off talking to themselves–confounded by the wisdom of The Lord.

Christians are, indeed, obliged to support the civil authorities; to obey the laws and to help pay for the costs of government.

In Romans 13:7, Paul instructs us to "pay taxes to whom taxes are due, revenue to whom revenue is due, respect to whom respect is due, and honor to whom honor is due".

Why? Because civil government is an institution ordained by God [1] so that "we may lead a quiet and undisturbed life (in our outward or physical state) and a peaceful existence in all godliness and honesty (in our inner or spiritual state)." [2] In other words, God established civil government so that His children could be safe and free on earth. In that way we could pursue our daily endeavours in peace and serve The Lord without fear of man.

For this protection from those who would violate our lives, our liberty and our property, we are to "render unto Caesar" his due.

The question is: "Just what is Caesar's *rightful* due?"

Caesar Demands Too Much!

All that we have belongs to God; our lives, our property, our liberty. We are His stewards in all that we have and do.

God asks us to tithe–to give at least ten percent of our substance and our time to His work.

But Caesar–he is not so easily satisfied!

He demands more than forty percent of what we have.

The total cost of all government today is estimated at forty-three percent of our nation's total personal income and 35 percent of our gross national product.[3] That's all government–federal, state and local. But, that tab does not include the most vicious tax of all, inflation.

It is estimated that the cost of government for fiscal 1974 came to $455 billion.* That is more than double the $186 billion cost of government in 1965, just nine years earlier. During recent years the cost of government has been increasing at a rate of 11 percent per year while personal income has been rising at a rate of 8 percent a year.[4] Over the past ten years the number of government employes has grown at the rate of 1,200 a day. At the beginning of 1975, there were 14.1 million government employes (not including the two million men and women in the nation's armed forces).[5] And, just about one out of every five in the nation's labor force (18%) is on a government payroll!

For years the government's appetite has been growing faster than the citizen's ability to produce. Thus, government continues to take a larger and larger piece of the nation's pie. To see just how that slice has increased, see the chart, *"Government Expenditures and Total Personal Income"*.

The Cost Per Producer

Customarily the cost of government is calculated on a *per capita* basis; so many dollars for each and every man, woman and child. Such computations are supposed to be more personal–"more meaningful". And, on that basis, the average cost of government in 1974 came to $2,146–for every man, woman and child in the United States.

But, that is actually a misleading bit of data. It is almost a "con" job. It does not really give the true picture of the cost-burden of government.

Take kids, for example. Kids are part of the "per capita" calculation–figured in there right along with everyone else. But kids don't pay $2,146 a year for government. They may pay a few taxes now and then when they buy some bubblegum, or comic books, or record albums–but not $2,010 a year. Someone else picks up that tab for them. It's the same with many elderly people who do not now carry a full $2,146 a year tax load; and it is the same for those on welfare and those who may be unemployed.

So, figure the cost of government a different way. Figure it on

* Economic Report of The President, Feb. 1975.

the basis of *per producer*—per working men and women in the labor force. **On that basis, it comes to $5,290.** That is the cost of government divided among the some 90 million men and women who work to produce the goods and services that make this nation go: $5,290 for each and every producer.

*GOVERNMENT SPENDING & PERSONAL INCOME**
1902—1974
(in billions)

Year	Total Pers. Inc.	Total Govt. Spend.	% to Govt.
1902	$20.2	$ 1.6	8.4%
1913	33.7	3.2	9.5
1922	62.0	9.3	15.0
1932	50.1	12.4	24.7
1940	78.7	20.4	25.8
1950	228.5	70.3	30.7
1960	398.7	151.3	37.9
1970	801.5	332.9	41.5
1974 e	1.055	455.0	43.1

Source: US Dept. of Commerce
Bank of Hawaii
Economic Report of The President, 1975

Those Hidden Taxes

Most folks will probably say they don't pay that much in taxes. Some don't but most do.

The truth is that many persons do not realize just how much they do pay for taxation. They forget to calculate the cost of *hidden taxes* and—as F. A. Harper wrote—"one cannot see what is hidden".[6]

A sizeable chunk of that forty-three percent of our total personal income going for taxes goes for those hidden taxes; taxes that are buried in the price of just about everything we buy and every

* All govts.—federal, state and local e—Estimated

service we procure. Someone once estimated that there are 502 taxes of one sort or another on a pair of shoes; each one levied at a different stage of production and distribution and sale by a different governmental agency.

"Business Taxes"

Many politicians, and quite a few economists, like to mislead folks into believing that companies and corporations pick up a sizeable share of the total tax tab. When they have reached the level of the taxpayer's endurance, and know that he would rebel at another tax hike, they grab for additional revenues by raising or instituting taxes on business and industry—with the boast that they are doing the working man a favor. Such expediency is dishonest; it is simply picking the citizen's pocket from another angle.

Companies and corporations do not pay taxes; *people pay taxes.* Companies and corporations simply act as tax agents. They collect the "business" tax as a part of the product; they collect it from the purchaser and they pass it along to the government—whether it's Uncle Gimmie or one of his state or local cousins.

"It may be popular to propose eventual tax reductions for individuals 'by tightening up on business', but this misses the point that business taxes are borne by individuals in the final analysis. Increasing the business tax would drain away sums from wages, rents, dividends and the creation of new jobs, in addition to jeopardizing future revenue growth." [7]

So, it is the people—*always the people*—who end up holding the tax bag. Today that tax bag comes to $455 billion and it is growing at the rate of about eleven percent a year.

Socialized Insecurity

It is not only income and sales and property taxes that have gone out of sight during recent years. Take a look at what has happened to the tax on employes and employers for "social security".

Many economists—and thousands of businessmen and millions

of wage earners—are increasingly concerned about the enormous increases in Social Security that are being financed by a regressive system of payroll taxes. These taxes chew away at the businessman's capital and the paychecks of the wage-earner in favor of the elderly and the retired.[8]

Back in 1935, when Social Security was established, Congress intended that it would be

1. purely a supplement to the individual's own retirement arrangements (and not a retirement plan in and of itself)—it would provide a "floor" but not the entire pension structure
2. fully funded by contributions from the employer and the employe (and not financed out of the taxpayers' general fund), and
3. honestly operated on an actuarily sound basis.

Even with those assurances, many Americans gagged at the idea. It was one more form of government control, one more pocket in government's tax bag. Many went along with the scheme; they believed that, at least, it would be operated on a financially sound basis. How naive! When, in recent history, has government operated its affairs on a financially sound and prudent basis?*

---

*In the beginning, 1937, "the maximum tax any person could have paid was $30 a year—1 per cent on the first $3000 of his yearly wages—for each of 13 years from 1937 through 1949. (The employer, of course, was matching those payments.) In 1950 he might have paid 1½ per cent on $3000, and in 1951 through 1953, 1½ per cent on $3600. Thus, if he had earned the maximum taxable income in each of those 17 years, he might have paid a total of $597 in social security taxes. His employer would have matched that amount, bringing their combined total to $1194.

"If that person had retired on January 1, 1954, having reached the age of 65, and if his wife had also passed her 65th birthday, they would be eligible for benefits of $127.50 a month. Thus, within 10 months, that man and his wife would receive more in social security benefits than both he and his employer could possibly have paid as social security taxes for his account over the 17 years since the program was initiated. But the life expectancy at age 65 is more than 10 months—about 13 years, in fact. By what twist of logic or of morality does any person expect to get from 10 to 15 or even more times the benefits for which he has paid? At whose expense, and why?" —*Paul L. Poirot, "Social Security"*, 1954.

Initially, Social Security taxes were put into a reserve trust that was always to contain enough money to cover at least three years of benefit payments. That worked for a while, but not for long.

You know how most bureaucrats are with someone else's money; the idea of all that reserve money sitting around drives them nutty. Pretty soon the Social Security reserves were being "borrowed"—a little for this and a little for that. Before long the system was in a financial mess.

Take Social Security's 1973 "operating statement", for example. In that year, the system had a total income (from employe-employer taxes) of $63.4 billion. Its expenditures (payouts for benefits and administrative costs) totalled $61.0 billion. Just about everything the system took in (through taxation of the now-employed) went right out in benefits (to those no longer employed).

In 1973, only $2.4 billion went into the Social Security reserves. At the start of 1974, the reserve fund (assets) stood at $52 billion—just about enough to carry the system for ten months. So much for the original concept (and legislation) that called for keeping three years of benefit payments in reserve!

If your friendly local banker handled his customer's trust funds that way, he'd be holed up in Leavenworth jail. But, too often these days what is considered crooked or unethical if done by the individual citizen is condoned or deemed appropriate when it is pulled by Caesar or his legions. And, the citizen is taxed to cover their mistakes and misfeasance.

The Tax of "Social Security"

In 1937, the Social Security tax rate was one percent on an annual income base of $3,000. The total tax was $60; $30 from the employe and a matching $30 from the employer.

By 1968, the Social Security tax had increased ten-fold (this was caused, in part, because more and more politicians no longer viewed the system as purely a supplemental pension aid but began to consider it a retirement program in and of itself). The tax rate in 1968 was 8.8 percent on the first $7,800 of earnings; annual taxes came to a maximum of $686 per worker—$343 from the employe and another $343 from the employer.

Since then the combined employe-employer Social Security tax has risen to $1,474.20 a year and the likelihood is that this will rise even higher; probably to $1,544 in 1975 or '76. That is more than four times what it was ten years ago.

Even with those tremendous tax increases–almost 25-fold since the system began–Social Security is in serious financial trouble. It is estimated that the system faces a long-term (75-year) deficit of $1.3 *trillion.* [9]

Nancy Teeters, budget expert at the Library of Congress, has pointed out that during the years 1969 to 1974, the cumulative across-the-board increases in Social Security payments have far exceeded the inflation in living costs.[10] Politicians, catering to pressure groups, have built in escalating benefits to the extreme; in the near future a worker will be able to draw more on Social Security than he gets on his job.[11]

Most of the increased tax to pay for those soaring benefits would be placed on the backs of fifteen percent of the work force–those Americans who earn between $14,000 and $24,000 a year. Middle America, already carrying the major burden of taxation and inflation, now faces at least a twenty percent increase in its Social Security taxation.

Ripping-off The Young

For young persons just starting out, Social Security is a giant rip-off. Through the coming years it will force them to hand over more and more of their earnings so that politicians can hand out larger and larger benefits to those already retired. Don't blame the retired, they tried: most of them saved, and paid their Social Security tribute in good faith. It's just that their dollars aren't what they used to be. But, that's another story–the story of inflation.

On a strictly financial-return basis, Social Security is a lousy investment. No doubt that is one of the reasons participation in the system is compulsory.

Suppose, for example, that in 1975 a young man gets a job earning $14,000 a year. Each month the young man and his employer chunk a combined $122 into Social Security. That's $1,474 a year. If his salary were to remain static (which it won't) and the Social Security tax take were to remain as is (which it won't), by the time he retires, the combined deposits in that Social Security fund would total about $62,000. If he lives 80 years, after he retires he and his wife can expect to draw about $124,000 (under the existing benefits table). Big deal? *No, a bad deal!*

Suppose our young friend had taken that $122 a month and invested it at four percent interest, compounded. When he reaches age 65 he will have about $178,000 tucked away. And, if he had invested his money at six percent, compounded, his kitty will come to about $300,000!

That would be his money. No politicians would be "borrowing" it to line pork barrels. No bureaucrats would be doling it out to him on a string. He could earn additional income, as much as he wanted to. Or, he could live on just the interest of his savings and still have a higher monthly income than he would if he were receiving Social Security benefits. And, when he passed on he could leave the capital to his wife and heirs–minus taxes, of course.

Reform Is Vital

Obviously reform of the entire Social Security system is essential; to protect those who have already been compelled to buy their way into the program, and to prevent further confiscation of the lives and works of those young persons entering the work force.

At the very least, Congress should get the system back on a **pay-as-you-go basis.** That may entail raising taxes, but it should also involve holding the line on or reducing benefits. It also entails controlling inflation–and the only way to control inflation is to eliminate it

Secondly, participation in Social Security should be put on a **strictly voluntary basis.** We cannot cop out on the contracts made with the present participants but we can certainly provide our young people with an option. New workers entering the labor force should have a choice: either to be a part of the Social Security system, or to invest in a private employe-employer funded retirement program. One of the obvious extra benefits of such a voluntary program would be that the funds invested in the private programs would be available for investments in the private sector–working capital that would enable business and industry to modernize and expand and get the economy of this nation moving again.

The Spenders and Taxers

There are those–the spenders and taxers, the planners and controllers–who would have us believe that a government can spend a nation *out* of poverty, out of a recession or depression. These spend-and-tax advocates are not at all disturbed about the soaring costs and tax-take of government. They are all for taxing Peter to pay Paul.

They belong to the Keynesian school of economics. "Purchasing power", regardless of its source, is the name of their game. If we followed their argument, we would praise the activities of the thief and the more he stole, the more he would be lauded. After all, when he robs us he has more purchasing power to spend at the corner bar. The fact is, of course, that his victims have exactly that much less to spend.

In these days, when government's hand is already so deep into our pockets, the spenders demand the hand go even deeper. These liberal friends–liberal with the working man's income–seldom equate increased government spending with increased taxation and run-away inflation. Yet, it is one of the hard, cold facts of life that everything government spends comes from our pockets–*either now, or later.* The *now* we call taxation, the *later* we know as inflation.

There ain't no free lunch. Every action has a consequence and the consequence of government spending is less spending by the private citizen who is working and earning his way.

The Growing Grab

Finally, our spend-happy advocates would have us believe that increasing government spending is simply keeping pace with the increase in our gross national product.

The record shows otherwise:

–in 1940, government took 18.5 percent of the GNP
–in 1950, it took 21.3 percent
–in 1960, 27 percent.

By 1970, it was 32 percent and it is estimated that government now takes 35 percent of our gross national product.

That is really rendering unto Caesar!

Suppose our liberal friends were correct. Suppose, over the past ten or twenty years government spending had simply kept pace with the increase in our gross national product.

Suppose, for example, that in 1974 government had taken only 21.3 percent of the GNP–as it did in 1950. Twenty one percent, one-fifth of all we produce; that's not being stingy with Caesar. And on that basis, the cost of government in 1974 would have been $275.8 billion instead of what it actually was–$455 billion.

Or, suppose that in 1974 government had taken only 27 percent of the GNP, as it did in 1960. That would have held the cost of government down to $350 billion. The per capita cost of government, then, would have been $1,660 rather than the actual $2,146–a savings of $486 for every man, woman and child. Imagine what the average family of four could do with an extra $1,944 right now!

Gross Statistics

Actually, to measure the heavy-hand of government spending solely on the basis of gross national product is somewhat misleading. GNP statistics, as generally presented, are inflated; about twenty percent of our GNP goes to support the governmental establishment–everything from paper clips and typewriters to automobiles and bombers. A great deal of that money goes to administrative overhead; government salaries, for example, are now running at an average cost of $11 billion a month.

Some of that spending is necessary–because certain functions of government are necessary. As Henry Hazlitt, one of America's soundest contemporary economists, wrote:

"Necessary policemen, firemen, street cleaners, health officers, judges, legislators and executives perform productive services. . . . They make it possible for citizens to function in an atmosphere of law, order, freedom and peace. But, their justification consists in the utility of their service . . . not in the purchasing power they possess by virtue of being on the public payroll." [12]

Many government expenditures are not necessary. The operating costs of the myriad bureaus and agencies, at virtually every level, that regulate our commerce and control our travel, to name a few.

And, some government expenditures and "services" are counter-productive. They restrict our liberty, our economic growth (the increase in goods and services and jobs in the private sector) and thus these governmental activities slow down, and often halt or reverse, the increase in our gross national product.

Fewer Guns, More Butter

One of the primary functions of government is to protect its citizens from its enemies abroad. Just as it is necessary to employ police to provide some measure of law and order in our communities, so it is essential that we maintain a strong defense apparatus to insure some measure of national security. And, in these unsettled days, eternal vigilance would seem not only prudent but vital.

Yet, it has not been "defense spending" that has caused the tremendous increase in our federal budgets.

In the period, 1961-1974—including that ill-fated and expensive endeavour in Southeast Asia—defense spending increased 145 percent. But, during those same years, non-defense federal spending jumped *350 percent!* In other words, during those 15 years, federal non-defense spending increased at a rate twice that of the increase in defense.

Further, in the five years, 1970-1974, while defense spending was holding at about $80 billion a year, non-defense spending continued to soar: from $116 billion in 1970 to $195 billion in 1974.

"What Kind of A Society?"

As they say in the puzzle palaces of the Potomac, "You ain't seen nothing yet; the past is only prologue."

When former director of the federal budget, Roy M. Ash, was previewing government spending for the fiscal year 1976, he set this warning before President Ford:

> *If the average nine percent rate of growth in public assistance and social security payments continues through the year 2000, federal and state-local budgets will account for two-thirds of the gross national product.!* [13]

The growth in government spending in those areas in recent years has been literally incomprehensible. Since 1959, "federal payments to individuals, plus aid to state and local governments to finance other payments to individuals, has jumped from $22.1 billion, or 24 percent of the U.S. budget, to $143 billion, or 44 percent, in fiscal 1975".[14]

Then Mr. Ash posed the question:

"What kind of a society will we have if two-thirds of the economy comes through government?"

Who Works for Whom?

There are those–including our friends of the liberal spend-and-spend school–who contend that if government did not spend so much money to employ and subsidize so many persons, those individuals would be out of work. Wittingly or unwittingly, they advocate that government be the nation's employer of "first resort".

When government becomes the employer simply for the sake of employing as many individuals as possible, government no longer works for the people–the people work for it; both those who "receive" and those who are "taken".

As has been noted, some government is necessary at every level–federal, state and local. Thus, a certain number of government employes will always be needed to perform legitimate functions; in that sense, government employes are productive rather than parasitical.

It is the illegitimate and the excessive in government that should concern us. These not only limit our liberty, they restrict our economic progress.

The excessive funds now siphoned from the individual (the private sector) could, and would, be used by the private sector to provide the greatest benefits for the greatest number of people. Those benefits would be far greater than any provided by government. Once "freed" from government's grasp, that money would

–provide the taxpayer with additional income and real purchasing power, thus to create an increased demand for goods and services

–supply additional investment capital for economic expansion and new jobs in the productive private sector to meet those increased demands

–enable individuals to save and invest in annuities and pension plans so that they need not be dependent upon government (other taxpayers) in later years

–create and accelerate the distribution of "new" wealth (thus to broaden the tax base and spread the tax burden).

Refuting the argument of those who advocate increased government "purchasing powers" through larger and larger government payrolls, Henry Hazlitt wrote:

"Once again it is forgotten that if these bureaucrats are not retained in office, the taxpayers will be permitted to keep the money that was formerly taken from them for the support of the bureaucrats. Once again it is forgotten that the taxpayer's income and purchasing power go up at least as much as the income and purchasing power of the former officeholders go down." [15]

The Dead Hand of State Capitalism

Individual enterprise and investment builds capital. State control and state spending destroys capital.

That is exactly what is happening in this nation today.

As government takes more and more of the nation's personal

income and a larger and larger chunk of our gross national product, the nation's economy slows and becomes stagnant:

Productivity lags, inflation balloons, prices rise, the growth rate of the GNP shrinks and disappears, unemployment increases, the ranks and raids of government increase–and the people suffer.

Leviticus 17:14 tells us that the "life of the flesh is in the blood thereof". Years ago physicians came to realize that. They stopped bleeding the sick and let the body manufacture new blood to cure the disease. The economic life blood of a nation is in its working capital–whether it be a single carpenter's investment in his tools or a corporation's investment in its machinery and other productive equipment. Such capital, such lifeblood, is essential to the health and growth of a nation. Yet, the "physicians of government" continue to bleed the patient.

And, how fares the patient these days? Well, check the chart:

–43 percent of the total personal income and 35 percent of the gross product go to government

–almost one out of every five (18 percent) of the labor force is on the government payroll [16]

–the ratio of producers to non-producers now stands at close to one to two. (For every productive–income earning and taxpaying–citizen there are 1.9 who are non-productive; i.e. not gainfully employed tax beneficiaries.)

–taxes now take more than two and one-quarter times as much as the amount of money we spend on our daily bread, more than three and one-half times as much as the cost of the roof over our heads, and more than five times as much as we spend for the shirt on our back. [17]

–in 1974, almost one-quarter of a million individuals declared personal bankruptcy because they could not keep their heads about the rising tide of inflation, and

–combined public and private debt in this nation now exceeds *three trillion dollars!*

Such is the devastation–with all its economic, social and moral ramifications–left in the wake of the so-called New Deals, Fair Deals, New Frontiers, Great Societies and New Federalism: controlled citizens, uncontrolled government, and debt, inflation and crime.*

A New Slavery

If someone were to suggest that this nation once again condone slavery, he would no doubt be glued together with tar and ridden out of the country on a splintered rail. Yet, consider this:

> *The amount of money government takes is equivalent to the total personal income of about 100 million Americans. Compare that present day "legalized" involuntary servitude with the four million slaves in America just prior to the outbreak of the War Between the States.*

Those four million slaves of the mid-1880s were "privately owned", forced to labor on private plantations. Today's slaves are "federally owned"; they labor on government plantations.

Since outright enslavement of 100 million of our fellow-countrymen would provoke rebellion, the bondage is distributed. Each of us is made part slave and each of us is left part free. That way we can live in our "own" home, work at our "own" job, attend our "own" church, and even go bowling on Friday nights . . . as long as we render unto Caesar that which he demands. Such a convenient arrangement should not blind us to the fact that involuntary servitude is being forced upon citizens by excessive government spending.

II.

An auto wrecking yard is not the most attractive of locations. It is, indeed, strange soil on which to take a stand for freedom.

---

*The wages of public extravagance are far greater than just economic. There is, for example, a definite relationship between inflation and rising juvenile delinquency, especially in the suburbs. As more and more mothers are forced to seek employment to help fathers make ends meet, more and more children are left unattended and on their own, after school and on weekends. Unsupervised and with "no one to care", many become easy prey for mischief, drugs and promiscuity.

But then, one cannot always choose the time or place to damn the tyrant. So, consider the case of the Internal Revenue Service versus one George Scott, proprietor of Scotty's Auto Wreckers, in Chico, Calif.[18]

Mr. Scott was delinquent in his federal taxes. In the forty days preceeding March 31, 1972, he had paid the government $3,400. There was a balance due of $1,450 and he needed more time to raise that money.

But, don't get hung up on the dollars and cents. Mr. Scott's particular money problem is not the central issue here. What is central is the manner in which the IRS seized his property.

At 11 A.M. on Friday, March 31, 1972, without court order, without judicial hearing or approval, agents of the Internal Revenue Service seized Mr. Scott's wrecking yard. They seized it and sealed it. They claimed it in the name of the Secretary of the Treasury of the USA, as if it were some foreign territory.

Just plain and ordinary citizens–the kind who fought or waited while their menfolk fought at Bunker Hill and Belleau Wood and Bataan and Baker Two–would like to claim those agents did not have such power; to claim that Articles IV and V of this nation's Constitution protect each citizen from such arbitrary confiscation by Caesar and his men.

Article IV–"the right of the people to be secure in their persons, houses, papers and effects, against unreasonable search and seizure".

Article V–"nor be deprived of life, liberty, or property, without due process of law." Due process before the fact. What good is due process after the fact?

Where, you may ask. At what time, and on what date in the history of this Republic, did Congress or the people ever give to the IRS the right to ride rough shod over the Constitution and the rights of freemen?

Well, Congress did. While we were looking the other way–fighting depressions and wars, attending to our daily chores–Congress did.

Title 26, Section 6331, US Code: the Secretary of the Treasury, or his designated agent, can seize your property. Seize it ten days after you are declared delinquent in your taxes. On his own, by administrative edict, the Secretary or his designated agents can seize and sell your property, place a levy on your wages, or use other methods to confiscate the fruits of your labor. And damn the Constitution!

When did this all happen? It happened in the darkness of 1939, when Franklin D. Roosevelt was president and Henry Morgenthau, Jr., was Secretary of the Treasury, and Americans were trying to climb out of the depression. It was reaffirmed, in 1954, and it was all done–both times–with the aid and consent of the Congress; those men and women who are elected to represent us, to serve us, and protect us.

The courts, upon occasion, have held the statute valid; have held *in summary* that the Internal Revenue powers do not violate those Articles IV, V, and XIV (equal protection under the law).

Peace officers, even with compelling reason to suspect a clear and present danger to public safety, cannot search or seize or confiscate without a court order or a judge's by-your-leave. But IRS agents can–on the allegation of a computer print-out that says a citizen is delinquent in his taxes.

Not Even King George

During the U. S. Senate hearings on Watergate and related matters, Senators Sam Ervin and Herman Talmadge made a great issue of the precious right of a citizen to be secure in his person and home and office.

The Senators, in front of nationwide television, traced that protection back to its beginnings; back through the Constitution, back through the early days of the American colonies–back to English Common Law and the Magna Carta.

Senator Talmadge concluded his effusion with a reading of the words of William Pitt, The Elder:

"The poorest man may in his cottage bid defiance to all the force of the Crown. It may be frail; its roof may shake; the winds may blow through it, the storms may enter, the rain may enter–but the King of England may not enter; all his forces dare not cross the threshold of the ruined tenement!"

In all their stout-hearted defense of the citizen's right to be secure, neither Senator Ervin nor Senator Talmadge made mention of the violations of that security in the name of "the government" and in the pursuit of the tax dollar. Can it be that neither legislator was aware of the ravages of Title 26, Section 6331? Would they uphold for Donald Ellsberg's psychiatrist that which they would not uphold for the average working man and common citizen?

Guilt Presumed

A similar type of tax arrogance exists in many states. There, too, when Caesar's tax agents say the citizen is wrong, he's wrong—until he proves himself innocent, or right.

In no other area of the law is the individual presumed guilty. In every other legal battle, the citizen is protected by the guarantee of presumed innocence until proven guilty beyond a reasonable doubt. Caesar's tax men are above that law and thus the citizen is beneath it. Can it be the almighty tax dollar ranks higher than the citizen's rights?

In California, one state senator tried to set things straight. James Q. Wedworth, of Inglewood, demanded that the burden of proof in tax matters be put where it belonged: on the government. Wedworth introduced SB 443 to do just that; to require the government to prove a taxpayer's guilt rather than to force the citizen to prove his innocence.[19]

Radio station KNX, Los Angeles, aired an editorial supporting that measure:

"We marvel at how many Americans continue to endure a tax system that is unfair; needlessly complicated; arrogant, and one that violates our ideal of justice.

". . . in no other judicial proceeding is the accused considered guilty until proven innocent. If the tax system charges you with violating the law, you have to prove yourself innocent or go to jail or pay a fine.

"At the heart of all this is the . . . men and women you elect to represent you. Year after year they let this unfair, complicated, arrogant, and un-American system endure. And, you let them let it endure."[20]

That editorial, and other citizen support, did not sway many legislators in Sacramento. A majority killed Senator Wedworth's bill of rights for taxpayers. They stomped on it in committee and threw it in the trash. A gaggle of bureaucrats–servants of the people, county tax assesors and tax collectors–lobbied the bill to death.

They rejected the suggestion that they be required to justify their claims and defend their assessments. That, they argued, would put an added burden on the establishment. After all, to a bureaucrat nothing is more sacred than the bureau.

What America needs is a taxpayer's bill of rights as well as honest-to-goodness tax reform. If men will not act on principle, surely they will act when their property is destroyed. And, at today's cost in both dollars confiscated and liberty lost, there is ample reason to demand relief, reform, *and justice.*

III.

History gives us the cold, hard warning:

> *When government takes 35 percent or more of a people's production, individual freedom is close to the point of no return. It is on its way out and from there on it's mostly a downhill exit. A one-way ride to socialism–the total tyranny of government ownership and control of the means of production and distribution. A totally-managed society, an Orwellian nightmare, with virtually complete government control of the citizen's existence.*[21]

Sir Flinders Petrie, the noted British archeologist, is recognized as an authority on the subject of individual liberty in relation to the rise and fall of civilizations. During his lifetime, Sir Flinders studied the records of the world's six great civilizations of the past 8,000 years. His probing led him to this conclusion:[22]

> Civilizations reach their peak when liberty is at its maximum. When economic "parasitism" sets in–when government and its allies of the special interest factions feast on the fruits of the working man's labors–civilizations slide into the abyss or a prolonged "dark ages". And, few recover.

Cut, Limit and Restore

Let someone suggest the restoration of individual liberty through the limitation of government and someone else is bound to pop up with that dog-eared challenge, "Okay, wise guy. Just what government functions would you eliminate?"

Obviously, before you can cut taxes you must reduce government spending; otherwise you end up with even more inflation and that means you're not really cutting taxes at all. And, before you can reduce government spending, you must eliminate, or curtail, the size and scope of government.

"So, what would you eliminate?"

That is not an easy question to answer. The thicker the crust, the more difficult to get to the core; the crust of government is mighty thick right now. Some politicians, elected to public office on well-intentioned and sincere promises to break through that crust have, instead, broken their picks. *The proponents of unlimited government are legion*—both inside and outside the establishment. They comprise bureaucrats and special interest groups who covet the working man's income and are adept at "legalized" plunder. They make for formidable opposition to any limits on government.

But, it can be done. Government can be brought down to its proper size and scope and powers.

Some federal legislators are already moving in that direction. They have introduced bills that would

—put a moratorium on new federal spending programs,
—reduce the federal budget by ten percent,
—place a three-year hiatus on all U.S. foreign aid,
—require a balanced federal budget for fiscal 1976, and
—call for a Constitutional amendment forbidding future federal deficits and requiring gradual repayment of the $500 billion national debt.[23]

The Uncontrollables

One of the difficulties in eliminating or curtailing federal spending programs involves so-called "uncontrollable" expenditures.

These "uncontrollables" are open-ended programs and fixed costs to which past Congresses have commited the taxpayer. In many areas, such back-door spending is not only improper but downright deceitful. Many of the commitments were pushed through by spend-and-elect congressmen who feared that future Congresses might resort to fiscal sanity and eliminate such programs. Thus, those congressmen foisted upon us–in effect and in fact–taxation without representation.

Some legislators argue that these "uncontrollable" expenditures cannot be eliminated–or even curtailed–without violating the public trust. The public trust has already been violated in such matters; what they are saying is that the elimination of such open-ended, *in perpetuum,* programs would fly in the face of promises and pledges they made to special interest blocs.

It is estimated that at least 56 percent of all federally budgeted expenditures are "uncontrollable".[24] And, that another 20 percent of current spending arises from expenditures of prior years that were budgeted into the future. Unless this strangle hold on today's and tomorrow's taxpayers is broken, citizens will not regain the freedom to make their own decisions as to how they wish to allocate future economic growth.[25] Until such freedom is restored, any future growth will simply serve as a vitamin pill for bigger and bigger government.

Commitments made must be undone if we are to avoid that disaster of which former budget director Roy M. Ash has warned: that day when 66 percent of our gross national product goes to Caesar.

What has been done can be undone. If not by those now in Congress, then by new representatives elected to release the citizen from such bondage. Legislators are chosen to reflect the contemporary wishes of the citizenry, not to simply parrot the decisions of previous bodies.

A Matter of Principle

It's not just the money, it's the principle.

And, if government is to be restored to its proper size and scope and cost, it must be done by standing on principle–not by getting bogged down in petty details or decimal points or pettifoggery.

What principles? The principle of individual liberty and limited government. A government that serves the people but a government that does not violate the citizen or his rights.

Leonard Read, president of the Foundation for Economic Education, is perhaps the leading expositor of such principles in America today—as he has been for the past quarter century.

"Just what government would you cut out?" Let Leonard Read answer that challenge: [26]

"I would favor the rescinding of all governmental action—Federal, state or local—which would interfere with any individual's freedom . . .

". . . to pursue his peaceful ambition to the full extent of his abilities, regardless of race or creed or family background;

". . . to associate peaceably with whom he pleases for any reason he pleases, even if someone thinks it's a stupid reason;

". . . to worship God in his own way, even if it isn't 'orthodox';

". . . to choose his own trade and to apply for any job he wants—and to quit his job if he doesn't like it or if he gets a better offer;

". . . to go into business for himself, to be his own boss, and set his own hours of work—even if it's only three hours a week;

". . . to use his honestly acquired property in his own way—spend it foolishly, invest it wisely, or even give it away. Beyond what is required as one's fair share to an agency of society limited to keeping the peace, the fruits of one's labor are one's own;

". . . to offer his services or products for sale on his own terms, even if he loses money on the deal;

". . . to buy or not to buy any service or product offered for sale, even if refusal displeases the seller;

". . . to agree or disagree with any other person, whether or not the majority is on the side of the other person . . .

". . . to do as he pleases in general, as long as he doesn't infringe the equal right and opportunity of every other person to do as he pleases.

"In short, instead of attempting to explain the thousands upon thousands of governmental agencies you would eliminate, let the author of the tricky question explain just one peaceful activity he would deny to the individual. Isn't that putting the burden of proof where it belongs?"

Indeed it is. Too often, today, government forces the individual to justify liberty rather than the individual demanding that government attempt to justify coercion.

Tax Reform

Come the usual election year and politicians–those in office and those who want into office–whisper sweet nothings about tax reform. By and-large, that is exactly what the citizen gets in the way of tax reform: *nothing.*

Once in a while we get a bone of tax relief and for such small favors we are grateful and momentarily pacified. Now and then, there is "reform" in the shifting around of tax levies; but that is not reform, that's a shell game. We end up paying just as much, or more, through different taxes on different transactions. Some taxes are reduced, others are introduced or increased; some loopholes are closed, others are created.

What we need at all levels–is reform. Not just expedient, squeaking-wheel revision but honest, bedrock reformation.

Take the federal income tax laws, for example. What started out as thirty words and one percent has proliferated and expanded into millions of words and progressive rates that patronize some and rip off others. It's the same in most states; a crazy quilt of add-ons and take-offs, loopholes and gimmicks; guaranteed, if not calculated, to drive the average middle income taxpayer up the wall and closer to the poorhouse.

Here are ten basic suggestions for tax reform.

1. *Taxes should be used to raise revenues for legitimate government activities, period. Taxes should not be used for social control or social reform.*

When taxation is employed to finance the proper and necessary functions of government, it is a legitimate extension of civil authority. When taxation exceeds those limitations, it becomes a license to plunder; it violates God's laws *(Thou shalt not covet, thou shalt not steal.)*

There are those who see the instrument of taxation as a means to achieve their concept of "social justice"—of redistributing income and wealth, of robbing Peter to subsidize Paul, and forcing individual initiative and reward down to the lowest uncommon denominator. "One of the prime functions of government is continually to redistribute market incomes so that incomes are in accordance with our social or collective judgements as to what constitutes a just distribution of economic resources." [27]

Where? Where in the Constitution is this "function" of government set forth? Where does it say that "redistribution of wealth" is a power given by the people to the government—at any level? It is inherent in the basic law of the land that government in its administration of taxation should be, as it is in the administration of justice, "blind"—according equal treatment and protection to each and every citizen.

Professor Irving Kristol suggests that the average taxpayer views the problem differently than his "self-appointed saviors": [28]

"The average American, no matter what he may sometimes say or what is said in his name, is not rebelling against tax inequities. He is rebelling against taxes, period. He is rebelling against increased property and sales taxes. He is rebelling against the hidden tax that inflation represents. He is rebelling against all those itemized deductions from his paycheck—(against the fact) that his hard-won wage increases seem to exist only on paper and never find their way into his pocket.

"The American worker . . . resents this whole process, which bureaucratically insists on improving his longer-term prospects at the expense of his shorter-term ones—on improving his general welfare at the expense of his specific well-being. In short, he resents the present structure of the welfare state, and his tax rebellion is an expression of this resentment."

What would happen—what has happened already—to work incentives, the market process, and the standards of living, if a compulsory and large-scale income redistribution is made through the tax system? The economic greatness of America—the wealth of any industrial nation—lies not in some static and socialistic distribution of income; it lies in the dynamic process of producing the greatest benefits for the greatest number by rewarding initiative and achievement and penalizing slothfulness.

2. *Taxes should be apportioned so that each citizen pays a fair share of the cost of government—no more and no less.*

Every citizen should help pay the cost of government—no matter how small the levy or how minute the share. Using the tax system as an appendage of the welfare program may seem to be efficient, but it can have deadly results. *When government is "free", its citizens seldom are.*

Tax rates should be proportional, not progressive. If the cost of government is, for example, thirty percent of total personal income, then a flat rate of 30 percent should be applied to all incomes. At the same time all loopholes and exceptions should be eliminated.

Further, any consideration of the impact of taxation should include tax "benefits" as well as tax payments. A review of the existing tax-and-spend system (ratio of taxes paid and benefits received) clearly demonstrates the existing inequities. A study by the Tax Foundation found that "those with income under $3,000 received benefits equal to two or more times their total tax burden. At income levels above $6,000, tax burdens exceeded benefits." [29]

A more recent survey by Miller and Herriott, of the U.S. Census Bureau, revealed an extremely progressive redistribution of income and tax burden.[30] "Families with less than $2,000 of earned income in 1968 paid an estimated 50 percent for all taxes—but received 106.5 percent in government transfers of money and services for a net benefit of 56.5 percent. In the $8,000-$10,000 group, taxes amounted to 29.2 percent of income and benefits to 5.5 percent—for a net tax of 23.7 percent. Median income in 1968 was $9,633."

3. *The amount of taxes government collects each year should be clearly established in advance, with a cast-iron lid on that amount.*

The citizen has a right to know that government will not take more than a set amount of his wealth and that no open-ended budgets at any level can cause taxation to exceed that limit during the stated (annual) period.

This could be pegged as a percentage of the gross national (or state) product, or a percentage of total national (or state) personal income.

Such a lid would force government to set a budget within the people's means—and stay within it. Bringing government spending down to that ceiling could be achieved within a certain period of years, year-by-year. For example, if it were agreed that the federal government should not take more than 20 percent of the total national personal income, the present level of 28 percent could be reduced to 20 percent in ten years by reducing government's take of the total personal income by .8 percent in each of those ten years. Revenues in excess of those totals, because of economic growth, would be applied to a reduction of government debt, or split between debt reduction and tax refunds.

4. *Property taxes should be levied at the local level only.*

Currently, there are moves in many states to institute statewide property taxation. This would not only serve to further weaken local governments, it would accelerate the growth of the "big state."

"When the power to tax (property) leaves the county, tyranny will then begin in the United States. Socialism or communism will be only a step away. The people of a county will be helpless as their property is taxed to the point of expropriation by a distant state capital." [31]

5. *Property taxes should be levied for "property-connected" services only (police, fire, sewer, special districts, etc.).*

Forcing property owners to pay taxes for general governmental functions (such as education, welfare, courts, etc.) is forcing them to pay twice—once through property taxation and again through taxes on income and/or purchases. Further, including those costs (education and welfare) in the property tax is forcing those taxes up to the point where many elderly persons can no longer keep their homes—and many young persons cannot afford to buy a home.

Additionally in this area, some means should be found—perhaps a "deflation factor"—to end the injustice of basing property assessments on inflated market values when the owner has no intention of placing his home on the market. Long-term residents should not be placed in the same category with speculators.

6. "People" taxes (income, sales, etc.) should be used to finance "people" services (general services such as education, public assistance, justice, etc.).

Relying on the property (real estate) tax to fund the major portion of public education is a hold-over from by-gone eras; it is no longer necessary and it has long since been inequitable.

Financing "people" services through "people" taxes would help to spread the tax burden so that it would be more equitable and easier for all citizens to bear.

Those who receive a service should foot the bill; as widely as possible, government should base its income on a fee-for-service basis and operate on a cost-price-market system.

7. Only those who are to pay a tax should be permitted to vote on the imposition and amount of that tax.

To some this will no doubt seem to be heretical. But, fair's fair!

"How long would Christianity last as an institution if unbelievers could vote in churches? Will non-owners respect property to any greater degree?" [32] Why is it right that someone who will not pay the tax should have the license to vote on the amount of tax others will be forced to pay?

"Is not private property as an idea abolished when the non-property owner becomes legislator for the owner? The property qualification for the vote is the ultimate political form of the recognition of private property." *So wrote a man named Karl Marx.*

8. Taxes should always be visible: no more "hidden taxes"—and, no more pyramiding of taxes.

The people have a right to know when, and how, and how much they pay out in taxes. Hidden taxes make for invisible government.

Further, hiding taxes tends to encourage pyramiding of taxes—taxing the tax on a product. A gross example of this: slapping a sales tax on gasoline that already includes in its price per gallon both state and federal excise taxes. Thus, the consumer is compelled to pay a tax on a tax.

9. Government representatives (federal, state or local) who seek to spend the taxpayers' money should be required to levy the tax

necessary to raise that money. With the power to tax should go the direct responsibility to answer to the taxpayers.

The common practice of state and local officeholders basing their spending programs on "federal" money invites extravagance and irresponsibility. It is a shell game that permits government officials to escape accountability.

Further, the technique of using federal taxation to raise revenues for state and local programs (financed by grants from Washington) is deadly; in addition to forcing the taxpayer to carry Uncle Sam's "brokerage fees", such dependence on the whims and wiles of federal legislators and bureaucrats hastens the day when states' rights will be spelled "r-i-t-e-s".

Public service responsibilities (taxing and spending) should be held at the lowest practicable level; close enough to the people so that their votes can have a direct, immediate and obvious effect.

10. ***All tax agencies and agents should be required to abide by and uphold all Constitutional guarantees and protections (due process, restrictions on search and seizure, presumed innocence, etc.).***

In a society of freemen, all individuals stand equal before the law and every man is entitled to his full day in court. No man is beneath the law, and no man–*not even The President and certainly not tax agents*–is above the law.

CHAPTER ELEVEN

Inflation Is Killing America!

Things aren't going too well for Joe Griffin and his wife.

Here they are, retired in the golden years of their lives, and everything keeps coming up crabgrass.

Fifteen years ago Joe and Dolly bought their home for $25,000. They planned to live there for the rest of their natural born days. Two years ago Joe retired and the Griffins now live on a fixed income of just under $10,000 a year. When Joe took out that annuity, years ago, he figured it would provide them with a comfortable old age.

Back in 1960, when Joe and Mrs. Joe bought their home, the property taxes were $325 a year. This year those taxes are $940. That's almost three times what they were and almost one-tenth of Joe's total annual income.

What's going on?

Did the Griffins add on to their home? Did they add a swimming pool? Or, a new garage? No. Aside from the normal maintenance there has been no change in the Griffin house.

What happened was this:

–over the years the property tax rate has more than doubled, and

–the assessed value of their home has exactly doubled.

According to the county tax assessor, the Griffin house now has a market value of $50,000. The Griffins have (or had) no intention of selling. That house is their home, not a speculator's sport. But, they are being taxed on the basis of what the tax assessor says they could get if they were to put it on the market.

And so they are hit from both sides. The tax rate goes up to pay the inflated cost of doing government. And the assessment rises to reflect the inflated prices of the market.

The Great Bubble Machine

All of this has hit the Griffins in their old age and at the same time that the cost of almost everything else has skyrocketted. For example, when they first moved in, it cost them $150 a year to heat their home. Today their monthly fuel bills are almost $75. The same thing has happened to the cost of electricity, and the cost of food, and the cost of the other necessities of life.

The bottom has dropped out of Joe's annuity. He still gets his monthly annuity check for $800, but he and Dolly are hard-pressed to make ends meet.

They are not alone in their financial anguish although the fact that they are on a fixed income makes it especially tough. Millions and millions of Americans are suffering on the rack of inflation. They stretch and stretch but it keeps getting harder and harder to make ends meet. Every now and then a group of housewives will whoop it up down at the supermarket, angered by the rising prices. They picket the store and boycott the butcher.

Their frustration and their anger is understandable. But, they boycott the wrong outfit.

High prices and shrinking dollars are not the cause of inflation, they are the consequences!

The ladies–and the Griffins–should be boycotting the Federal bubble machine—the one back in Babylon-by-the-Potomac that keeps turning out the fake money and turning on the fake credit.

That is the source of inflation.

That is the cause of their economic miseries.

Just What Is Inflation?

Politicians keep passing the buck!

They say it's worth sixty cents (based on what the dollar bought in 1958). If they were honest, they'd at least admit that the dollar is worth maybe twenty-five cents (based on what the dollar bought in 1940).

We are being had—we have been had—by something called inflation.

Just what is inflation?

Inflation is an increase in the supply of money—an increase in the amount of currency and credit.

That's what it is, pure and simple.

Inflation is *not* higher prices.

Inflation is *not* higher wages.

It is *not* an increase in the cost of living, or the shrinking value of the dollar.

Those are the consequences, the symptoms, the visible signs of inflation. The disease itself is something else. Scratch five economists and you're likely to get six different definitions of inflation. But, consider what these prominent individuals have to say.*

Henry Hazlitt: "Inflation is the increase in the supply of money and credit . . .".[1]

Lawrence Fertig: "monetary inflation is always and everywhere the cause of price inflation." [2]

Wilhelm Roepke: "It should be clear by now that the quantity

*Each of the individuals quoted has written outstanding books and articles on the relationship of money, government and inflation. Some are listed in the bibliography that appears in the back of this book. The person who wants to pursue this important subject in greater depth should take advantage of the genius of those men.

of money in circulation decisively affects the purchasing power of money, an increase in the supply of money lowering its purchasing power (inflation), a decrease raising it (deflation)." [3]

Gary North: "There are two basic definitions: (1) an increase in the money supply and (2) a rise in the general level of prices which is caused by an increase in the money supply. I prefer the first definition: inflation is simply an increase in the supply of money." [4]

Harry Browne: "Inflation is the issuance of paper currency for which there's no gold (or other commodity) in storage . . . inflation is nothing more than the counterfeiting of paper money." [5]

Leonard Read: "Inflation is nothing more or less than the printing of what government has declared to be legal tender, that is, printing ever-increasing quantities of fiat money." [6]

There you have it. Each individual in his own words is saying just about the same thing:

> *Inflation is an increase in the supply of money. The more money government pours into the system, the less each unit of money is worth.*

Money! Money! Money!

The key word in the definition of inflation is money.

What is money?

Many persons equate money with wealth.

Is money wealth? No!

Wealth is what exists–what you own, for example–in real goods, in tangible items, in property. The market value of those items is wealth, inherent or intrinsic wealth.

Money is a medium of exchange. And in that sense, wealth is not how much money you may have but what your money will buy.

Here, let Henry Hazlitt, one of America's most articulate economists, explain:

> *"The most obvious and yet the oldest and most stubborn error on which the appeal of inflation rests is that of confusing 'money' with 'wealth'.*

Where Did All The Money Go?

Most of the money stolen by inflation went to feed the leviathan of government. Here are a few of the items it paid for:

• *interest on the federal debt*–since the end of World War Two, *just the interest* on the debt has cost taxpayers more than $318 billion.

• *social welfare programs*–costs of these programs have skyrocketed from $23.5 billion a year in 1950 to $251 billion in 1973.

• *foreign aid*–$170 billion, from 1946-74 (plus an additional $94 billion in interest charges on those borrowed funds).

• *wars*–more than $150 billion for the Vietnam war, alone.

• *farm programs*–$25 billion for "farm price and income stabilization" from 1968-72–mostly to corporate and wealthy farm interests.

• *housing programs*–$12 billion in urban renewal, 1949-71 (that $12 billion built 200,687 housing units and destroyed 538,044 units–for a net loss of 337,357 units).

• *give-away programs*–more than 10,000 of them as listed in the 1,000-page *Encyclopedia of US Government Benefits,* W. H. Wise & Co., 1965, and

• *general funds* for the swollen costs of government (that have mushroomed from $20 billion a year in 1940 to just about $500 billion in 1975). Included in those rising costs were such little dillies as . . .

. . . $35,000 to chase *wild boars* in Pakistan, $70,000 to study the smell of *sweaty Australian bushmen,* $250,000 a year to run the *Interdepartmental Screw Thread Committee* (established in WWI), $6,000 to study *bisexual frogs in Poland,* $20,000 to research *cockroaches in Germany,* $20,234 to analyze *the mating call of Central American toads,* $84,000 to study why people fall in love, $260,000 to investigate the seeds of "passionate love", and $2 million to buy *a luxury yacht* for Marshal Tito of Yugoslavia.

"Real wealth, of course, consists in what is produced and consumed; the food we eat, the clothes we wear, the houses we live in. It is railways and roads and motor cars; ships and planes and factories; schools and churches and theaters; pianos, paintings and books. *Yet, so powerful is the verbal ambiguity that confuses money with wealth that even those who at times recognize the confusion will slide back into it in the course of their reasoning.*

"Each man sees that if he personally had more money he could buy more things from others. If he had twice as much he could buy twice as many things; if he had three times as much money, he would be 'worth' three times as much.

"And to many the conclusion seems obvious that if the government merely issued more money and distributed it to everybody, we would all be that much richer." [7]

Welcome to the age of inflation!

As Hazlitt goes on to point out, the fallacy of such reasoning is this: simply increasing the amount of money does not increase one's wealth, it only increases the amount of money–other factors take over from there.

For an extreme example of what happens when money is poured into the system, look at Germany during the years 1919 to 1923. During the close of that period the German people had lots of money. They had so much money that they literally carted their *marks* to the market in wheelbarrows. A loaf of bread cost 1.25 *trillion* marks.

American tourists visiting Germany at that time had much less money. Did that mean they had less wealth? Not exactly. *In 1923, an American could get 11.7 trillion marks for one dollar.* And, an overnight stay at a hotel cost one thin dime!

Legalized Counterfeiting

What occurred in Germany is, perhaps, an extreme example (although not an isolated one; many countries have experienced such *hyper-inflation*–such massive counterfeiting of currency). Yet in the extreme can be found the fact:

It is not the quantity of money alone that counts, it is the quality.

If the quantity is arbitrarily increased, the quality will automatically decrease.

In his *Introduction to Christian Economics,* Gary North emphasizes that inflation is counterfeiting:

> "If individuals do it, the State must intervene and punish the violators, since fraud and theft are both involved. Yet, the State is also to be limited by the law of honest weights and measures; it must not force citizens to accept a unit of money which is worth less in exchange than its face value.
>
> "In short, legal tender laws* are immoral; currency debasement is immoral; printed unbacked paper money is immoral." [8]

From Merchandise to Manipulation

Obviously it would be impossible to give a comprehensive history of money in a few short paragraphs or even a few short books. But, let these few lines that follow suffice to sketch its genesis, its evolution and its degradation.

1. In the beginning, *the medium was the merchandise;* the fish that was traded for the stone axe, the canoe that was bartered for the cave.

2. Soon *the medium* (of exchange) *was confined to various recognized commodities*—beads, jewels, salt, tobacco, women—and *finally precious metals* such as gold and silver. Metal was then weighed and stamped and used as money.

3. *Paper IOUs were introduced* as a matter of convenience to the metal money owner—it was easier to carry around a pocket full of paper than a bag full of gold. But, each IOU was worth its face value in gold; *redeemable at any time . . .* as good as gold.

4. *Government arbitrarily divorced the paper IOUs (money) from metal (gold).* It repudiated any claim the holder of the paper substitute had on specie money. It declared that the paper, in itself, was money (fiat). Why was it money? Because the State said it was. *Sic semper tyrannis.* Sic, sic, sick!

---

* Legal tender laws dictate that certain specified "money" (i.e. Federal Reserve notes) must be accepted at its face value for the payment of any debts.

5. *Government can now print money at will and without any regard to species or existing wealth.* Thus, easy money replaces sound money and thus the State manipulates the individual by manipulating his money.

As Dr. Hans Sennholz has observed, it is not money that is the root of evil, it is the *manipulation* of money–that is the evil. Money manipulation is, without question, the major cause of our economic slavery; it is responsible for the involuntary servitude impressed upon the citizen by those who see the State as Supreme and the individual as servant.

A Quickie Quiz!

To understand what has happened to the value of your dollar, keep these two things in mind:

1. Money is not wealth. It is a medium of exchange.
2. Inflation is an increase in the supply of money.

Now, how about a quickie quiz!

Who can increase the supply of money (check one)?

( ) Business
( ) Labor
( ) Government

Answer: only government can increase the supply of money!

One of the prevailing fallacies about inflation is the so-called "wage-price spiral"–the myth that higher wages and higher prices are the causes of inflation. Wage and price hikes are not the cause of inflation; *they are the consequences.*

As Henry Hazlitt explains, "If it (the wage-price spiral) were not preceded, accompanied, or quickly followed by an increase in the supply of money, an increase in wages above the 'equilibrium level' would not cause inflation; it would merely cause unemployment. And an increase in prices without an increase in cash in people's pockets would merely cause a falling off in sales. Wage and price rises, in brief, are usually a consequence of inflation. They can cause it only to the extent that they force an increase in the money supply."

In his book, *Prosperity Through Freedom,* Lawrence Fertig underscores the point:

"It is a common misconception that increased wages *always* mean higher prices and inflation. This is not so unless the government acts to inflate the currency in order to support uneconomic wage rises. Otherwise the result of such increases would be curtailed production and unemployment."

So much for the argument that high prices or high wages are the cause of inflation. Business cannot print money. Labor unions cannot print money.* Government (or its designee) is the agency of inflation. *Its monetary policies have been and are now the root cause of inflation.*

Money and Credit

There are basically two ways government increases the supply of money.

First, it just plain prints more money.

Creates it out of paper and ink, and backs it up—not with wealth but with words.

Take, for example, the anticipated federal deficit of $60-100 billion for the fiscal year 1975-76. Where will all of that money come from? It will come from the government's printing presses. *From the federal bubble machine!*

As the need arises to finance the deficit, the Treasury will print and issue debt security notes. It will then sell those securities (and thus compete with others–individuals and businesses–who are trying to borrow money). Next, it will have the Bureau of Engraving print the necessary paper money and hand that over to the Federal Reserve which will use that fiat to buy the securities from the brokers and the public who purchased them from the Treasury. The whole process is nothing but "creating" money out of thin air.

That "new" money–ultimately $60-100 billion–will pour into the

---

* Because of organized labor's monopoly powers and its disproportionate political influence, it can (and does) impress its inflationary demands on spend-easy liberal politicians. Through its influence on such politicians, it does have a hand in increasing the amount of money (currency and credit) pumped into the system. Thus it participates in the perpetuation of inflation.

economy. There is no real wealth backing it. It is in essence worthless. But, the government will say it is worth 100 cents on the dollar and so we will be forced to accept it at face value. We take our financial licking later when we spend the money and find out it's worth maybe twenty cents on the buck, in terms of purchasing power.

Fractional Reserves

Second, the government can increase the supply of available credit–which is in reality just another form of money. As a matter of fact, there is far more credit-money in the economic system today than there is currency-money.

Enter, again, the Federal Reserve–the privately-owned and controlled central bank that received from Congress back in 1913 the power to regulate the value of our money.* "The Fed" establishes the percentage of cash reserves its member banks must keep on hand to cover their customers' demand deposits. These are called "fractional reserves".

Suppose you deposit $100 in your local bank, subject to payment (withdrawal) on demand. How much of that deposit do you suppose the bank is required to keep on hand against the possibility you will walk in and withdraw your money?

$100 $75 $50 $25 $10

The answer is $10. *Ten percent.* That is the cash reserve required; on the calculation that ten percent of such deposits is all that is required to meet the normal demands for payment. (Of course, if everyone demanded their money at the same time, the bank would be in trouble–"deposit insurance" notwithstanding. When it happened in 1929, 9,000 banks went kaput.)

What does the bank do with the other ninety percent of the deposits–yours and all the others? It loans it out. *A single deposit*

---

* Most congressmen try to disown the actions of the Federal Reserve, saying that what it does is beyond their control. *That is a cop out.* Congress has the power to strip the Federal Reserve of its authority and to regain the Constitutional powers granted the Congress anytime it members have the guts to do so.

of $100 can be used to create $900 worth of loans throughout the entire banking system.[9]

Professor Wilhelm Roepke explains how it works:

"There is yet another angle from which we can observe how the modern banking system affects the supply of money. A businessman, for instance, may establish a demand deposit (checking account) not only by depositing hard cash, *but by getting the bank to extend him a loan for this purpose.* Thus, by adhering to a proportion of 1:10 between cash reserves and outstanding demand deposits, with 90 percent of the actual currency paid in being loaned out, the bank can by granting credits create new checking accounts (demand deposits) *to an amount nine times greater than that which has been paid into it.* . . . (The bank) grants credits not out of preceding savings, but from additional resources *obtained by the creation of credit.*"[10]

Fractional reserve banking has vastly outstripped the State's printing of money as a means of inflation.[11]

Warns Dr. Roepke, "It is of great importance that we thoroughly understand (this) . . . for without such understanding we cannot adequately comprehend the perils and problems which currently beset our economic system."[12]

The Big Red Balloon

The following table (covering the years 1940—1974) reveals how government has increased the supply of money—and how the purchasing power of the dollar has declined:

	Federal Spending	Federal Debt	Money Supply*	Pur. Power of Dollar
	(In billions)			
1940	$ 9.1	$ 42.9	$ 66.0	100¢
41	13.3	48.9	73.4	95
42	34.0	72.4	80.1	86
43	79.4	136.7	102.1	81
44	95.1	201.0	116.6	80
45	98.4	258.7	138.4	78

	Federal Spending	Federal Debt	Money Supply*	Pur. Power of Dollar
	(In billions)			
46	60.4	269.4	157.8	72
47	39.0	258.3	164.1	63
48	33.1	252.3	165.7	58
49	39.5	252.7	165.6	59
1950	39.6	257.3	169.9	58
51	44.1	255.2	174.7	54
52	65.4	259.1	184.9	53
53	74.3	266.0	192.6	52
54	67.8	271.3	198.5	52
55	64.6	274.4	207.7	52
56	66.5	272.8	213.6	52
57	69.4	270.5	219.4	50
58	88.9	279.1	NA	48
59	91.0	286.6	210.9	48
1960	92.2	290.9	217.0	47
61	102.1	292.9	228.6	47
62	110.3	303.3	242.8	46
63	113.9	310.8	258.9	46
64	118.1	316.8	273.8	45
65	118.4	323.1	301.1	44
66	142.8	329.5	314.0	43
67	158.3	341.3	345.7	42
68	178.8	369.8	378.0	40
69	184.5	367.1	386.8	38
1970	196.6	382.6	425.0	36
71	211.4	409.5	473.0	35
72	231.9	438.1	526.0	33
73	246.5	493.2	572.2	32
74 (e)	298.6	528.0	613.9	25

* Total money (currency in circulation and demand and time deposits).

Source:
Library of Congress
Statistical Abstract, US Dept. of Commerce

There! Is that not a picture of inflation during the past thirty-four years? Is it not a record of what happened to the purchasing power of your hard-earned dollars—and why? *It's a big red balloon!*

$1 Trillion 410 Billion!

The American Institute for Economic Research estimates that *inflation has robbed 42 million of the nation's families of $1 trillion 410 billion during the years 1940-1975!* That was the loss in value of the various forms of savings and investment held by those individuals.[13]

*$1,410,000,000,000!**

That staggering loss averages out to a loss of about $33,600 for each of those 42 million families. It is also approximately equal to forty-three percent of the total federal tax take during those same 34 years. And, it is actually only a small part of the total loss of monetary value suffered by all Americans during that period.**

Inflation robs the working man. Even those whose salaries or wages were "adjusted" from time to time to make up for the rising cost of living (i.e. the declining power of the dollar). Because the

* The AIER based its estimate on the losses calculated in nine principal forms of investments, including: life insurance and annuities, trust funds, savings (or time) deposits, savings-and-loan and credit union accounts, government bonds, corporate bonds, mortgage loans held by individuals, and currency in checking accounts.

** Many readers may recall the tremendous losses suffered during the Great Depression (1929-30s). Yet few realize that those losses were "mild" when compared with the losses due to inflation during the ensuing years. The American Institute for Economic Research, in its Jan., 1974, *Economic Education Bulletin* reports: "During the early years of the Great Depression, from the end of 1929 through 1933, nearly 40 percent of the Nation's banks (more than 9,000) failed. Loud were the lamentations when depositors lost $1.3 billion (in then-current dollars) as a result of those bank failures. However, the losses to savers and holders of life insurance during the past 35 years in relation to total wealth was more than 100 times the relative loss suffered by depositors whose banks failed during 1929-33.

theft has been so subtle, and sustained over such a long period of time, few working persons realize the full extent of their loss. *It is quite likely that inflation, over the past thirty years, has cheated the average working man of just about thirty percent of the value of his total earnings.*

Lifetime Earnings—and Theft!

Take a hypothetical—but entirely realistic—case. Consider what inflation did to Bill Bagadonuts.

Back in 1954, Bill was graduated with a degree in engineering. He started out earning $10,000 a year. A pretty good salary back in those days. Bill's employer raised his salary periodicially. In 1974, after twenty years with the firm, he was earning $20,000; double what he earned when he started in 1954.

Over those years the value of the dollar—*its purchasing power*—was chopped in half by inflation. Calculated on a purchasing power index of 100 for the 1954 dollar, the 1974 dollar was worth 54 cents. So, Bill was just a little better than even. In terms of real purchasing power, he earned $10,800 in 1974; *only $800 more a year than when he started out.*

That, in itself, is enough to drive a fellow up the wall. And think what it does to the wife who has to make ends meet! And the kids who were counting on help from dad when they went to college!

You may have a fairly definite idea of what inflation steals from you, and your family, over a year's time. But, have you considered what inflation has done—or is in the process of doing—to your *lifetime* earnings?

Eight Percent, Compounded

In his essay, *Is Inflation Here To Stay?,* Morris J. Markowitz suggests "A 35-year-old man now earning $20,000 a year may need $200,000 a year or more by the time he retires." [14] Mr. Markowitz used the term "may need"—may need $200,000 a year by the time he retires. May need for what? To satisfy increased appetite? To luxuriate in splendid new creature comforts? To amass great wealth?

No. He is saying that the fellow "may need $200,000 a year" just to stay even, financially speaking, with where he was in 1975.

Comments Mr. Markowitz, "Note that a mere 8 per cent annual increase (in inflation) amounts to over 1000 percent in 30 years, when compounded." [15]

Inflation Is A Tax . . . Is A Tax . . . Is A Tax

Inflation is a tax.

It is the most insidious tax of all. Whoever cast their ballot for inflation?

> "The loss of purchasing power of the dollar is the invisible tax that pays for the increase of (government) expenditures. *The inflation tends to hide the actual burden of taxation; what we do not pay for on April 15, we pay for in higher prices. The government cannot get something for nothing; when it increases expenditures the public must reduce its consumption or investment.* Higher prices accomplish this goal: the citizens reduce their purchases as the government increases its purchases. That is why inflation is a tax." [16]

Inflation is a hidden tax. There are no reports to fill out, no printed forms to complete, no deductions itemized on the paycheck stub. But, it is there—just as real and just as destructive as any other form of confiscation.

Inflation is an open-ended tax. There is no fixed rate of confiscation. There is no way to figure, "If I earn so much, the rate will be X percent of Y dollars." What will it be, that tax? Eight percent? Ten percent? Fifteen? How can you know? Not even the perpetrators know; they have lost control.

Inflation is a flat tax: "tantamount to a flat sales tax of the same percentage on all commodities, with the rate as high on bread and milk as on diamonds and furs." [17]

Thus, inflation is a regressive tax. It hits hardest at those who are the least able to pay. Inflation is butchering the lower and middle income groups. Destroying not just their todays, but their tomorrows.

Is it not strange that those politicians who pretend the greatest concern for the little people are the very champions of the spending and deficit programs that destroy the individual's earnings and savings and hope and opportunities? You know who they are: the "inflation fighters" who insist that government is not doing enough; that it can buy our way to prosperity!

We have wandered in their wilderness for forty years and now we know: all their glitter is fool's gold!

II.

This gigantic swindle, this hoax, this immorality of politics and economics . . .

. . . how did it come to happen, here in America?

We, the people, never voted for inflation.

We never passed an initiative on the proposition, "Shall we employ inflation?". There was never a referendum on the matter.

Yet, here it is. A national way of life. It has been with us, creeping up on us, accelerating its take, for more than forty years.

Our federal representatives will claim *they* never voted for inflation. And, they didn't. Not *per se.* Not in so many words.

Many campaigned on it. Many promised it. When they were elected, and re-elected, they voted for it. But, not once did they utter the word–except to oppose it. Not once did they say, "We are voting to destroy the value of your dollar."

Instead, they voted for the roots of inflation.

This is what they did:

–They voted to *knock the dollar loose from gold;* to discard that measure of monetary discipline. Thus they changed money from a medium of exchange to a political tool.

–They voted to delegate *to a private banking corporation the power to regulate the value of our money.* They handed that right to dictate "legal tender" to a central entity not answerable to the people, or to the people's elected representatives. Thus they tossed the Constitution into the ashcan and with the help of the Court rewrote Article 1, Section 8, Part 5 of the law of the land: *"Congress shall have the power to coin money and regulate the value thereof, and of foreign coin, and fix the Standard of Weights and Measures."* Standards of weights and measures are important to a people, but what good are they if they do not also apply to money? Where is the protection to the people if a quasi-governmental, independent bank can manipulate their money?

–They voted to take *billions, and hundreds of billions, of the people's dollars* and spend them for subsidies and social programs, give-aways and foreign aid. But, seldom did they have the guts to vote the full measure of taxation to fund such spending. They hid beneath the elastic ceiling of an ever-rising federal debt. So it is the federal debt today is about $500 billion; $5,800 for every working man and woman.

No, they never voted for inflation, per se. They voted rather for the root cause of inflation. That is what they did to America.

We Let Them Do It!

In retrospect we ask, "How did it happen? How did these politicians get away with it?"

Part of the answer is, trickery. Deceit. Sleight-of-hand. The art of those economic messiahs who led them, and us, in dark directions.

But, the other part of the answer is this: they got away with it because we, the people, let them. When we stopped believing that government was the responsibility of the people and bought the line that the people were the responsibility of the government. *That was the green light.* From then on Caesar and his costs were magnified; faith in God and His abundance was put in second place, or third–or maybe fourth.

> *"Behold the fowls of the air; for they sow not, neither do they reap, nor gather into barns, yet your heavenly Father feedeth them. Are you not much better than they?"* [18]

Somewhere along the line we seem to have forgotten that!

Some Resisted

There were those, in and out of Congress, who fought the planting of inflation's roots. They tried to prevent the rape of the working man and his family.

These were the ones whose intelligence and integrity compelled them to speak out for monetary discipline; to say that it was essential to the survival of the Republic. The ones who preached that a nation cannot go on spending what it doesn't have. That someday we would pay the catastrophic consequences.

Slow down, they urged. If government needs more money, stand up and say so. Be honest with the people. Tell them what the tax bill will be and be guided by their response.

Watch out, they pleaded. Inflation will destroy America!

Take heed, they warned. Those who control the money system control the nation.

But they were the minority. Their words were truth but they were not popular. Some of the men who spoke them were defeated at the polls. *We will punish them,* the voters decided; but they were only punishing themselves. They would get the due bill at a later date.

Dupes and Do-Gooders

There were some congressmen, the greatest number, who simply gave the people what they knew they wanted. Where the public's heart was, that was where they put the public's treasure.

To suggest that they had some evil intent–or that they knew they were tearing the heart out of America's economic structure–would be untrue and unfair. In that regard they did not know what they were doing. They were simply dupes and do-gooders; more concerned with staying in office than in preserving the nation.

They failed to recognize the unholy powers of the "new" economics and the "new" politics that were taking advantage of the situation and taking over the system. So they went along helping to plant and cultivate the roots of insidious inflation. Some, in retrospect, saw the error of their ways. Sumner Slichter, he of the New Deal, was one. He looked back and cried, *"Who will reform the reformers?"* But, the damage had been done.

Those Who Knew

And what of those elected or appointed to high office, and those who serviced the men in high places, who knew exactly what they were doing and where they were taking America?

For them, inflation was the economic means to a political end and the end was revolution.

This is what they knew about inflation:

at the outset economic disruption is important but in the long run monetary ruin is secondary; it is the ensuing moral decay that leads the way to raising the State above the individual.

In *The People's Pottage,* Garet Garrett laid bare their purpose and design:

"Those who take the New Deal to have been the beginning of revolutionary change in the character of government are wont to cite its laws, and its many innovations within the law, and to forget that if it had been without the means to enforce them all of its intentions would have died in the straw. *It had to have money; and not only a great deal of money, but freedom from the conventional limitations of money. It knew that.*

"Unerringly, therefore, its first act was to prepare inflation; and this was to be a kind of inflation we had never imagined before; that is, inflation for premeditated political purpose." [19]

What would be the path and the consequences of such inflation? Garrett outlined it, step by step:

"When, in the conquest of power and for political ends, a government deliberately engineers inflation, all the monetary evils occur as before—and then to those you add such consequences as:

"*first,* that as the government expands explosively, the people will lose control of it;

"*secondly,* as the people receive millions of checks from the automatic printing machines in the United States Treasury they learn to become dependent upon government for aid and comfort;

"*thirdly,* people are first enticed by the benefits and then obliged to exchange freedom for security, and

"*finally,* the revelry of public money, which for a while seems to cost nobody anything, brings to pass a state of" immorality that permeates every level of society.[20]

Thus was mapped the course to change the character of American government. Thus was inflation engineered to serve the pagan view that man was born to serve the State. The citizen was invited to finance the funeral of his own freedom; inflation bought the casket.

> "Monetary destruction breeds not only poverty and chaos, but also government tyranny. *Few policies are more calculated to destroy the existing basis of a free society than the debauching of its currency.* And few tools, if any, are more important to the champion of freedom than a sound monetary system." [21]

Slogans and Money

At no time, except within the inner circles, did the quiet revolutionaries admit to such design. Publicly they talked of economic growth, of everlasting progress and full employment. They boasted that their new economics could spend the nation out of depression into never-ending bonanza; a perpetual boom with ever-higher plateaus. That was their promise; that was their deceit; that was their "people's pottage".

They coined new slogans the way a Pied Piper pipes new tunes. They coined new money even more rapidly. And under such auspices inflation came; *a thief in the night* leaving behind the seeds of revolution. While the people were in the parlor counting all their "free" money, inflation crept through the back window. While the people were listening to political flim-flam, inflation stole the family valuables–not just their gold and silver, but their moral fiber and the parchment proclaiming their right to be free. From then on they would gradually be more and more dependent, and more and more enslaved.

P. T. Barnum was right!

Gross Products

It wasn't long before most people bought the line.

Why worry about the federal debt? We only owe it to ourselves. It's not as if some foreign potentate held the mortgage.

And so they went on letting government spend their tomorrows to pay for their yesterdays. Now the interest on that federal debt–just the interest–costs $30 billion a year and comes to just about

$350 from every working man and woman in the land.

*Besides, boasted the spenders, look at the gross national product! See how it grows. Inflation hasn't hurt a bit; in fact it helps!**

That was another argument backed by error . . .

. . . by duplicity.

The boasters seldom pointed to the ever-greater part of GNP *being taken by the government:*

—18 percent of $99 billion in 1940,

—35 percent of $1.4 *trillion* in 1974.*

They seldom referred to the *massive accumulation of debt, both public and private.*

—$190 billion in 1940.

—$3 *trillion* in 1975.

Three trillion dollars! What was it the Apostle Paul advised the Romans? "Owe no man anything, but to love one another." [22]

Running Wild

The people largely ignored the early symptoms of the cancer.

Even when it took larger and larger doses of fake money and stretched-out credit to alleviate the economic pains. Even when it took increasing hordes of bureaucrats to staff the mushroomed agencies and bureaus. Even when the controls and interventions multiplied. They were slow to acknowledge how deeply the malignancy had eaten into the national marrow. Who likes to admit he is sick and take the cure?

It was not just the economic cancer; it was also the political cancer: both were running wild. Physicians have a word for it, when cancer runs wild. They step out into the hall and whisper, *"It has metastasized!"* And they shake their heads and walk away.

That is what has happened. The cancer of inflation has metastasized. What part of the body national—what organ, what appendage, what function—is not now affected? *Name one!*

---

*And, as Dr. Elgin Groseclose of the *Institute for Monetary Research* points out, GNP totals include "services". Services may contribute to our comfort, convenience and well-being, but how much do they really add to the gross national product?

Those Higher Prices

The symptoms are not recent; they began to show themselves years ago. The higher prices, the economic dislocations, the shift of capital from individual to the State, the slow and steady erosion of savings and annuities, the rising unemployment.

What about those higher prices? That loss of purchasing power? The difficulty in stretching the family budget to make ends meet? What about that symptom?

After a while the people began to ask:

What's going on here? We have more money but we're sliding backward? How come?

The manipulators were ready for that one, too. They had their scapegoats pre-selected.

It's those greedy businessmen! That's what's causing the higher prices. Those guys aren't satisfied with a reasonable profit. We try to fight inflation and they keep raising prices.

That's right, agreed the public. It's those greedy businessmen. They keep raising the prices. All they care about is profits. It's just like they taught us in school–those guys are greedy!

(Few bothered consider the cause of the higher prices–the rising costs of inflation. And, few bothered to check the profit structure. If they had they would have found that in general and in constant dollars profits had not increased; that by-and-large profits were dropping–that over the years profits averaged from four to seven percent of total sales.)

The public took the politicians' propaganda at face value and in such a frame of public mind it was no trick at all to add more controls and more shackles to free enterprise. That, of course, increased the costs and raised the prices even more. And so the people howled again.

In defense, businessmen put forth a scapegoat of their own.

Look, they countered, it's the labor unions. They keep demanding higher wages. They hold down productivity. How can we keep a lid on prices when they keep doing that?

Yes, that's true, agreed the people. The labor unions keep demanding unrealistic and higher wages. And, look at those make-work rules. The high cost of labor must be a part of the high cost of living.

So the public blamed both, and business and labor blamed each other, and few blamed the government; the politicians, the manipulators, and the money changers who kept pumping bad money after bad and debt on top of debt.

Rising Unemployment

And now, of late, the people ask:

"If these 'new economics' are so great, how come this rising unemployment? What's causing that?"

Well, inflation is causing it—that's what.

The spenders and the socializers may not like this, but it is fact:

> "This recession and all its symptoms—rising unemployment, falling commodity prices, lower production, and the like—are the *direct* result of the previous roaring inflation. . . ." [23]

When waste is rewarded and thrift is penalized, when speculation means gain and investment means loss, then capital disappears and production declines. When production declines, prices soar and unemployment rises.

> "Rampant inflation (i.e. two-digit inflation) destroys the capital markets which are the very wellspring of productive enterprise. Business capital, especially long-term capital, becomes very scarce, which precipitates economic stagnation and recession." [24]

What happens when such cracks appear? When recessions keep niggling at the door and unemployment rises?

> "The Federal government comes to the rescue with record budget deficits and new bursts of currency expansion. After all, this is the basic recipe of the 'new economics' that has shaped Federal economic policy since the 1930s and has given us 'inflationary-recession', i.e. simultaneous inflation and recession." [25]

"The Federal government comes to the rescue." Politicians talk about tax cuts and increased deficits and Santa Claus rides again—down the hill of inflation, taking our dollar down to a dime. And the people cheer.

Or, do they? Are more and more of us finally catching on to

the false prophets? Are more and more of us ready to run the money changers out of the temples of our government?

Only the people can raise the demands that will restore monetary discipline to the system and rebuild the value of the dollar . . . and return integrity to our private and public contracts.

Only the people can make it clear this nation is willing to make the sacrifices to halt the binge of inflation and economic immorality.

> *"The nation which permits monetary inflation to persist, as if it were not a terrible moral evil, will suffer the consequences described by Isaiah and Ezekiel."* [26]

If the people do not do it, surely God will.

> *Isaiah 1:25*—"I will turn my hand upon thee, and purely purge away thy dross and take away all thy tin."
>
> *Ezekiel 22:21-22*—"Yea, I will gather you, and blow upon you in the fire of my wrath, and you shall be melted in the midst thereof. As silver is melted in the midst of the furnace, so shall you be melted in the midst thereof; and you shall know that I the Lord have poured out my fury upon you."

III.

It is up to us . . .

. . . *to "we, the people."*

We will either stop inflation, or

we will continue down the slide to economic chaos and the social, political and moral bankruptcy it always brings.

We cannot depend on the politicians, or the bureaucrats, or the other vested interests to do it for us. If this Republic is to be saved, the people must save it.

It will not be done by budgetary gimmicks or tax refunds, or add-ons or rip-offs. It will only be achieved through a complete and honest overhaul of the way things are now being done—*or, undone.*

It will take courage, stick-to-itiveness, and a willingness to make some short-term sacrifices.

The Pain without The Cure

How do we stop inflation?

Many experts are quick with advice on that. Some good. Some bad.

One thing is sure:

we will not stop inflation with more inflation.

If that were the cure—if simply printing more fiat money and increasing government spending were the answer—we would have been whole long ago! The fact is: the more government takes from the people, the deeper go the roots and the more deadly the cancer grows.

There is only one way to stop inflation and that is to stop it. To chop out its roots—to lay them bare and dig them out.

Among those who resist putting an end to inflation are those who argue, "If we take that cure we will have serious economic dislocations! We will have recession. We will have unemployment. We will have suffering."

Are they blind? Do they not see the pain that already exists—without the cure? We already have recession, or "stagflation". Unemployment is already rising. The economic dislocation is already there; it has been brought about by inflation! The cure would not be the cause of the illness; it would be the elimination of the disease before the disease eliminates the patient.

It will not be easy, and it will not be pleasant. But it can be relatively short-term; especially in comparison with the long, drawn-out and terminal malignancy that now chews at our core and guarantees destruction.

Those who refuse to face such facts, and refuse to level with the people, do the public no service—they help to prolong and compound the problem.

First Things First

Advocate the ending of inflation and there will be those who respond, "Yes! Let's return to the gold standard!"

Is it necessary to restore gold as the measure of our currency if we are to halt inflation, and prevent it in the future?

The answer is, "Yes, it is."

But, there are other things that must be accomplished *first.*

"The gold standard is not important as an isolated gadget but as an integral part of an economic system." [27]

We must take first things first.

The first step we must take is to demand economy in government. Not just demand it, but enforce the steps necessary to see that it is done!

How can we do it?

Cutting the cost of government will not be accomplished by messing around with bits and pieces of the government. Trying to reduce the cost of government by tackling one department, or one area of the government's budget, is like wrestling with a rubber life raft: the more you squeeze on one end, the more the other end balloons.

There is only one way to really cut the cost of government:

–cut the "take" of government–reduce its revenues.

Therefore, this must be the first step:

Put a limit on government spending. Slap a lid on the amount of our money the government may have–can take–in any one year.

Down to Twenty Percent?

The federal government now spends approximately twenty-eight percent of the nation's total income. (State and local governments spend another fifteen percent, bringing the total of all government spending to about forty-three percent of the total personal income in the nation.)

Since 1940, government spending has increased almost twice as rapidly as the rate of growth in total personal income. The per capita cost of the federal government has increased from $77 to more than $1,400 in 1974.

Where do we draw the line?

What is a reasonable percentage of total personal income to pay for the operation of the federal apparatus?

10%? 15%? 20%? 25%?

Or, the twenty-eight percent it now takes?

The answer to that should be decided by the people; in a society of free people, it would be. Yet, seldom do the people have an opportunity to vote directly on what they want the cost of government to be!

But here, for the sake of illustration, let's say that the cost of the federal government should be *no more than twenty percent* of the nation's total personal income. That would mean that Washington is now taking eight percentage points—or about twenty-five percent—more than it should.

Those who urge continued and increased government spending will go through the roof at the thought of returning so much money to the people from whom it came! (Although for the sake of political expediency they promote "tax cuts" while calling for larger and larger federal deficits!) They will tell you such a reduction in government revenues is impossible. What they mean is this: *such reductions would make it impossible for the gargantuan federal government to continue living in the style and on the scale to which it has become accustomed.* It would force the elimination, or abortion, of their pet projects; it would force the reduction of other projects now bloated, and it would mean fewer bureaucrats and fewer extras in Babylon. Well, is that not part of the task that must be tackled?

One "liberal" Republican senator recently chastised "conservatives" for trying to force "quart-sized" problems into "pint-sized jars". That was a neat turn of a phrase but it was off the mark. *What conservatives really object to is the political propensity of liberals to turn pint-sized problems into gallon-sized spending programs.*

Over A Ten-Year Period?

Why not put a lid on the cost of government and make it a definite chief aim to cut spending to or below that level within a period of ten years?

If that lid were, for example, a maximum of twenty percent

of the total personal income in any one year, why not require the federal government to reduce its present twenty-eight percent by .8 percent a year, for ten years? That would affect a total reduction of eight percent of the take by the end of the ten-year period, and cut government spending to the mandatory twenty percent limit.

Even under such a program of reduced percentages, the federal government's revenues would continue to increase during those years. How? Because even though the government would be taking a reduced percentage of total personal income each year, *that total personal income would be increasing!* In other words, the government would be taking a smaller piece of the enlarging pie.

Total personal income in the nation has been increasing, recently, at a rate of about five percent per year. If that rate of increase were to continue over the ten-year period, the federal government–while "suffering" an eight percentage point reduction in its take–would actually realize a *seventeen percent increase* in annual revenues by the eleventh year!

And, the important point is this:

> *The people would have realized a net savings of some $660 billion that otherwise would have been confiscated by the federal government, through taxation–and that is without considering any increase in taxation, direct or indirect!*

$660 billion! That would be enough to pay off the entire federal debt and still return almost $100 billion to the taxpayers' pockets and paychecks. That could be done by commensurate and concurrent tax reductions, or rebates, as the plan progressed through the ten-year period.

How The Plan Might Work

On a strictly estimated and overly-simplified basis, this is the way such a plan to limit the government's "take" might work. Let's use the eleven-year period 1974-1984 as an example.

	1. Total Pers. Inc.*	2. Present 28% "take"*	3. Reduced %tage of take	4. Max. Take Under Plan*
1974	1055	295.4	28.0	295.4
1975	1108	310.2	27.2	301.4
1976	1163	325.6	26.4	307.0
1977	1221	341.9	25.6	312.6
1978	1282	359.0	24.8	317.9
1979	1346	376.9	24.0	323.0
1980	1413	395.6	23.2	327.8
1981	1484	415.5	22.4	332.4
1982	1558	436.2	21.6	336.5
1983	1636	458.1	20.8	340.3
1984	1718	481.8	20.0	343.6
TOTALS		$4196.2		$3537.9

* All $ in billions

Col. 1–Total pers. income, est. at 5% inc. per yr.

Col. 2–Amt. fed. govt. would take under existing 28% rate

Col. 3–Proposed reduction of .8% per yr. to reach 20% max.

Col. 4–Amt. fed. govt. would take under proposed limitation

....

Some readers will recognize this proposal as being similar to the tax reform initiative prepared in 1972-3 for Gov. Ronald Reagan by a task force directed by Lewis K. Uhler, a Sacramento (Calif.) attorney. Actually, the original concept, modified and applied by the Reagan group, was put forth back in 1960 in the Herlong-Baker Tax Reform bill. Its purpose then was to use government revenues realized from economic growth to reduce progressive federal income surtaxes and also reduce the federal debt.

There is little chance that such root-reform legislation would ever come out of the present Congress with its liberal majorities. It is not the nature of spend-easy politicians to cut themselves apart from the taxpayers' pocket. *Thus, any such ceiling on federal spending can come only through the election of congressmen who are committed to fiscal responsibility.* Men and women elected by citizens who care enough to get to work in the precincts and in the congressional districts.

That would take work–lots of work, and sweat, and volunteers. But, surely it would be worth it to gain control of the expenditures of the federal government. Once a responsible majority were elected to the Congress, it would then be possible to instigate a Constitutional Amendment–*to make permanent such a ceiling on federal spending*–so that future Congresses could not revert to excessive spending, excessive taxation, heavy debt and insidious inflation.

Outlaw Deficits

It is also essential to outlaw deficit spending.

Government must begin to live within a balanced budget. We can no longer abide these annual, and ever-greater, federal deficits.

As long as irresponsible politicians can take the easy way out by indulging in deficit spending, we shall not regain a real measure of control over our personal earnings, or the value of our dollar. *Government overspending is a cause of inflation; until it is stopped, inflation will not be stopped.*

It should again be obvious–on the record–that such fiscal responsibility will not come from the present Congress. Thus again, it is up to the people:

> *If they really want to gain control of the monster that is government, and its spending and taxing ways, they must gain control of the Congress. The route to fiscal sanity–the way to restore the value of the dollar–starts in the precincts and aims toward election day.*

Only a responsible Congress will outlaw deficit spending. And only with a responsible Congress is there any hope of legislation that would make such a prohibition of debt a permanent part of the federal operation.

"Yes, But . . ."

There will be those who rise to say, "Yes, but . . .".

They will argue, "What if an emergency arises and a deficit is necessary? What if government needs money in a hurry and cannot obtain it quickly enough through a tax increase?"

Such occurrence is highly unlikely in a well-run House, or Senate. Funds can usually be obtained through transfers–through reducing expenditures or appropriations for one program and increasing another; that is a matter of priorities–the time for "buying everything in the store" is over. Then, too, through the device of withholding that has been foisted upon the people, if a situation were urgent enough Congress could enact a tax increase and have additional tax revenues flowing into the treasury in short order.

It is always the better part of wisdom–and best for the citizens–to restrict the convenience with which government can increase the national debt.

Yet, if it were necessary to gain support for the basic prohibition of deficit spending, a provision for handling emergency situations could be included. Such an emergency provision, however, should stringently limit time and procedure:

–the period of the deficit should be limited to the current fiscal year in which the emergency provision was exercised, and

–the provision should be exercised only after a call of the President and approval of two-thirds of both houses of Congress (not two-thirds present and voting, but two-thirds of the entire membership of both the House and the Senate).

Tough? Perhaps, but not as tough as it is becoming for individuals to pay their taxes and live within incomes decimated by the ravages of inflation.

Monetary Discipline

Let us suppose, for the moment, that we have succeeded:

–that we have put a limit on the amount of money the federal government can take from the total personal income (or gross national product) in any given year, and

–that we have outlawed deficit spending and forced government to live within a balanced budget.

Now, for the third step in achieving monetary discipline:

We must return to the gold standard.

Why? Because as long as the government can print money and rig credit, we will still be short of the goal of preventing inflation.

The gold standard–gold payments–is "the capstone of the arch of building sound money." [28]

The money changers and the political exploiters do not like the idea of returning to the discipline of gold. It would clip their wings–and their coupons. It would tie their hands and take away the tools they have used to whipsaw the working men and women of America.

"The gold standard functions with the force and inevitability of natural law, for it is the money of freedom and honesty." [29]

And, was not freedom and honesty–certainly honesty on the part of government as well as individuals–to be part of the bedrock of the American Republic? Should it not be so again?

The Gold Standard

The rejection of gold as the basis of freedom and honesty in monetary systems and affairs is a relatively new advent. It has occurred during the past three to five decades. That rejection came as a companion to the "new" economics and the "new" politics–those twin plagues that have torn this nation loose from its moorings and pushed it to totter on the brink of fiscal and moral insolvency.

Why do the advocates of the "new" in economics and politics reject gold? *Because it is impossible to debauch a nation's currency as long as it is on the gold standard.* And, the debauching of currency opens the door to inflation, which opens the door to the silent revolution. The new economic and political messiahs reject gold because it restricts their movements and impairs their license. It deprives them of their role in the planned society and the managed economy.

Dr. Charles E. Weber, professor at the University of Tulsa and an authority on history and monetary matters, writes it this way:

"Gold strongly restricts governmental intervention in the economy and the redistribution of wealth from the productive to the non-productive components of the population.

"We appreciate the role of gold as an honest, constructive monetary medium when we consider the nature of its enemies. Keynes, whom Lenin lauded before the Second Congress of the Communist International, considered gold a barbarous relic. Typically, the people who are shouting most loudly that gold is a barbarous relic are the very ones who are most adamant in their demands to suppress the monetary use of gold by force. (Who really are the barbarians?)

"These 'experts' must know full well just how powerful gold is in spite of their public denials that it should play a role in the monetary system and in spite of their claims that it is worthless except for filling teeth and the like." [30]

History makes this much clear:

> *unless we resume gold backing of our currency, inflation will go on and on, and this nation will go down, and down.*

As Dr. Howard E. Kershner of the Christian Freedom Foundation warned, years ago, "no civilization has long survived the disappearance of trusted money." Let a nation leave the gold standard, he admonished, and it will soon relegate God to second place. The first and great commandment will surely then be revised to read: *"Thou shalt have no other gods before the State."*

The worship of fiat money is the root of many evils.

Not "If", But "How?"

The purpose here is not to attempt to detail any step-by-step, or time certain, plan for returning to the gold standard. Many outstanding free market economists and freedom-oriented philosophers have written on that, and those works are available. For the layman, perhaps the best explanation and proposal is to be found in Chapters 15 through 19 of Henry Hazlitt's *What You Should Know About Inflation.*

However, it is important to emphasize that any "overnight" return to the gold standard could be counter-productive and injurious to the overall effort to restore monetary discipline to the nation. To return to the gold standard without reflecting the tremendous changes in our economic picture–our monetary situation and the real growth in our national product in the past forty years–could create havoc.

Consider this, for example:

When we were forced off the gold standard on April 5, 1933, the amount of US currency in circulation was approximately $10 billion and the total money supply (currency and credit) was about $40 billion.* As of the end of 1974, we had something like $68 billion in currency and a total money supply of close to $614 billion.

What, then, should be the price of gold at that time we return to the gold standard?

It would seem obvious that the best way to determine that is to let the free market speak. As Hazlitt proposes, announce (well in advance) that on a date certain the United States will return to the gold standard. The value of gold will at that time be whatever the free market has determined it to be; that price will be the "official" price of gold for conversion of dollars.

(As of Jan. 9, 1975, France revalued its gold at $170.40 an ounce. Bankers, who bought the largest amounts of gold when the "right of ownership" was restored in this nation in Jan., 1975, paid an average of $165.50 an ounce. The US Treasury, obviously, recognizes that $42.70 an ounce is unrealistic; it would accept no bids for gold for less than $153 an ounce.)

To repeat: the purpose here is not in any way to suggest the manner or method by which we return to the gold standard, that is left to those who have studied the problem and formulated the various plans; the point being made here–clearly and purposefully–is this . . .

. . . if we are to conquer inflation, we must return to the monetary discipline of the gold standard.

---

*At that time the "going price" for gold was $20.67 an ounce. The $35 "peg" was subsequently–and arbitrarily–set by Franklin Roosevelt.[31]

End Fiat Money

The fact that the "right to own gold" has been restored in January 1975, is heartening. However, it does not really restore those rights that were lost on April 5, 1933. On that day, this nation went off the gold standard. On that day, gold was no longer legal tender; paper was, whatever the US Treasury decided–that was "legal tender".

Since then, and even now, the American dollar is not convertible into gold. The use of gold as money is forbidden. The absolute and monopolistic power of the federal government to enforce fiat money remains. That hoax should be ended.

The Federal Reserve

There are those who insist that there is no need to return to gold. Those who will assure you that the Federal Reserve System can keep our economy stabilized through managing our money and our credit. *Such an argument, in and of itself, is reason enough to return to gold!* Let Dr. Hans Sennholz tell you why:

"Experience alone would dictate an immediate inactivization of this central command post over the economic lives of the American people. *In the sixty years of its existence the Federal Reserve System has presided over unprecedented economic instability*–over two depressions of which one was the longest and most severe in American history, over seven booms and recessions, and an inflation that reduced the American dollar to less than one-fifth of its pre-Federal-Reserve value. *This is indeed a long record of money mismanagement.*" [32]

What America needs is not a managed currency but an honest currency. What Americans need is not a planned economy but a vital, strong economy based on the energies and efforts of free citizens engaged in free enterprise and employing the free choices of the free market.

Dr. Sennholz offers this truism:

"Its (the Federal Reserve System) very premise of central

management of money and credit is alien to economic freedom and contrary to stability."[33]

Raise The Fractional Reserve

As has already been noted (page 11-11), fractional reserve banking has vastly outstripped the federal printing presses when it comes to causing inflation. Those reserve requirements now stand at ten percent. They should be raised to forty percent, at least.* That could, and should, be done through a series of gradual and annual steps so as to ease the adjustment to a more responsible credit base. If Congress were ever to want to demonstrate its opposition to further inflation, here is the way!

Five-Part Program

What has been briefly outlined here is a five step program to
–put a lid on the cost of government
–prohibit deficit spending
–restrict the printing of fiat money
–restore to 40 percent the fractional reserve requirements, and
–return to the gold standard.

It is the path that must be followed–the course that must be taken–if we are to halt inflation, restore value to our money, and regain the economic freedom of Americans.

Can it be done?

That answer rests wholly with the people.

Politicians will not embrace it (until they see the people taking the lead).

The money exploiters will fight it–every inch, every foot, with every dollar at their command.

Speculators will lambast it. Easy-spenders and special interests will damn it.

---

* The pre-World War II level.

Only those who will benefit will endorse it and work for it.

And, who are they?

They are "the forgotten Americans". The working men and women, the retired who exist on fixed incomes, the young who desire to look forward to some measure of security without becoming wards of the State, and the emerging minorities who want to believe there is still a ladder to climb.

To them, the end of inflation and the return to the gold standard is the way to a future in which their earnings will have value and their holdings, no matter how small, will be secure.

The decision rests with us:

we will either stop inflation, or
inflation will stop America.

CHAPTER TWELVE

These Are The Peacemakers

As children of God—as Christians—we are instructed to be at peace.

To have the peace of God.

To be at peace with our fellow-man.

To love one another; to be of good will and good works.

And, as extensions of ourselves,

to establish and support civil government and

to enact and support laws that make for peace here on earth.

The Apostle Paul, in Romans 13:3, assures us that "civil government is not a terror to people of good conduct but to those of bad behavior".

The coming together in civil government to protect the individual and to punish those who would violate his person or his rights . . .

. . . that was what it was all about when our founding fathers formed this "more perfect union"—this one nation under God.

The defense of the individual, whether it be from the front office thief or the back-alley hood or a foreign power—that is the first and foremost function of government in a society of freemen. That is why we willingly render unto Caesar that which is Caesar's.

First Things First

In recent years, things have been getting out of whack.

In many of the affairs and functions of government, first things are no longer first.

For decades, government has been so involved and so embroiled in secondary—and often improper—activities that it has neglected its most important function, its reason for being: *peace, law and order and justice.* When government meddles in the affairs of men that are not its legitimate concern—when through force it intrudes upon areas of private domain and private responsibility—it tends to neglect those first tasks it was given to do. It spends its time and attention and the people's resources on matters of relatively lesser importance and gives short shrift to things of first priority.

Such disarray in Caesar's palace tends to condone—and, in fact, breed—disorder throughout society. More and more legislators feel free to coddle the criminal, under the guise of humanism, and to play footsies with the enemy abroad—under the guise of peace. To paraphrase Edmund Burke, their passions forge our fetters.

Farewell, Young Man

Consider, for example, the tragedy of young Jeff Adams of Springfield, Ore.

Mourn for a moment at his grave and shed a tear in his memory.

Jeff was sixteen and full of life and laughter and all the things a young man is full of at that magical age. But there is no more laughter in Jeff Adams—and no more life.

He was shot down by a felon's bullet. Struck during a gun battle between a cheap hood from California and the police who were trying to apprehend him.

Jeff and his dad were driving along when a slug slammed through the door of their car and for Jeff life on earth was over.

He was killed as much by government as he was by bullet.

The hood who shot it out with the police should not have been in Springfield. He should not have been at-large. At the very least he should have been in San Quentin prison.

Charles Hein had already been convicted and sentenced for first degree murder. But, no capital punishment for him. A majority of the California Supreme Court had ruled the death penalty out of order. Life imprisonment, they decreed, was sufficient to serve the people's purpose.*

Life imprisonment? Parole officials interpreted that to mean a few years in the pen, and Hein was due for release. As part of his "life adjustment" before release, Hein was given a 24-hour pass so that he could look for a job.

Charles Hein never went job hunting. He fled to Oregon and that is where the police finally caught up with him. And that is where Jeff Adams paid the price:

Here lies Jeff Adams, aged 16,
Shot down by a felon's bullet;
But killed in part by soft-headed judges
And a parole board's game of roulette.

Jeff Adams was made a sacrifice–one of many–on the altar of the "new morality"; a strange sense of values that slaps the killer on the wrist and stabs the innocent in the back.

Distorted Values

In 1974, state and local governments spent a total of $176 billion on all of their activities. *Only four percent of that*–$6 billion–went for police protection and prisons.[1]

Such relatively low-level expenditures can hardly be defended on the basis of a prevailing domestic tranquility. The nation's

*The people of California, by a margin of two-to-one, subsequently voted to restore the death penalty for certain crimes and classes of crime.

crime rate in 1974 was seventeen percent higher than it was in 1973. An *increase* of 1,470,000 reported crimes in one year.[2]

In 1972, state and local governments spent more on "financial administration" than they did to provide police protection for their citizens.[3]

- They spent $5 per capita on police protection and $92 per capita on welfare programs.[4]
- *They spent two and one-half times as much on environmental protection as they did for "people" protection.*[5]

Of the roughly 12.5 million persons on the payrolls of state and local government in 1974, only 616,000–about five percent–were employed to keep the peace and maintain law and order.[6]

And, consider this:

–it is not unusual for states to pay $15,000–$20,000 a year to legislative aides who run hither and thither in panelled offices and marbled halls

–while they pay $10,000 a year to police officers who live in the shadow of death–and pay for their own uniforms.

Can it really be that those who keep our public files and do the politician's chores are more highly valued than those who protect our lives and property?

No Peace without Law

In this "enlightened" age–in which old values fade and young victims die–"law and order" seems to be a discarded, antiquated term. Words to be avoided lest they conflict with the semantics of some "new morality".

Even the President of the United States was prompted to skirt the issue. In a "tough" speech on violent crime, President Gerald Ford was moved to comment:

> "In thinking about this problem (of violent crime) I do not seek vindictive punishment of the criminal but rather protection of the innocent victim. . . . *(That is) why I do not talk about law and order* and I return to the constitutional phrase–insuring domestic tranquility."[7]

Does the President equate law and order with "vindictive punishment"? Vindictive punishment is not law and order; it is vengeance. It is not vengeance the people long for, it is law and order–and justice.

How does a society preserve domestic tranquility without a foundation of law and order? How do we measure the crime and mete the punishment without law? If there were more attention paid to the punishment of criminals, there would be fewer innocent victims.

Sleep well, Jeff Adams.

The Plastic Jungle

The thin blue line that holds back the jungle of barbarism grows proportionately thinner as the crimes increase. It is not that these officers of peace are any less dedicated to their task; if anything they are even more committed, better trained and more capable. It is that the tide of appetite and violence is rising. It is Sodom and Gomorrah in quadrophonic sound and living color–full blast and no holds barred.

Hear the acrid, acid music. The blatant, blatting beat of the parade of sex and drugs and violence. Televised, romanticized and headlined by the media that is upon occasion void of conscience.

The situational ethics of the classroom (and sometimes the church) slop over into society and the permissiveness of a thousand homes becomes the promiscuity of a hundred streets. Narcotics permeates the grammar schools and forty-five percent of the nation's high school students boast they have been drunk on alcohol.

And so the whirlwind grows and reaps.

Authority is flaunted.
The police are villified.
Morality goes out the window and values down the drain.
Justice becomes a sick joke and peace a cop-out.
The miscreant is excused and the malcontent is pampered . . .
. . . and society is faulted because life is not a silver platter and the scene is not a bed of roses.

It's society that is sick. We are all to blame. That's what the new moralists assert. And, in part, perhaps they are correct—but for a different reason. We have let things go too far. We should have yanked things straight, long ago.

Individuals commit crimes—not societies.

Societies do not molest children. Individuals do.

Societies do not rape elderly women. Individuals do.

Societies do not murder shopkeepers for the dollars for drugs. Individuals do.

Society is at fault because it has excused and coddled too many of the individuals that commit the crimes. *That is our crime.* The silent majority was voiceless while soft-heads and bleeding-hearts used "peace" to make crime.

The great god humanism measures with a rubber yardstick and the state too often governs with a double standard. Social adjustment becomes the synonym for justice. *Accountability is a dirty word.*

> Where are those who will stand and insist that each and every individual is indeed equal before the law and that equality includes accountability? When will they point out that he who is not held accountable is demeaned, belittled, and considered un-important?

And what of the so-called "victimless" crimes that are being pawned off on us these days? The term itself is contradictory. If there is no victim, there is no crime—*but there are victims.* Consider these:

> The children who go hungry when the money goes for a bottle or a hit. The abandoned wife, the abandoned husband, the abandoned child. The rape victim of the drug addict. (Is it that the rape is criminal but the cause is not? What specious reasoning!) And what of those who are led astray, those who imitate, those who get hooked on drugs or pushed into prostitution? Are they not victims?

Does no one care for them?

What has happened to the soul of America?

The Righteous Mourn

The righteous mourn. Let them express concern. Let them challenge the laxness. And hear the retort:

"Hey, man. You can't legislate morality!"

Perhaps not. Morality is of the spirit.

But at the very least we can stop legislating immorality.

The records are clear: when "Thou shalt not" is changed to "Whatever turns you on" the flock is scattered and the sheep are led astray.

If it's legal it must be moral, right? *Wrong!*

Coddling the criminal and excusing the crime—or making the act an un-crime in the eyes of the law does not lead to law and order. It does not lead to domestic tranquility. It leads to crime, and violence.

And in that there is no peace.

No peace with God.

No peace among men.

It Ticks for You

Small wonder the crime rate soars.

In the past ten years

violent crimes have increased 174%

murder—up 129%

rape—up 192%

robbery—up 226%, and

aggravated assault—up 139%.[8]

Now, the time clock ticks more rapidly:

In 1973, 8,638,400 crimes reported . . .

. . . every 3.5 seconds, *a serious* crime

. . . every 36 seconds, a *violent* crime

—one *aggravated assault* every 76 seconds

—one *robbery* every 82 seconds

—one *forcible rape* every 10 minutes

—one *murder* every 27 minutes.[9]

And the time-lapse between violence grows even shorter!

In 1974, 10,107,000 crimes reported.[10]

As you were reading these statistics, *at least eight more crimes* were committed.

When will the bell toll for thee?

Get The Facts, Get To Work

The issue of crime and violence deserves–*demands*–the citizen's attention. Law enforcement agencies at all levels–from the local police department to the FBI–have public information programs on both the cause and the cures for lawlessness. Concerned citizens should get these facts, and get to work on those constructive efforts to see that the necessary laws are enacted and upheld to keep the peace and protect the law-abiding. In the final analysis the call for law and order and justice must come from each citizen at every level and on every occasion. Only in that way can our people be safe and free.

The problems dealing with crime and violence are complex and many-facetted. The solutions will be found on many fronts and at many levels–starting with the inner-self and reaching up to Jesus. And through prayer, and good works in His name.

At the same time, and on the governmental action-line, here are some suggested laws and law-reforms:

automatic death penalty upon the conviction of *killing any peace officer or prison guard on duty*

–strong penalties for criminals who *carry or use a firearm during the commision of a crime* (10-year minimum mandatory prison sentence without possibility of probation or parole)

–increased penalties for *convicted peddlers and pushers of hard drugs* (10-year minimum on first conviction, life imprisonment for repeat offense)

–*total embargo* (foreign aid and trade) on nations that continue to produce and export illicit drugs.

(In 1971, six "pusher" nations produced more than 1,000 metric tons of opium worth $22 billion at New York street prices. Since World War Two, the taxpayers of this nation have shelled out almost $7 billion to those six nations–almost $500 million of that in 1973.[11] That is madness!)

–automatic revocation of parole for *any first-time offender who commits a second felony.* (Police officials estimate that approximately thirty percent of violent crimes are committed by felons out on parole.)

–revocation of driving privileges for a specific term of any person convicted of *operating a vehicle while under the influence of narcotics.*

–automatic one-to-three days in jail, without exception, for conviction of *operating a motor vehicle while under the influence of alcohol*–i.e. a blood alcohol content of 0.10 percent or higher. (Highway safety authorities report that had-been-drinking drivers are involved in approximately fifty percent of all accidents resulting in traffic fatalities.)

Suffice it to comment here that not all crimes are committed in the streets and back alleys! Refusal to adopt laws that protect the law-abiding, refusal to enact laws that give the peace officer a fighting chance, refusal to mandate appropriate penalties upon those who would prey upon the innocent, their lives and property–*these, too, are crimes!* Crimes committed by legislators who refuse to protect the citizen and who insist on coddling the criminal.

In a society of freemen–in a republic–we insist that each individual be held accountable for his actions. Should not such legislators be held accountable for theirs?

Capital Punishment

The Scriptures make it clear that the death penalty is proper and necessary. Further, the Scriptures delineate between accidental killing (manslaughter) and purposeful killing (murder).

Capital punishment is not prescribed for manslaughter:

"As in the case of manslayer . . . (who) strikes his fellow man without knowing it and was not a hater of him formerly; or when he goes with his fellowman into the forest to gather wood, and his hand has been raised to strike with the ax to cut the tree, and the iron has slipped from the wooden handle and it has hit his fellow man so that he died . . . (that man) must live . . . there is no sentence of death for him, because he was no hater of him formerly . . ." [12]

But, murder. That is a different matter. It demands the death penalty:

". . . in case there should happen to be a man hating his fellow man and he has lain in wait for him and has risen up against him and has struck him fatally and he has died . . . the elder men of his city must deliver him unto the avenger of death and he must die." [13]

Moses also set forth the reasons for the death penalty. It was a punishment but it was more–it was a protection to the innocent, and a deterrent to those who might feel impelled to murder their fellow man:

"You must also do to him as he schemed to do to his brother, and you must clear away what is bad in your midst. So those who will remain will hear and be afraid, and they will never do anything bad like this in your midst." [14]

That is the law. God's law.

Ah! some will protest. That is the law that was. That is the Old Testament. Christ removed us from that law.

No so!

Christ came to fulfill the law as well as the prophecies. He did not come to waive the law, or destroy it.

"Think not that I came to destroy the law, or the prophets; I am not come to destroy, but to fulfill. Verily I say unto you, Till heaven and earth pass, one jot or tittle shall in no wise pass from the law, till all be fulfilled. Whosoever shall break one of these commandments, and shall teach men so, he shall be called the least in the kingdom of heaven . . .". [15]

Many who oppose the death penalty may be well-intentioned, but they are also misguided. Repealing the death penalty may end it for the murderer–*but not the victim.* The victim still dies. Those who argue that capital punishment is not a deterrent take a gamble . . . they gamble with the lives of future victims.

Clean up The Prisons

There is a real need, right now, for prison reform.

Not the permissive, country-club, let-the-inmates-run-the-institution reform so many liberals and some experiment-minded penologists advocate. We have been that route and it hasn't worked. Years when the experiments pre-empted experience and knowledge and common sense. In too many instances the mistake was paid for in blood; the blood of guards, the blood of peaceful inmates, and the lives of unsuspecting citizens who were set upon by felons let loose to roam the streets.

The reform that is needed in our prisons is to make them decent, habitable places in which to house those convicted of crimes. An individual does not lose his basic human rights when he is imprisoned. Prisons should have adequate facilities for sanitation, medical care, privacy, wholesome meals—and personal safety.

Jails should not be hell-holes. And too many of them are.

Consider, for example, what happened to a 38-year-old mother who had been charged with obstruction of justice. Because she could not make bail, she was placed overnight in the Washington, D.C., women's detention center. During that one-night stay, she was sexually assaulted "innumerable times" by other inmates. That is not justice; that is the jungle! [16]

That is not an isolated case. Such shocking incidents occur with increasing frequency—many times each day—in prisons across this nation.

The vicious, and the unrepentant, and the radical, must be separated and held apart from the peaceful and defenseless inmates. Surely the youthful and the first-offender should be isolated from the hardened criminal and the pervert and the violent.

Our Brother's Keeper

The purpose of prison is three-fold (and in this order of importance):

—to protect the public

–to punish the law-breaker, and

–to help (rehabilitate) those inmates willing to be helped.

We are reminded, in I Peter 2:14, that government is sent for the "punishment of evildoers" as well as the protection of the law-abiding.

In her book on prisons, Jessica Mitford demands that penal institutions be shut down and closed up. To serve her tirade, she tried to twist a phrase:

"Are we our brother's keeper?" (Meaning, what right does the public have to judge and imprison others.)

Well, indeed we are our brother's keeper. And especially so when it comes to protecting the lives and the welfare of the defenseless and the law-abiding.

The society that refuses to imprison those who would prey upon others is not humane, *it is just plain stupid.*

Christians not only have a responsibility to obey the law–God's laws and the laws of society–they have a responsibility to help and minister to those in prison. Our Savior set the example and He counsels us to do likewise.[17] There is comfort to be given, hope to be shared, skills to be taught, knowledge to be imparted and there are souls to be saved. We should be about our Father's business in this regard. If we are not able to do so ourselves, then surely we should support those individuals and those organizations that can and will.

The Real Peacemakers

It had been a long and sometimes acrimonious legislative hearing. The lights in the stately old California capitol had burned far into the night. An endless stream of well-rehearsed witnesses–including several clergymen–had argued militantly against the proposed stiffer penalties for violent crimes.

As the session moved toward a close, State Senator Clark Bradley removed his spectacles and aimed his remarks toward the soft-on-crime group. He knew its members well; they were usually on hand to oppose any tough crime-fighting laws.

"You have all spoken for the criminal. Now, is there not one among you who has a kind word for the victim . . . past or future?"

Those who are not willing to provide the proper protection for the innocent and the defenseless and the law-abiding . . .

. . . those who are eager to excuse the criminal and the crime . . .

. . . those who work to weaken our system of law and order and justice . . .

. . . they are not peacemakers.

They are, in effect if not in fact, party to the crime and partly responsible for the increased number of victims in our land.

Who are the peacemakers?

They are those who walk in peace.

Those who will not violate the lives and rights of others.

Those who stand to protect and defend the helpless, the innocent, and the law-abiding.

Those who insist that civil authorities uphold the right of each individual to be secure in his person, his property and his lawful activities.

Those who help to preserve law and order and justice.

They are the builders of domestic tranquility.

They are the providers of the common defense.

They are the peacemakers.

Blessed are they!

II.

The world is now engaged in a deathly struggle

–the forces of darkness against light

–the forces of war against peace

–the tyrants of slavery against the children of liberty.

We cannot ignore this battle, any more than we can ignore the criminal in our streets. To ignore either is not to keep peace; it is to entertain the enemy.

Thus, as we assess current–and unfolding–world affairs, we must face this question:

Can a Christian be a pacifist?

Or, should a Christian be a pacifist?

If, by the term "pacifist", we mean someone who prays for peace, someone who walks in peace and works for peace, someone who is willing to take a stand for a just peace and pay its price, then all Christians should be pacifists.

But, if by "pacifist" we mean

–those who would buy peace by selling themselves, and us, to the tyrant

–those who are not willing to protect their loved ones

–those who will not defend the defenseless

–those who will not keep strong this land that shields their lives and liberty, or

–those who permit others to fight the battle and then come forth to enjoy the fruits of victory . . .

–those who yield to the atheistic forces that suppress the freedom to proclaim the Gospel . . .

. . . if this is what it means to be a pacifist, then the Christian cannot go along!

Christianity? Or, Cop-out?

Are we not urged to love one another?

Are not all men our brothers, all women our sisters, in Christ?

Where is the love in sitting back while your brothers and sisters are slaughtered by a godless tyrant? Where is the love in standing by while barbarians invade, enslave, ravage and ruin? Where is the love in being mute and motionless while others are fed into gas ovens or machine-gunned at the side of some communal grave?

To mutter pious mouthings in the face of such depravities is not love, it is total selfishness. It is not Christian, it is a cop-out. And in it there is no honor, and no true peace.

Some may rationalize that such indifference and such indolence is peace–and peaceful. Pacifism that permits others to be sacrificed on the altar of despotism is, at the very least, mis-directed piety:

It is born of the same stupidity and fear that gave us Munich.

It spawns the same myopic mentality that would have us coddle the criminal in our streets and prisons and throw the victim to the ground.

It promotes the distorted reasoning that we should unequally yoke ourselves with the forces of darkness—that we should play footsies with our enemies and abandon ourselves to their holocaust.

Defensive Force

Let this be clear.

Crystal clear.

Christians are not—must not be and cannot be—warmongers.

There are basically two types of force:

Defensive force, to protect and defend, and

Aggressive force, to attack, to capture and enslave.

As Christians we oppose the use of aggressive force—whether it be against an individual, or a nation.

But, as Christians, we have a right to seek—to insist upon—defensive capabilities for our civil authorities. So that our local police department and our nation's armed forces have the means by which to defend us if that need arises.

Thus, our call for military preparedness is not for aggression, or economic gain or employment—it is for defense. For survival!

Pacifism that denies the propriety and availability of such defensive force is either mis-guided or subversive. It invites the use of aggressive force by the public enemy—at home and abroad. It excites the barbarian and encourages the bandit. It jeopardizes the lives and liberty of all within our land.

Abram's Lot

Let's go back a few thousand years. Back to the time of Abram, before he became Abraham. Back to that day when the enemy kings conquered the cities of Sodom and Gomorrah and ran off with Lot, Abram's brother's son.[18]

When Abram learned that Lot had been taken captive, what did he do? Did he hang his head and shed a tear and murmur, "Isn't that sad?" and go on about his business? No way!

Abram gathered and armed his trained servants—all three hundred and eighteen of them—and went in pursuit of the aggressors. He caught up with them on the other side of Damascus and God gave him the victory against vastly superior forces.

Abram loved Lot enough to rescue him. He was willing to pay the price to defend him and set things straight.

Ah, some will argue. That was before Christ came. Christ brought love. And the commandment of love.

Yes, He did. He loved enough to give His life for us. He loved enough to be the sacrifice through which God's wondrous gifts of justification, and salvation, and atonement could be for all who believed on Him.

But, think about this.

On that final evening—after the last supper—when it seemed there was a possibility that some untoward incident might prevent Him from fulfilling His mission, what did Jesus do?

It's all there. In the Scriptures, in Luke 22:36-38:

> *"Then said He unto them (His disciples) . . . he that hath a purse, let him take it, and likewise his scrip: and he that hath no sword, let him sell his garment and buy one."*

A disciple with a sword? How come?

> *"For I say unto you, that this that is written must yet be accomplished in me, 'And He was reckoned among the transgressors': for the things concerning me have an end."*

Christ had a mission to fulfill. Nothing was to be permitted to prevent the completion of His gift through Calvary and resurrection.

> *"And they said, Look, Lord, here are two swords. And He said unto them, it is enough."*

Enough for what? Enough to conquer by the sword? Enough to drive away the soldiers who came for Him? No. Enough to be ready to defend Him should there be a scuffle or an attempt on His life before the appointed hour and the appointed cross.

In the light of that passage of Scripture, cannot this be said?

> *Christ loved the world so much that He was willing to have done whatever might be necessary to buy time and make sure that all men were given—through Calvary—the opportunity for salvation and eternal life.*

If called upon, can His followers do any less?

When Do We Stand?

As long as there are men of evil intent and diabolical design
freemen must be willing to take a stand:
a stand for that which is right
a stand for freedom under God.

A strong and vigilant defense is one of the requisites of freedom. The greater the threat of evil, the stronger that defense must be. That which is right does not survive unattended; it, too, must have its defenders.

When do we take our stand?

When do we attend to our nation's security?

When do we mend our defenses?

Is it when the enemy is miles away?

Is it when his forces start toward our shores, or our skies?

Is it when his troops approach our beaches and his planes are over the horizon and his missiles target our cities?

When? When do we erect our defenses to protect those we love and defend this land where God can still be worshipped in truth and safety?

When?

Suppose that you were nearby when some thug, some depraved maniac, threatened your wife. What would you do? When would you move to protect her?

Before the attacker made his advance?

When he held a knife at her throat or a gun in her ribs?

When he began ripping the clothes from her body?

When?

What would you do?

Would you call, "Come, let us reason together"?

Would you say "Go so far, but no further"?

Would you shut your eyes and turn away and hope the thug will have a change of heart?

Or would you do everything you could, use everything at your disposal–including your own life, if need be–to save her?

And, if by the grace of God, she were spared would you not do everything possible to make sure that such barbarians were never again permitted to prey on helpless victims?

Suppose you were nearby when someone of criminal intent threatened a friend, or a neighbor, or a stranger? What would you do then?

Would you rush to their aid, to their defense? Or, would you do as the neighbors did that night young Kitty Genovese was brutally attacked?

From house to house she ran, screaming through the darkness, pleading for help, begging for someone to protect her from her assailant. The murderer hid in the bushes, ready to run or ready to continue his attack if no one came. Lights went on in houses along that street. But not one person came to Kitty Genovese's rescue. Not one person bothered to call the police. And the murderer finished his job. Kitty Genovese was slain because the good folks on the block did not want to get involved. *They would not take a stand.* Not for her—and not for themselves, not for their loved ones who could have been the next victims on another street on another night.

When the people of Athens sought freedom from responsibility, Athens ceased to be free.

The Minds and Souls of Men

We mourn for Kitty Genovese.

But this nation faces a far greater enemy than the criminal who murdered her.

That enemy is communism.

It poses the severest threat, the most sustained threat, this nation and the free world has ever known.

In *Creed or Chaos?*, Dorothy L. Sayer spelled it out—coldly, clearly:

> "Christendom and heathendom now stand face to face . . . The people who say that this is a war of economics or of power-politics, are only dabbling about on the surface of things. . . . At the bottom is a violent and irreconcilable quarrel about the nature of God and the nature of man and the ultimate nature of the universe; it is a war of dogma." [19]

Dr. James Roy Smith, in *God Still Speaks in The Space Age,* emphasizes the spiritual and psychological nature of the war that is upon us:

> "The germ of the conflict is anchored in religion, and the battle is an ideological battle between atheism and theism. It is a battle not only for the minds of men, but also for their souls. Communism is atheistic. Communist Russia is the first nation in history which has officially adopted atheism as its national belief. Its motives and its methods are the result of a denial of God. Because there is no God, there is no moral judgment and there is no personal accountability." [20]

The Communists have given us fair warning:

We will bury you.

That death sentence has yet to be repealed or recanted.

Today's Communists say "Peace, peace" but it is the peace of the slave labor camp they have in mind, the "peace" of total enslavement of the United States plus what little is left of the free world.

Those Who Will Not See

Yet there are those, within our midst–even within the churches and councils–who tell us there is a softening in the Communist drive; that there is a change in the Communist design.

"In reality, those scholars and statesmen who are best informed about Soviet intentions argue that the Russian revolution, as designed by Lenin and Trotsky, is no longer operative. . . . The system which Stalin built was neither socialist nor revolutionary, but rather a form of state capitalism based upon authoritarian of planning and economic centralization." [21]

Who are these "scholars and statesmen who are best informed about Soviet intentions" who would claim the USSR has suddenly become a benign and benevolent pussy cat? Certainly one who is *not* in their ranks is Alexsandr Solzhenitsyn.* Solzhenitsyn, the great contemporary Christian libertarian, who knows from long and personal experience–rather than propaganda–the true nature

* Author of *Gulag Archipelago, Cancer Ward, August 1914,* etc.

and design and goal of Communism. Solzhenitsyn, who documents—in devasating detail—the fact that terror and tyranny "was not just a wave in Soviet history, but the whole ocean" . . . even unto this day.

Where is this "softening" in the Communist that those who disagree with Solzhenitsyn profess to see?

Do they see it in the constant persecution and imprisonment of Russian Christians? Or in the refusal to allow Jews to emigrate to Israel?

Do they see it in the spread of those tentacles that reach out to smother emerging nation after emerging nation?

Do they see it—this "softening"—in the arms and ammunition, the planes and tanks and technicians that were supplied all through those years to Hanoi and the Viet Cong? And the Khmer Rouge?

Or, do they see it in that fact that—over the past decade—the Soviet's military expenditures have risen by at least forty percent?

Where is this change of heart in Communism these "scholars" see?

> Is it in the arming of the Arab nations so as to bring those countries into its orbit and cause chaos in the Middle East by cutting off oil to Europe and the United States?
>
> Is it in the subversion of Portugal? Or, in the $1,000,000 a day going to Castro who harbors Soviet submarine facilities and missile pads just ninety miles from our shores?
>
> Or, now that Vietnam has fallen, is it in the Communists' encouragement of their "patriots" in South Korea to press their drive so that North Korea can aid them in their plans to take over that republic?

Is it time for these gentlemen to pay more attention to what the Communists are doing, and less attention to what they are saying!

When the survival of a nation—and an idea and a way of life—is at stake, what the adversary does is more important than what he says. By his fruits shall you know him!

If there has been any softening during recent years, it has been here—in the United States. And not in Communism.

"We will bury you!"

That threat still stands.

We live in its shadow.

III.

It is the first—and foremost—duty of our civil government to protect and defend us from those forces that would prey upon us and destroy our nation.

Yet, in the face of the most severe—and the most prolonged, and increasing—threat against our national survival, Caesar diverts his attentions and our resources to other matters.

In 1973, total government outlay for social welfare was $215 billion and rising. In 1974, this nation's expenditures for defense and national security were $81 billion.[22]

". . . the antidefense trend has accelerated in recent years. In 1975, the smallest part of the Federal budget since 1940, pre-Pearl Harbor, will go for national defense. In 1975, the Defense Department's money . . . will buy the lowest amount it has been able to purchase since 1951. Further, national defense spending represented 9.7 percent of the GNP in 1956; 6 percent of our GNP was consumed by military spending in fiscal 1974; in fiscal year 1976, it will be an estimated 5.2 percent."[23]

"To put it another way, the portion of the Federal budget outlays consumed by the Defense Establishment has dropped by almost thirty percent since 1956."[24]

Those who would claim that defense spending is taking more and more of our national purse should get their facts straight.

Consider this:

- –in the past ten years, social security and other retirement and disability programs have increased by 283 percent;
- –health services—including Medicaid and Medicare—have increased by 4,418 percent, and
- –public assistance costs went up 365 percent.[25]

Since 1968, the total federal budget has risen seventy percent and state and local government spending has climbed 131 percent . . .

. . . during those same years, defense costs rose nine percent.[26]

Reviewing this record, Edward Luttwak, an expert on the state of America's defenses, made this comment:

> "American military expenditures have in fact declined quite drastically over the last decade. . . . It is a curious reflection

on the supposedly pervasive and skillful propaganda of the Pentagon that the vast majority of the public continues to believe that military expenditures have been steadily increasing relative to everything." [27]

Those "Softening" Soviets

And what have the Communists been doing all this while? Have they been cutting back their military expenditures while the anti-defense claque in this nation has been reducing ours?

In his analysis of the federal budget for The Heritage Foundation, Dr. Charles Moser wrote:

> *"(Edward) Luttwak points out that over the last decade the defense expenditures of our chief political and military antagonist, the Soviet Union, by the most conservative estimates, have risen by some 40%, and its military manpower has increased; while at the same time U.S. defense outlays have declined almost 20% from 1964 in real terms, and military manpower has declined roughly the same percentage."* [28]

What has that forty percent increase over the past ten years done for the Soviet Union, in terms of might? What has that twenty percent decrease done to us, in terms of strength? The tables in this section tell part of that tale. Their message can hardly be of comfort to freedom-loving Americans.

In its 1974-75 edition, the authoritative *Jane's Fighting Ships* concluded:

> "The Soviet navy leads the world in seaborne missile armament, both strategic and tactical, both ship and submarine-launched. Their short-based air force is second to none, and they have mine-warfare forces and a considerable amphibious capability." [29]

Former Chief of Naval Operations, Elmo Zumwalt, has warned that it is becoming *increasingly unlikely* that the United States Navy

COMPARATIVE CAPABILITIES: U.S.–USSR

Mid-1964 [1]			*April 1975* [2]		*U.S. Net ±*
U.S.	USSR		U.S.	USSR	
		STRATEGIC OFFENSE			
630	190	Long Range Bombers	498	160 [3]	
700	1100	Mid-Range Bombers	0	700 [4]	
834	200	ICBM Launchers	1054	1590	
416	120	SLBM Launchers [5]	656	340	
2580	1610	Total	2208	2790	–1282 [6]

Mid-1966 [7]		SURFACE COMBAT SHIPS	*April 1975* [7]		
15	0	Aircraft Carriers	14	0 [8]	
8	0	Anti-Sub Warfare-Carriers	0	0	
7	0	Helicopter Carriers	7	2	
14	17	Cruisers	5	31	
232	81	Frigates & Destroyers	91	84	
42	87	Escort Ships	64	106	
0	133	Missile Patrol Craft	0	135	
4	695	Other Patrol Craft	14	550	
152	103	Amphibious Ships	58	100	
84	404	Mine Warfare Ships	3	270	
246	575	Auxiliaries	127	750	
2	0	Command & Control	0	0	
806	2095	Total	383	2028	–356

1. International Inst. for Strategic Studies report.
2. Secy. of Defense, Annual Report to Congress, Feb., 1975.
3. Includes 20 supersonic aircraft of B-1 type already in service.
4. Int. Inst. for Strategic Studies (data used in SALT talks).
5. Submarine Launched Ballistic Missiles.
6. Relative U.S. net loss during period reported here.
7. Adm. H. Rickover, statement to US Congress, reported in *Defense Space Business Daily*, 4/28/75.
8. USSR has two aircraft carriers under construction.

can perform its primary task of keeping the sea lanes open against Soviet naval opposition.[30]

The reports of Soviet superiority in regard to air defense is equally grim. This nation has permitted its air defense to deteriorate. As of April, 1975, the USSR had 10,000 surface-to-air missiles (SAMs), the United States had none. According to reliable estimates the Soviets have 2,500 fighter-interceptor aircraft, the U.S. has 405; the USSR has 4,000 surveillance radar installations, the U.S. has 67.[31]

SUBMARINES: U.S.–USSR[1]

(As of April 1975)

		U.S.	USSR	U.S. ±[2]
Attack Subs	Nuclear	64	40	+ 24
	Non-nuclear	12	158	– 136
Ballistic Missile Subs	Nuclear	41	50	– 9
	Non-nuclear	0	22	– 22
Cruise Missile Subs[3]	Nuclear	0	40	– 40
	Non-nuclear	0	25	– 25
Totals	Nuclear	105	130	– 25
	Non-nuclear	12	205	– 193
		117	335	– 218

1. Testimony of Admiral H. Rickover before Congress as reported in *Defense Space Daily*, Apr. 28, 1975.
2. U.S. lag or lead in category.
3. Shorter-range missiles for use against ships but could be used with nuclear warheads against port cities and naval bases.

The Constitutional Mandate

To add to the picture of our weakening defense posture, consider this:

> In 1962, when the United States forced Premier Nikita Khrushchev to back down during the Cuban missile crisis, we had a nuclear superiority over the USSR of eight-to-one (megatonnage). *Today, the Communists hold that superiority, by five-to-one (some experts assert it may be as high as eight-to-one).*[32]

There are still those who prate about "parity"–a balance of weaponry with the Soviet to "preserve the peace". Any such point of parity has long since been passed–in our disfavor. In many categories of defense capabilities the balance has shifted to the enemy.

To have permitted this to occur was sheer madness; the height of irresponsibility. It was not the route to peace; it is the chute of suicide!

Yet even now, in the face of an implacable foe and our weakened defense, there are still those–including some of our Christian brethren–who militantly oppose virtually every defense expenditure and insist the defense budgets be slashed even more. They charge that we spend too much on defense. The facts are otherwise; we spend too little. They claim we have become a nation of warmongers. The record contradicts them; we have tried to keep the peace.

> *It is not the United States that has enslaved nation after nation since the end of World War Two. It is not the United States that foments and rides on revolution throughout the world. It is not the United States that has declared, or has any intention, of world domination.*

Yet, in the face of such events, we are advised: "Instead of leading the anti-Communist forces, Evangelicals should be in the vanguard of promoting a proper understanding of the nature of the Russian system so that they may aid their fellow citizens in overcoming the national paranoia concerning Communism."[33]

Evangelicals should, indeed, be in the vanguard of helping their fellow-Americans understand *the true nature of Godless Commu-*

nism; its tactics, its design, its goals.

Sounding the alarm on the floor of the House of Representatives, Congressman Bill Young of Florida said:

> "I am determined that we must have a quality force, sufficiently capable of 'providing for the common defense'. For the Congress to allow this defense to become vulnerable would be to desecrate our constitutional mandate." [34]

Amplifying that concern, Congressman Jack Kemp of New York set forth the task if we are to remain free:

> "Our high priority, then, must be the support of defenses for the Nation which will ensure its sovereign survival in a still risky and dangerous world. The maintenance of internal and external order is the first responsibility of government. When that responsibility is met, we may concern ourselves with the other objectives of government." [35]

IV.

No one can fault the ideal of a world at peace. It is one of man's loftiest aspirations.

Christians know that peace is coming—coming through The Living God; our Heavenly Father through whom and in whom all men are brothers.

What a glorious day that will be!

> *And nations shall beat their swords into plowshares and their spears into pruning hooks. Nation shall not lift up a sword against nation, neither shall they learn war any more.*[36]

Praise God!

> *And every man shall sit under his vine and under his fig tree and no one shall make them afraid . . . all the peoples do now walk in the name of their god but (then) they shall walk in the name of Jehovah our God for ever and ever.*[37]

Amen!

When shall that be, Lord? How shall it come to pass?

> *"In the last days it shall come to pass that the mountain of the house of The Lord shall be established in the top of the*

mountains, and it shall be exalted above the hills; and people shall flow unto it. And many nations shall come and say, Come, and let us go up to the mountain of The Lord, and to the house of the God of Jacob; and He will teach us of His ways, and we will walk in His paths . . ." [38]

One World! But, Whose?

Surely, the United Nations does *not* fit that prophecy.

It does not serve God.

It denies God!

It is no house of God.

God is officially *personna non grata* there.

Back in the beginning, back in 1945, the UN made its choice.

It chose man. It chose the Super State. *It rejected God.*

"He who is not with Me–who is not definitely on My side, is against Me, and he who does not gather with Me, scatters." [39]

The United Nations does not gather with God. It is the ultimate expression of humanism–the delusion that man, in and of himself and without God–can solve the problems of this world and keep the peace. But, as the age of humanism fails and fades and falls apart, so the United Nations comes undone.

That should come as no surprise. The Psalmist told us, years-upon-years ago that *"Except The Lord build the house, they labor in vain that build it; except The Lord keep the city (the nation, the world) the watchman waketh in vain."* [40]

False God, False Start

The United Nations does not serve God. It does not serve man; not the men of peace, and not the quest for justice.

Those who are truly concerned, those who truly search for peace on earth among men of goodwill, should consider the facts. And, any honest assessment of the UN and its twenty-eight years must come to this conclusion:

It is a failure, another pursuit of a false god, another false start by men who rejected God.

"Peace," men cry. But there is no peace.

In the first twenty-five years of the United Nations history, there were more than seventy-five wars around the world. Since the time its charter was signed in San Francisco, more than one billion persons have been enslaved by Communism.

As John Chamberlain wrote, "The UN, as it has evolved, has become the happy hunting ground of all the two-bit bully boys who talk about liberty and use stolen property to bolster their one-party regimes." [41]

Words and Mis-deeds

The UN talks of human rights and dignity

but it stood mute when the USSR raped Hungary and Red China practiced genocide on the Tibetians.

The UN declares for the worth of the human person

but its blue-helmeted mercenaries, under its blue banner, murdered and maimed and pillaged and ravaged the helpless of Katanga.

The UN speaks of the equal rights of nations "large and small" *but it looked the other way when Nigeria forced starvation on 800,000 children in Biafra.*

The UN talks of trust and justice and goodwill

yet it entertains the butchers and the tyrants and the pistol-packing demi-gods of the world and lends them the platform of its podium and cheers their wild-eyed ravings.

The UN prates about man's inhumanity to man

yet it refused to act in the face of incontrovertible proof that the Communists of North Korea deliberately machine-gunned more than five thousand American prisoners and buried them in mass graves.

"Peace, peace," men cry. Where is the peace?

There is no equity in the representation at the United Nations, no such thing as one-man, one-vote. More than half of the nations in the UN have fewer people than the population of New York city. One-fifth of all the UN members have populations of less than two million each. Yet, each of their votes in the General Assembly is equal to that of the United States and most of the time their votes go with the Communist bloc . . .

> . . . as they did on the expulsion of Free China, as they did on the admission of Red China, and as they did and still do on those votes of censure against Israel.

On that day when the UN voted to expel Free China (a charter member in good standing) the record of that world body was forever marred with bigotry and bias. The U.S. Ambassador to the UN, George Bush, was moved to protest, "Never have I seen such hate!"

Ask yourself: How can hate be an instrument of peace?

And is not the United Nations dedicated to peace? Whose peace?

The Fox in The Hen House

In his analysis of the federal budget for possible cost-savings, Dr. Charles A. Moser made this suggestion concerning the U.S. membership in the United Nations:

> "In fiscal 1973, the United States contributed more than $138 million to the UN, a major portion of that organization's budget;* in fiscal 1975, the (Ford) administration proposed to increase that contribution to more than $155 million. In view of such recent UN actions as the semi-recognition of the Palestinian Liberation Organization, the expulsion of the Republic of China and South Africa . . . and the continuing UN pressures on Israel, the United States would be well advised to reduce its contribution to the UN by, say, half. . . . It is likely that a sharp reduction in United States financial support for the United Nations would lead to increased respect . . . for our point of view. Even if it did not, our position in that organization could hardly be worse than it now is." [42]

There are many deeply-concerned Americans—and their numbers

---

* Approximately one-third.

grow daily—who think that Dr. Moser's suggested cut to one-half is only half of what should be done. In addition to all the other grievous shortcomings of the UN . . .

its denial of God
its failure to live up to its own charter
its silence in the face of murder and enslavement and violence
its lack of equitable representation

. . . in addition to all that, and the fact that the United Nations is now virtually a captive of the Communist-bloc nations, they point to this:

From the very beginning, the military affairs of the United Nations have always been in the hands of the Communists. Since 1945, eleven men have held the post of Undersecretary-General of Political and Security Council Affairs. Ten of those men (including the incumbent, Arkady N. Shevchenko) have been Russians and one was a Yugoslavian.

What are the duties of this undersecretary?

To control all military and police functions of the UN
To supervise all disarmament programs of member nations
To control all atomic energy placed under UN care for peaceful and other purposes.

Since 1945, a Communist has held that post. The fox has been guarding the hen house. *And, we are the chickens!*

The Tower of Babel

Remember the tower of Babel?

The one the sons of Noah built there on the plains of Shinar?

Remember how they wanted to make a name for themselves, to be on a par with God?

"They refused to acknowledge God's power in the world. They thought they were wiser than God." [43] *Isn't that a good description of today's statism-humanism?*

"They wanted the security of being together. They tried to achieve security and unity through organization. But unity does not come through visible organization. Real unity is internal, not external." [44]

But, they builded themselves a tower—a temple of idolatrous

worship. These sons of Noah put other gods before The Living God; they enthroned themselves rather than The Lord.

The result was confusion, and chaos, and a scattering of the people far and wide.

Is not the United Nations today's Tower of Babel?

Is it not the same with that tower of glass and stone and steel? Does it not deny The Lord and worship the false gods of man, and humanism? Did it not seek unity, and security, in organization devoid of Spirit?

They builded their UN tower on sand–the sands of idolatry; a pagan temple that puts man above God, and the state above man.

Small wonder God confuses them and scatters them through the land!

"Be Ye Not Unequally Yoked . . ."

It is time for concerned Americans–and especially Christians–to honestly and seriously and prayerfully consider the United Nations, its Godless conception, its record, and its actions in these days. To do it, not only in regard to the defense and security of this republic but also in regard to our spiritual well-being as a nation. To do it, perhaps, in the light of this Scripture:

"Be you not unequally yoked with unbelievers–do not make mismated alliances with them, or come under a different yoke with them. For, what fellowship has righteousness with unrighteousness? And what communion has light with darkness? And what concord hath Christ with the devil? Or what part has he that believeth with an unbeliever? And what agreement has the temple of God with idols? For you are the temple of the living God; as God has said, I will dwell in them and walk in them; and I will be their God, and they shall be my people. Wherefore, come out from among them, and be you separate, saith the Lord, and touch not the unclean thing; and I will receive you,

> "And will be a Father unto you, and you shall be my sons and daughters, sayeth the Lord Almighty." [45]

What a tremendous promise.
What a mighty fortress is our God!

"Stand fast therefore in the liberty wherewith Christ has made us free, and be not entangled again with the yoke of bondage." [46]

God's Strategic Agent

These hours may seem dark but from the darkness emerges a glorious light.

It is a challenge to all Christians—and it is a special responsibility to all Christians fortunate enough to be Americans. Dr. Charles W. Lowry, in *Communism and Christ,* raises the banner and sounds the call:

"America today has the mightiest opportunity in history. It is not merely the chance to throw back the forces of reaction and to repel the evil and demonic dream of a single, man-governed totalitarian world. Nothing negative will suffice. Simple condemnation will not stem the tide of a dynamic advance.

"The opportunity of our great country, which God has so wonderfully led and so richly blessed, is to lead faltering mankind beyond the twilight and the hovering darkness into the sunshine of a larger, happier day. It is to use our vast resources and inspiring inheritance under God to usher the whole earth into a period of abundance, freedom, and brotherhood. It is to be a strategic agent in continuing God's recreative work in Christ.

"It is to extend and ever-more to consolidate in the affairs of men the Christian Revolution." [47]

EPILOGUE

"Choose You This Day!"

Not too long ago a group of 120 humanists hung a "Closed" sign on the world.

In their foreboding *Humanist Manifesto,* they intoned that God was dead. They assured America that any search for Divine Guidance in these troubled times was a bunch of hokum. Voodooism in twentieth century garb.

"No diety will save us.

"We must save ourselves."

That was their message of hope.

Religion that places God above man does a disservice to the human species.

That is what they said.

Let us be your shepherds.

That was their invitation.

Well, for years this nation has been wandering in the wilderness of the humanist and his cohort the statist.

And, look where we are!

The whirlwind we reap is not of God. It did not come from following God.

It comes from man cut loose from God. From man denying God.

If, as a nation, we would return to God's eternal truths, and to the Faith of our fathers, we could get out of the fix we're in.

But the darker it gets, the louder the humanists propound their paganistic propaganda. Religion, they say, is only an escape mechanism. We've heard that before. "Religion is the opium of the masses." Karl Marx came up with that one.

Sorry, gentlemen. No sale!

Our God is not dead!

We tried to warn you about yours.

The unholy alliance of humanism and statism has always been a failure. It is now.

The world trembles from its errors.

As Rev. R. J. Rushdoony points out, what we now witness is the breaking up of the pagan proposition. The thieves fall out and their order disintegrates.

The question is, what will take its place?

The light and the love and the power of The Living God?

It waits to be re-asserted! Re-applied!

It is the power that can change men's hearts. The power that can move nations. The power that can end famines and still the raging seas. The power that makes all things possible . . . through prayer . . . and faith . . . and works.

If we are to restore America . . .

if we are to make it once again a home of righteousness and freedom

. . . we must return to God. Obey His laws, and do His works.

Dr. Charles Malik summed up the challenge:

"When the tears and joy of Christ come to perfect fruition in this land, the America will utter her word."

There! There we are!

Christ is the answer. For each individual. For America. For the world.

America has a choice to make. And, that choice starts with you.

It is the choice that God's prophet Joshua put before the people of Israel:

"Choose you this day whom you will serve."

Joshua made his choice:

"As for me and my house, we will serve The Lord."

What about you?

Have you made your choice? Do you have a personal commitment to Christ? Do you know Jesus? As your Savior? Your Master? Your Light and your Way?

That's the first step. To put Him first.

Then, join with others of like-mind.

In prayer. In praise. In action.

Put your faith to work!

In your church. In study groups. And, in public affairs.

Yes, even in the affairs of civil government. Join with others to help elect God-directed men and women to public office at every level. To hang back, to do nothing, is to let others—even Caesar—run things for you.

There's the choice:

One nation under God? Or, one big superstate under Caesar?

That is the decision America must make. And now.

The children of Israel made their choice:

"God forbid that we should forsake The Lord to serve other gods."

America's choice starts with you.

What will be be?

One nation under God!

REFERENCES & SOURCES

Chapter One—"THE CHRISTIAN IDEA OF GOVERNMENT"

1. Slater, Rosalie J., *Teaching and Learning America's Christian History,* p. 202.
2. I Samuel 8:10-18.
3. Bradford, Wm., *History of Plimouth Plantation* (1647 1901 edition).
4. Eggleston, E., *The Beginners of a Nation* (1896).
5. *Ibid.*
6. Hall, Verna M., *Christian History of the Constitution.* Preface p. iii.
7. Morley, F., *The Power in the People,* p. 41.
8. Atwood, H.F., *Back to the Republic,* pp. 28-29.
9. *Ibid.,* p. 37.
10. John 3:16.
11. Rushdoony, R.J., *The Nature of the American System,* pp. 2-3.
12. Partridge, J.A., *The Making of the American Nation* (1866).
13. John 15:17.
14. Matt. 7:12.
15. Matt. 6:33.
16. Mark 8:36.
17. Morley, F., *The Power in the People,* p. 47.
18. Locke, J., *The Reasonableness of Christianity* (1695).
19. Webster, D., *Works of Daniel Webster,* (1851).
20. Gen. 8:15 et seq.
21. Scofield, C.I., *The New Scofield Reference Bible,* cf3pp 13-14.
22. *Ibid.,* cf1 p. 94.
23. Prince, Derek, *Shaping History Through Prayer and Fasting,* p. 42.
24. Montesquieu, *The Spirit of Laws* (Colonial Press—1900).
25. Bacon, L., *Genesis of the New England Churches* (1874).
26. Hall, E., *The Puritans and their Principles* (1846).
27. Webster, Noah, *First Edition of An American Dictionary,* 1828.
28. Hall, E., *The Puritans and their Principles.*
29. Neal, D., *History of the Puritans* (1731).
30. *Ibid.*
31. Bancroft, Geo., *History of the United States* (1850).

32. Henry, Patrick, Speech in Virginia Convention, Mar. 23, 1775.
33. Frothingham, R., *The Rise of the Republic of the United States* (1890).
34. *Ibid.*
35. Slater, Rosalie J., *Teaching and Learning America's Christian History,* p. 187.
36. Eph. 6:12.

Chapter Two—FALSE GODS, STRANGE PROPHETS

1. Madison, James, *The Federalist Papers.*
2. Platform of the Democratic Party, 1932.
3. Garrett, Garet, *The People's Pottage,* p. 26.
4. Rushdoony, Rousas J., *The Nature of The American System,* p. 9.
5. *Ibid.*
6. Soderling, H.E., *National Observer,* 9/74.
7. Garrett, Garet, *Opus cit.,* p. 132.
8. Soderling, H.E., *Opus cit.*
9. Alfange, Dean, *My Creed.*
10. Hall, Verna M., *Christian History of The Constitution,* Preface iii.
11. Chambers, Whittaker, *Witness,* foreword.
12. Matt. 12:30.
13. Joshua 24:15.

Chapter Three—GOD'S BED-ROCK LAWS FOR FREEDOM

1. I Peter 2:16.
2. II Cor. 3:17.
3. Gal. 5:13.
4. Thomas Jefferson.
5. Justice Learned Hand.
6. Hayek, F.A., *The Constitution of Liberty,* p. 17.
7. Read, Leonard C., *Accent on the Right.*
8. Thomas Wolfe.
9. Read, Leonard C., *Deeper Than You Think,* p. 16.
10. Morley, Felix, *Christian History of the Constitution,* p. ix, Intro.
11. Hall, Verna M., *ibid.,* p. iii, Preface.
12. Slater, Rosalie J., *Rudiments of America's Christian History and Government,* p. 61.
13. *Ibid.,* p. 61.
14. Bastiat, Frederic, *The Law,* p. 24.
15. Matt. 22:37.
16. Prov. 3:6.
17. Psalms 22:28.
18. Matt. 19:19.
19. Luke 6:31.
20. James 1:25.
21. Gal. 5:22,23.
22. Psalms 33:12.
23. Harper, F.A., *Liberty, A Path To Its Recovery,* p. 27.

Chapter Four–"COERCION–BY PROXY"

1. John 15:12,17.
2. Romans 13:10.
3. Harper, F.A., *Liberty, A Path To Its Recovery,* p. 147.
4. Romans 13:3.
5. 1 Peter 2:14.
6. Rushdoony, R.J., *The Nature of the American System,* p. 8.
7. Constitution of the U.S.A., Article X.
8. Bastiat, Frederic, *The Law,* p. 6.
9. Read, Leonard, *Meditations on Freedom,* p. 27.
10. Von Mises, Ludwig, *In Brief: The Individual in Society,* p. 8.
11. Harper, F.A., Liberty, A Path To Its Recovery, p. 104.
12. *Ibid.,* p. 105.
13. Bastiat, Frederic, *The Law,* pp. 73-75.

Chapter Five–"GOD'S 'SUPER' STRUCTURE: THE FAMILY"

1. Slater, Rosalie J., "Teaching and Learning America's Christian History", *Foundation for American Christian Education,* p. 3.
2. 2 Cor. 3:17.
3. Prov. 22:6.
4. Phillips, Rev. S., quoted by Rosalie J. Slater, *Opus cit.,* p. 10.
5. *Ibid.,* p. 10.
6. *Ibid.,* p. 11.
7. Eph. 5:25.
8. Col. 3:18.
9. Eph. 6:1-3; Ex. 20:12.
10. Eph. 6:4; Col. 3:21.
11. Cairns, Earle E., *The Christian in Society,* pp. 156-157.
12. *Ibid.,* p. 157.
13. Prov. 4:1.
14. Ortega y Gasset, Jose, *The Revolt of the Masses,* p. 11.
15. Phillips, Rev. S., *Opus cit.*
16. Ex. 20:13.
17. Jer. 1:5.
18. Isa. 49:5.
19. Psalm 139:14-16.
20. Isa. 44:24.
21. Johnson, Dr. Thomas, "Abortion: A Metaphysical Approach", *The Freeman,* August 1972, pp. 498-505.
22. *Ibid.*
23. Gen. 6:20; 7:3.
24. Pear, Robert, "New, Unashamed Attitude for Women With Abortions", *Washington Star,* April 7, 1975, p. A-1.
25. Matt. 27:24.
26. Pear, Robert, *Opus cit.*
27. *Ibid.*

28. Statistical Abstract of the U.S., 1974, p. 62.
29. Rhett, Dr. Barnett M., as quoted by Robert Pear, *Opus cit.*
30. Pear, Robert, *Opus cit.*
31. *Ibid.*
32. *Ibid.*
33. Johnson, Dr. Thomas, *Opus cit.*
34. Eph. 5:25; Gen. 2:24.
35. Col. 3:18; 1 Peter 3:1-6.

Chapter Six—"ARE PUBLIC SCHOOLS RUINING OUR CHILDREN?"

1. El Cajon (Calif.) *Daily Californian* 4/27/72.
2. Rushdoony, Rousas J., *The Messianic Character of American Education,* p. 322.
3. Proverbs 22:6.
4. Hall, Verna M., *Christian History of The Constitution,* p. 240b.
5. Graham, Dr. Billy, California Assembly Daily Journal, 7/6/71, p. 6468.
6. Rushdoony, R.J., *Opus cit.,* p. 323.
7. Radio Station K-POP, Roseville, Calif., 2/25/72.
8. Ventura (Calif.) *Star Free Press,* 5/21/74.
9. Ortega y Gasset, Jose, *The Revolt of The Masses,* p. 23.
10. Saginaw (Mich.) *News,* 9/25/74.
11. *Ibid.*
12. Flor, Lee, Washington (D.C.) *Star News,* 1/6/75.
13. Matthews, John, Washington (D.C.) *Star News,* 11/18/74.
14. *Ibid.*
15. *Ibid.*
16. Jones, Jenkins Lloyd, *This Is Literature?,* Washington (D.C.) *Star News,* 2/15/75.
17. Matthews, John, Washington (D.C.) *Star News,* 11/18/74.
18. Jones, Jenkins Lloyd, *Opus cit.*
19. *Ibid.*
20. *Ibid.*
21. San Rafael (Calif.) *Independent Journal,* 1/10/73.
22. Walton, Rus, KNBC, Los Angeles, *Sunday Show.*
23. Simpson, Gordon Gaylord, paleontologist and foremost contemporary proponent of evolution, quoted in the Oroville (Calif.) *Mercury,* 12/18/72.
24. Oroville (Calif.) *Mercury,* 12/18/72.
25. *Ibid.*
26. Morris, Henry M., *Introducing Creationism Into The Public Schools,* Institute for Creation Research Impact Series #20.
27. *Ibid.*
28. State of Tennessee Education Code, *Selection of Textbooks,* Section 49-2008.
29. Statistical Abstract of the U.S., pp. 109-110 *(US Office of Education).*
30. *Ibid.*
31. Biggs (Calif.) *News,* 12/21/72.
32. Feinberg, Lawrence, Sacramento (Calif.) *Bee,* 4/30/72.
33. Read, Leonard, *Government, An Ideal Concept,* p. 116.
34. Hodge, A.A., *Popular Lectures on Theological Themes,* as quoted by R.J. Rushdoony in *The Messianic Character of American Education,* p. 335.

35. Read, Leonard, *Opus cit.*, p. 115.
36. *Ibid.*, p. 116.
37. Rushdoony, R.J., *The Nature of The American System* p. 21.
38. Hayward (Calif.) *Daily Review*, 8/27/73.
39. Read, Leonard, *Opus cit.*, p. 114.

Chapter Seven—"STEWARDSHIP OR SOCIALISM?"

1. I Chron. 29:14.
2. Prov. 10:24.
3. Deut. 28:2-3.
4. Deut. 28:5
5. Phil. 4:19.
6. Matt. 25:14-30.
7. John 13:34.
8. Sheen, Bishop Fulton J., *N.Y. Journal-American*, 5/7/61.
9. Clark, Fred G., and Rimanoczy, Richard, "Christianity and Capitalism", *Bulletin*, July-August, 1952.
10. Sheen, Archbishop Fulton J., *Opus cit.*
11. *Ibid.*
12. Comparative International Statistics, *Statistical Abstract of the U.S.*, 1974, p. 814.
13. *Ibid.*, pp. 814-844.
14. *Ibid.*
15. *Ibid.*, pp. 351-356, and Cameron, Juan, "Black America: Still Waiting for Full Membership", *Fortune*, April 1975, p. 162.
16. Cameron, Juan, *Opus cit.*
17. *Ibid.*
18. Hazlitt, Henry, "The Story of Negro Gains", *The Freeman*, Nov. 1971, p. 697.
19. Strother, Robert S.,
20. Gorton, John, as quoted in "The Good Things About The U.S. Today", *U.S. News & World Report*, 9/2/1968
21. Dewhurst, Frederic, as quoted by Lawrence Fertig in *Prosperity Through Freedom*, p. 12.
22. The Library of Congress.
23. "Report on Russia", *U.S. News & World Report*, 4/2/73, p. 30.
24. *Ibid.*
25. Nightingale, Earl, "The Old Story", *Our Changing World.*
26. "Report on Russia", *U.S. News & World Report*, 4/2/73, p. 30.
27. Sheen, Archbishop Fulton J., *Opus cit.*
28. Keyser, Carl A., "Freedom's Bounty", *The Freeman*, Sept. 1974, p. 563.

Chapter Eight—"CONTROLLED PEOPLE AND UNCONTROLLED GOVERNMENT"

1. Bureau of Labor Statistics, U.S. Dept. of Labor, *Handbook of Labor Statistics*, 1974.
2. *Ibid.*

3. *Ibid.*
4. National Association of Manufacturers.
5. The Conference Board.
6. Chamber of Commerce of U.S., "Employee Benefits Jump 27%", *Washington Report,* 10/21/74.
7. U.S. Dept. of Labor, *Handbook of Labor Statistics,* 1974.
8. Economic Report of The President, 1975, p. 324.
9. Smith, Charles H., Jr., "The Future Price of Neglect", *Vital Speeches of The Day,* Oct. 1974.
10. Economic Report of The President, 1975, p. 153.
11. *Ibid.,* p. 154.
12. *Ibid.,* pp. 156-157.
13. Smith, Charles H., Jr., *Opus cit.*
14. Federal Environmental Protection Agency, June 14, 1972.
15. Walton, Rus, *Sunday Show,* KNBC, Los Angeles, 10/29/72.
16. Walton, Rus, "Parathion More Deadly Than DDT It Replaced", San Rafael (Ca) *Independent Journal,* 9/27/72.
17. Sennett, Richard, "The Hidden Injuries of Class" as reported in *Time,* 11/4/74, p. 102.
18. Natl. Commission on Productivity and Work Quality, *Productivity: An International Perspective,* Sept. 1974, p. 77.
19. Natl. Commission on Productivity and Work Quality, *Productivity and The Economy,* 1973, p. 28.
20. Economic Report of The President, 1975, pp. 35-37.
21. *Ibid.,* p. 37.
22. Gross, Hon. H.R., *Congressional Record,* 12/16/74, p. E7187.
23. Economic Report of The President, 1975, p. 41.
24. *Ibid.,* p. 350.
25. *Ibid.,* p. 350.
26. *Ibid.,* p. 350.
27. Fertig, Lawrence, *Prosperity Through Freedom,* p. 46.
28. *Ibid.,* p. 46.
29. Natl. Commission on Productivity and Work Quality, *Productivity and The Economy,* p. 48.
30. Smith, Charles H. Jr., *Opus cit.*
31. Natl. Right To Work Committee, *Some Comparisons,* 1974.

Chapter Nine, "THE GREATEST OF THESE IS LOVE"

1. Rom. 13:10.
2. Luke 10:30-37.
3. Matt. 22:39.
4. Mayer, Milton, *What Can A Man Do?,* pp. 39-40.
5. Clinchy, Russell J., *Charity, Biblical and Political,* Foundation for Economic Education, p. 12.
6. *Ibid.,* p. 10.
7. *Ibid.,* p. 10.
8. Matt. 14:15-21.

9. Haake, Dr. Alfred J., "Is Private Enterprise Compatible with Christianity?" Speech before Economic Club of Detroit, 1950.
10. Niehbuhr, Reinhold, quoted by Rev. Edmund Opitz in speech before Maine Farm Bureau, Portland, Maine, Nov. 16, 1959.
11. Opitz, Rev. Edmund, *Opus cit.*
12. Bennett, John C., quoted by Rev. Edmund Opitz in *Opus cit.*
13. Read, Leonard, "If government doesn't relieve distress who will?", *Cliches of Socialism,* FEE.
14. Statistical Abstract of the U.S., 1974, p. 265.
15. *Ibid.,* p. 298.
16. Conlan, Hon. John B., statement to the press, Mar. 30, 1975.
17. Tax Foundation, Inc., "The Financial Outlook for State & Local Governments to 1980," p. 55.
18. *Ibid.,* p. 49.
19. Ash, Roy, *Washington Post,* Nov. 26, 1974.
20. Hazlitt, Henry, "Welfarism Gone Wild," *The Freeman,* May, 1972, p. 267.
21. *Ibid.*
22. 2 Thess. 3:10-12.
23. 1 Tim. 5:8.
24. Summers, Brian, "Charity and The Welfare State," *The Freeman,* Dec., 1971, p. 712.
25. Shumiatcher, Morris C., "Welfare Fifty Years Hence," *The Freeman,* March 1974, p. 174.
26. Luke 18:27.
27. Author's estimate based on report from American Assn. of Fund-Raising Counsel, Inc.
28. American Assn. of Fund-Raising Counsel, Inc., "Giving, USA, 1974 Annual Report."
29. 1 Chron. 29:14.
30. Engstrom, Ted, in letter to author, April 17, 1975.
31. World Vision International, "Our Malnourished World," *World Vision,* Jan. 1975, p. 13.
32. *Ibid.*
33. Wolfbein, Seymour, "Managing Adjustments to Technical Change," *Conference on An Agenda for Economic Research in Productivity,* Natl. Commission on Productivity, April 1973.

Chapter Ten—"TAXES AND THE POWER TO DESTROY"

1. Romans 13:1.
2. I Timothy 2:2; I Peter 2:14.
3. Rowen, H., *Washington Post,* Nov. 24, 1974; *Economic Report to the President,* Jan., 1973.
4. Hillendahl, W.H., *Bank of Hawaii,* April 1973.
5. Associated Press, *New York Times,* Dec. 11, 1974.
6. Harper, F.A., *Liberty, A Path To Its Recovery,* p. 108.
7. NAM, *Wealth, Taxation and Fiscal Policy,* Sept. 1972.
8. Rowen, H., *Washington Post,* Nov. 24, 1974 (Interview with Roy Ash).

9. Wall Street Journal, *Response on Social Security,* Nov. 26, 1974, p. 26.
10. *Washington Post, Opus cit.,* 11/24/74.
11. *Wall Street Journal, Opus cit.,* 11/26/74.
12. Hazlitt, Henry, *Economics in One Lesson,* p. 48.
13. *Washington Post, Opus cit.,* 11/26/74.
14. Ash, Roy, *Washington Post,* 11/26/74.
15. Hazlitt, H., *Opus cit.,* p. 48.
16. Will, George F., *Washington Post,* Oct. 24, 1974.
17. *Industry Week,* Sept. 26, 1974, pp. 51-52.
18. Walton, Rus, *Oroville (Ca.) Mercury,* April 17, 1972.
19. Walton, Rus, *Fullerton (Ca.) Daily News Tribune,* May 21, 1973.
20. KNX, Los Angeles, April 15, 1974.
21. Harper, F.A., *Liberty, A Path To Its Recovery,* p. 107.
22. *Ibid.,* p. 112.
23. Conlan, Hon. John B., M.C.
24. The Heritage Foundation, Inc., *Federal Spending and Budget Control, An Analysis and Review,* March, 1974., p. 29.
25. NAM, *Wealth, Taxation and Fiscal Policy,* Sept. 1972, p. 10.
26. Read, Leonard C., *Cliches of Socialism No. 5,* Foundation For Economic Education.
27. Thurow, L.C. and Lucas, R.E.B., *The American Distribution of Income: A Structural Problem.* Joint Economic Committee, March 17, 1972.
28. Kristol, I. "Of Populism and Taxes", *The Public Interest,* Summer 1972, p. 5.
29. Tax Foundation, Inc.: *Tax Burdens and Benefits of Government Expenditures by Income Class,* 1967.
30. *New York Times,* March 19, 1971.
31. Rushdoony, R.J., *The Nature of the American System,* p. 9.
32. *Ibid.,* p. 16.

Chapter Eleven—"INFLATION IS KILLING AMERICA"

1. Hazlitt, Henry, *What You Should Know About Inflation,* p. 11.
2. Fertig, Lawrence, "The Political Costs of Price Inflation", *The Freeman,* Feb. 1975, p. 138.
3. Roepke, Wilhelm, *Economics of The Free Society,* p. 101.
4. North, Gary, *An Introduction to Christian Economics,* p. 20.
5. Browne, Harry, *You Can Profit From A Monetary Crisis,* p. 42.
6. Read, Leonard, "How To Stop Inflation", *The Freeman,* Nov. 1973, p. 675.
7. Hazlitt, Henry, *Economics in One Easy Lesson,* p. 115.
8. North, Gary, *An Introduction to Christian Economics,* p. 6.
9. *Ibid.,* p. 12.
10. Roepke, Wilhelm, quoted by Gary North in *An Introduction to Christian Economics,* p. 12.
11. North, Gary, *Opus cit.,* p. 12.
12. *Ibid.,* p. 13.
13. *Economic Education Bulletin,* American Institute for Economic Research, Great Barrington, Mass., Jan. 1974 (updated to March, 1975).

14. Markowitz, Morris J., "Is Inflation Here To Stay?", *The Freeman,* April 1974, p. 238.
15. *Ibid.,* p. 240.
16. North, Gary, *Opus cit.,* p. 24.
17. Hazlitt, Henry, *Economics in One Easy Lesson,* p. 123.
18. Matt. 6:26.
19. Garrett, Garet, *The People's Pottage,* pp. 1-3-4
20. *Ibid.,* pp. 101-2.
21. Sennholz, Hans, "The Causes of Inflation", *The Freeman,* May 1972, p. 284.
22. Romans 13:8.
23. Fertig, Lawrence, "The Political Costs of Inflation", *The Freeman,* March 1975, p. 138.
24. Sennholz, Hans, "Two-Digit Inflation", *The Freeman,* Jan. 1975, p. 23.
25. *Ibid.,* p. 28.
26. North, Gary, *Opus cit.,* p. 8.
27. Hazlitt, Henry, *What You Should Know About Inflation,* p. 26.
28. Burgess, W. Randolph, as quoted by Henry Hazlitt, *Ibid.,* p. 26.
29. Sennholz, "Gold Is Honest Money", *The Freeman,* Feb. 1975, p. 92.
30. Weber, Charles E., "A Closer Look At Gold", *The Freeman,* Sept. 1972, p. 541.
31. Garrett, Garet, *Opus cit.,* p. 106, and Jones, Allen A., in letter to editor, Phoenix *Arizona Republic,* Jan. 1975.
32. Sennholz, Hans, "Gold Is Honest Money", *The Freeman,* Feb. 1975, p. 91.
33. *Ibid.*

Chapter Twelve—"THESE ARE THE PEACEMAKERS"

1. *Statistical Abstract of the United States,* 1974, p. 251.
2. FBI report, May, 1975.
3. *Statistical Abstract of the United States,* 1974, p. 257.
4. *Ibid.,* p. 257.
5. *Ibid.,* p. 252.
6. *Ibid.,* p. 265.
7. Ford, President Gerald, "Ford Takes a Hard Line", *Washington Star,* May 2, 1975.
8. FBI report, May, 1975.
9. *Ibid.*
10. *Ibid.,* (preliminary data).
11. Walton, Rus, "Those Drug-Pushing Nations", *Piqua (Ohio) Daily Call,* May 24, 1973.
12. Deut. 19:4-6.
13. Deut. 19:11-13.
14. Deut. 19:19-21.
15. Matt. 5:17-19.
16. *Washington Star,* Nov. 13, 1974.
17. I Pet. 3:19 and Matt. 25:36,43,44.
18. Gen. 14:11-16.
19. Sayer, Dorothy L., as quoted by Dr. James Roy Smith in *God Still Speaks*

in The Space Age, p. 60.
20. Smith, Dr. Charles Roy, *Opus cit.*, pp. 60-61.
21. Clouse, Robert G., "The Christian, War and Militarism", *The Cross and The Flag*, Creation House, p. 230.
22. Young, Hon. C. W. Bill, *Congressional Record*, Mar. 25, 1975.
23. *Ibid.*
24. *Ibid.*
25. *Ibid.*
26. *Ibid.*
27. Luttwak, Edward, as quoted by Dr. Charles A. Moser in "Another Budget: Toward a Re-ordering of National Priorities", *The Heritage Foundation*, 1975.
28. Moser, Dr. Charles A., *Opus cit.*
29. Young, Hon. C. W. Bill, *Opus cit.*
30. Moser, Dr. Charles A., *Opus cit.*
31. Rickover, Admiral H., as reported in *Defense Space Business Daily*, April 28, 1975.
32. American Security Council data, May, 1975.
33. Clouse, Robert G., *Opus cit.*, pp. 230-231.
34. Young, Hon. C. W. Bill, *Opus cit.*
35. Kemp, Hon. Jack, *Congressional Record*, March 25, 1975.
36. Mic. 4:4.
37. Mic. 4:4.
38. Mic. 4:1-2.
39. Luke 11:23.
40. Psalm 127:1.
41. Chamberlain, John, "A Reviewer's Notebook", *The Freeman*, Nov. 1974.
42. Moser, Dr. Charles A., *Opus cit.*
43. Sollenberger, Kucille, "Christ in Genesis, Vol. I", *Living The Life Home Bible Studies*, pp. 72-73.
44. *Ibid.*
45. 2 Cor. 6:14-18.
46. Gal. 5:1.
47. Lowry, Dr. Charles W., *Communism and Christ*, p. 101.

SELECTED BIBLIOGRAPHY

(Alphabetical, by Author)

Ballve, Faustino, *Essentials of Economics*, Foundation for Economic Education (FEE).
Bastiat, Frederic, *The Law*, FEE.
Cairns, Earle E., *The Christian in Society*, Moody Press.
Cantelon, Willard, *The Day The Dollar Dies*, Logos.
Fertig, Lawrence, *Prosperity Through Freedom*, Henry Regnery.
Garrett, Garet, *The People's Pottage*, Caxton.
Graham, Billy, *Peace With God*, Doubleday.
Hall, Verna M., *The Christian History of The Constitution*, Foundation for American Christian Education.
Harper, F. A., *Liberty—A Path To Its Recovery*, FEE.
Hazlitt, Henry, *Economics in One Easy Lesson*, Harper and Row.
Hazlitt, Henry, *What You Should Know About Inflation*, VanNostrand.
Morley, Felix, *The Power in The People*, VanNostrand.
North, Gary, *Introduction to Christian Economics*, Craig Press.
Ortega y Gassett, Jose, *Revolt of The Masses*, Norton.
Possony, Stefan, *Waking Up The Giant*, Arlington House.
Prince, Derek, *Shaping World History Through Prayer & Fasting*, Revell.
Read, Leonard, *Government: An Ideal Concept*, FEE.
Read, Leonard, *Anything That's Peaceful*, FEE.
Read, Leonard, *Accent on The Right*, FEE.
Read, Leonard, *Deeper Than You Think*, FEE.
Roepke, Wilhelm, *Economics of The Free Society*, Henry Regnery.
Rueff, Jacques, *The Age of Inflation*, Henry Regnery.
Rushdoony, Rousas J., *The Nature of The American System*, Craig Press.
Rushdoony, Rousas J., *The Messianic Character of American Education*, Craig Press.
Schwarz, Fred, *You Can Trust The Communists*, Prentice-Hall.
Slater, Rosalie J., *Teaching and Learning America's Christian History*, Foundation for American Christian Education.
Sutton, Anthony C., *National Suicide*, Arlington House.
Weaver, Henry Grady, *Mainspring of Human Progress*, FEE.

. . . and first, last and always . . .
THE LIVING WORD, THE HOLY BIBLE!

NOTES

(Bible Verses, Special References, Etc.)